GBC

GOVERNMENT BEYOND THE CENTRE

SERIES EDITORS: GERRY STOKER AND DAVID WILSON

The world of sub-central governance and administration – including local authorities, quasi-governmental bodies and the agencies of public–private partnerships – has seen massive changes in the United Kingdom and other western democracies. The original aim of the **Government Beyond the Centre** series was to bring the study of this often-neglected world into the mainstream of social science research, applying the spotlight of critical analysis to what had traditionally been the preserve of institutional public administration approaches.

The replacement of traditional models of government by new models of governance has affected central government, too, with the contracting out of many traditional functions, the increasing importance of relationships with devolved and supranational authorities, and the emergence of new holistic models based on partnership and collaboration.

This series focuses on the agenda of change in governance both at sub-central level and in the new patterns of relationships surrounding the core executive. Its objective is to provide up-to-date and informative accounts of the new forms of management and administration and the structures of power and influence that are emerging, and of the economic, political and ideological forces that underlie them.

The series will be of interest to students and practitioners in central and local government, public management and social policy, and all those interested in the reshaping of the governmental institutions which have a daily and major impact on our lives.

Government Beyond the Centre
Series Standing Order
ISBN 0–333–71696–5 hardcover
ISBN 0–333–69337–X paperback
(outside North America only)

You can receive future titles in this series as they are published by placing a standing order. Please contact your bookseller or, in the case of difficulty, write to us at the address below with your name and address, the title of the series and the ISBN quoted above.

Customer Services Department, Macmillan Distribution Ltd
Houndmills, Basingstoke, Hampshire RG21 6XS, England

GOVERNMENT BEYOND THE CENTRE

SERIES EDITORS: GERRY STOKER AND DAVID WILSON

Making Local Governance Work

Networks, Relationships and the Management of Change

Sue Goss

palgrave

First published 2001 by
PALGRAVE
Houndmills, Basingstoke, Hampshire RG21 6XS and
175 Fifth Avenue, New York, N. Y. 10010
Companies and representatives throughout the world

PALGRAVE is the new global academic imprint of
St. Martin's Press LLC Scholarly and Reference Division and
Palgrave Publishers Ltd (formerly Macmillan Press Ltd).

ISBN 0–333–91787–1 hardback
ISBN 0–333–91788–X paperback

This book is printed on paper suitable for recycling and
made from fully managed and sustained forest sources.

A catalogue record for this book is available
from the British Library.

Library of Congress Cataloging-in-Publication Data
Goss, Sue.
    Making local government work : networks, relationships,
    and the management of change / Sue Goss.
        p. cm. — (Government beyond the centre)
    Includes bibliographical references and index.
    ISBN 0–333–91787–1
    1. Local government—Great Britain. 2. Organizational change–
    –Great Britain. 3. Local government. 4. Organizational change.
    I. Title. II. Series.
    JS3095 .G67 2000
    352.14'0941—dc21
                                                    00–048356

10   9   8   7   6   5   4   3   2   1
10   09   08   07   06   05   04   03   02   01

Printed in China

Contents

The importance of organisational forms   73
The limits to structural change   74
Systems   75
Managing change   77
Opportunities and constraints – the inevitability
  of unintended consequences   80
The creation of hybrids   82
The relationship organisation   84
The challenge of information technology   87
New forms for public organisations?   87
Alternative models for local governance?   89

5 **Networks and Partnerships**   **91**
Pressures towards cross-boundary working   91
Experience elsewhere   93
Are partnerships or networks working?   94
Practical solutions at the local level   97
We've heard all this before ...   100
Making sense of cross-boundary working   101
Systems thinking   103
Underlying forces in partnership working   105
Are we experiencing a paradigm shift?   112
Rules of engagement for partnerships   113

6 **Politics and Politicians**   **117**
The democratic deficit   118
Old town hall structures   120
Changing the structures of local politics   123
Real and imaginary structures   126
Political systems   128
Political culture   130
New roles and relationships   133
Real and imaginary community leaders   136

7 **Why is Change so Hard?**   **138**
Changing organisations   141
The manager as hero   141
The problem with culture   144
Attitudes, behaviour and identity   147
The public manager as hero?   148
The role of the professional   149

Lists of Tables, Figures and Boxes

Tables

Figures

Boxes

Acknowledgements

I am grateful to the Office for Public Management for giving me time to write this book. Many people helped with the thinking that went into it. Colleagues within local authorities, police and health authorities, partnerships, voluntary sector agencies and government departments provided insights into the problems and dilemmas they faced. Courageous and pioneering public managers, including Carol Hassan, Alan Clarke, Leisha Fullick, Michael Lyons, Rob Hughes, Mel Usher and Keith Barnes provided inspiration. Rory Barke at York City Council and Dick Hackett at Walsall helped with case-studies.

My colleagues at the Office for Public Management are a perpetual source of new ideas and challenge. In particular, conversations with Greg Parston, Robin Douglas, Helen Brown, Laurie Mcmahon, Kai Rudat, Paul Tarplett and David Albury proved invaluable. I am indebted to Anne Bennett for the description of the 'leaderful' case in the conclusion, to Stephen Thake for an invaluable conversation about social capital, and to Professor Paul Thompson for thinking about 'identity work'. Professors Gerry Stoker and David Wilson provided expert criticism and feedback during the writing of the book, and Steven Kennedy was a supportive publisher. I would like to thank Aleth Abadie for her patient and efficient support with producing the manuscript. All the mistakes are of course mine.

SUE GOSS

The author and publishers are grateful to the following for permission to use copyright material: the Office for Public Management for a diagram from Clive Miller in *Managing for Social Cohesion* (1999) and for a diagram from Mark Moore in a contribution to the OPM's *1999 10th Anniversary Symposium on the Future of Public Services* (1999); the Copyright Unit of Her Majesty's Stationery Office for permission to reproduce two diagrams from Stewart and Goss *et al.*, *Cross-cutting Issues Affecting Local Government* (DETR, 1999), a diagram from Lowndes *et al.* Enhancing Public participation in Local Government (DETR, 1998) and a diagram from the Urban Task Force Report *Towards An Urban Renaissance* (1999). Kogan Page gave permission to reproduce a diagram from Goss (eds) *Managing Working with the Public* (1999). Crown copyright is reproduced with the permission of the Controller of Her Majesty's Stationery Office. Thanks also to Robin Douglas, David Halpen and Gerry Stoker for permission to quote unpublished material. Every effort has been made to contact all the copyright-holders, but if any have been inadvertently omitted the publishers will be pleased to made the necessary arrangement at the earliest opportunity.

1 Introduction – Making Local Governance Work

The change from traditional local government to a more complex network of agencies involved in 'local governance' is no longer theory. It has become practice. Initiatives to tackle unemployment, to improve health, to reduce crime and to build communities are being taken across old boundaries. Action is planned and executed in neighbourhoods and regions, in city boards and community development trusts as well as in town halls and civic offices. Networks and partnerships are as much part of the organisational map as single government agencies. Learning is taking place very fast, as managers, politicians and citizens begin to make sense of a more complex world. The conversations within neighbourhoods are alive to the different communities that inhabit shared space, to the conflicting sets of interests to be balanced.

But progress is slowed by outdated mental models and institutional maps. Individuals and organisations struggle to make things happen in the fog of overlapping objectives, multiplying plans, competing departmental interests. The slogan 'what matters is what works' does not help us to understand why things work, and what needs to change when they do not. Government policy inhabits an imaginary world in which interests never conflict, outcomes never contradict each other, and power is never used by the powerful for their own ends.

The reforms of the 1980s and 1990s broke the bureaucratic complacency of public institutions. Competition from the private sector has sent a cold chill through almost all public agencies, and begun to create the conditions for innovation, new product development and consumer responsiveness. Change has been slow, but simple privatisation has not offered a palatable alternative. The private sector has often failed the public during the same period, for example through the miss-selling of pensions and endowment mortgages, or the abandoning of rural transport. The 1980s revolution in government travelled down a bleak cul-de-sac, one from which policy-makers and citizens are only just beginning to return. The construction of

1

the public as consumers created narrow and artificial limits to our ability to think through new relationships between government and civil society. The importation of private management culture failed to take account of the unique roles and values of public agencies. The simplification of central–local relationships to top-down control failed to recognise how things really get done.

From theory to practice

This book draws on research and consultancy experience in the UK – which has become something of a pathfinder in the emergence of new relationships and new forms of governance, in much the same was as it was earlier a laboratory of privatisation. Intended to meet the needs of anyone who works in, makes policy for, or studies in the field of local governance and management, it assesses the experience of local councils and partnerships to illustrate emerging relationships of local governance in practice, explore emerging dilemmas and demonstrate how networks can be made to work.

There are now many exciting governance experiments in the UK; everywhere, there is substantive change. But the obstacles are formidable, and without attention to them the flow of energy and creativity driving change could falter and dry up. The intention throughout this book has been to link theory to practice. Academic theory often misses the real-life dramas unfolding in day-to-day encounters. At the same time, relentless activity by public organisations without an understanding of the forces at work can be ineffectual. The absence of appropriate theoretical work simply means that old theories serving particular interests can be presented as 'common sense'.

I have drawn upon a range of theoretical debates – from within sociology, political science, social psychology and organisational theory – in order to connect changes in civil society, in politics and in public organisations. The book has been ten years in the making, ten years of working as an organisational change consultant in the public sector, working alongside managers, politicians and staff as we found that the conventional 'tools' of organisational change broke off in our hands and juddered to a halt against the solid walls of lived reality.

Research into local governance concentrates, sensibly, on local authorities. Local authorities have democratically elected politicians, and have a generally accepted role in community leadership. New legal powers to promote 'social, economic and environmental well-being' reinforce this. I have paid specific attention to local authorities for this reason, but have also attempted to reflect the extent to which other public, private and voluntary-sector agencies are now absorbed into governance, and to pay attention to the other levels where governance takes place; the local authority is not the only site. The region itself is a de facto site of governance, as is the neighbourhood. Decision-making at neighbourhood level involves the same dilemmas and conflicts, trade-offs and compromises that face local councils. Regional, locality-based and neighbourhood structures are often still struggling with old ways of doing things, and have not yet found ways of working that fit the emerging realities.

Making connections – new roles and relationships

The most important change in local governance is that of changing roles and relationships. I set out to show the importance of the connections between three different sets of changes:

- First, changes in the relationship between government and people, between citizen and the state. This relationship is being redefined in practice, renegotiated on all sides. But community engagement in the past has been over-designed, and heavily controlled from the top. Citizens have been invited to take part in meetings or events dominated by an organisational timetable and organisational needs. Conversations between public agencies and local people have often involved both sides talking and no one listening. But new sorts of interaction are emerging which do not involve local people off-loading their problems onto local agencies; instead they involve a shared or negotiated process of planning action requiring very different behaviours from all concerned. This raises new questions. What are the rules of engagement? What are the governance behaviours expected of citizens? Such rules cannot be imposed by government; they are subjects for future conversations. Much of the debate about local governance has been 'blind' to the implications of social and economic inequality. If local governance is to play a role in community leadership, these questions have to be faced head on. The politics of these interactions are also important; do they intensify inequality or reduce it? Local politicians are coming to terms with new structural arrangements, with partnerships, with executive and scrutiny roles. But they are also struggling to find a role within new, more negotiated relationships with local citizens. Is the nature of local politics changing? And how are politicians changing in response?

- Second, changes in the roles of managers and staff inside local public agencies. As they begin to engage more with each other, and with the public, they face a series of dilemmas about the purpose of government, about the roles of citizens, about the construction of legitimacy, about the nature of identity and belonging, about freedom and responsibility, about autonomy and power. These are not 'management' problems in any sense that would be recognised by traditional management textbooks. But they need to be explicitly tackled within the management relationships of governance. Nor can they simply be 'solved' – since they are not caused by inefficiency, or by technical or systems failure. The political and social dilemmas of our society are translated into the management of public services. It is precisely because governance offers the possibility of breaking through professionally-based, bureaucratically-sealed thinking that they emerge so clearly into view. They can no longer be 'boxed' into issues of 'politics' or 'sociology'; they are the substance of ordinary decisions in the everyday practice of governance. New relationships, by breaking through old barriers, offer a space within which these debates become the day-to-day subjects of conversations between the people who work in public organisations, and citizens. This changes the role of a public manager, and sets up new and contradictory pressures which public managers have to understand in order to cope.
- Third, changes within public organisations themselves. Public managers are coming to terms with structural and systems changes within their organisations and with new partnership and network relationships. As one manager vividly put it in Vivien Lowndes' admirable summary 'we are learning to accommodate mess' (Lowndes, 1998). The transition is not simple or smooth, there is no 'new management' to juxtapose with 'old management'. New organisational forms are emerging, including strategic alliances, partnerships, co-located organisations, virtual organisations, city boards, partnership webs and capsule organisations – but at the same time, centrally-determined performance indicators reinforce departmentalism and traditional delivery systems. Managers and staff are learning to live in a world of mixed messages and contradictory pressures.

By understanding how these sets of changes interact, we can begin to recognise the potential for successful governance, and to create organisations capable of responding.

However, old ways of doing things are becoming obsolete before new ways are fully-established. This means that the immediate experience for many of those participating is that of muddle and mess. The process of 'learning to accommodate mess' is characterised by multiple initiatives, by ineffectual consultation with the public, by weak partnerships, and by unfinished change programmes. Unintended consequences often include a waste of energy and resources, poor understanding at all levels, or failure of focus. The preoccupation of central government with 'keeping control' of local governance is a bit like trying to control the responses of every individual in the country to the weather. The amount of planning knowledge or system control needed is disproportionate to the gains. Lack of knowledge about what is happening on the ground means that civil servants constantly try to suck up 'best practice' from the field and then design delivery systems which can then be imposed. It is impossible to know enough at the centre to do this well. However, there are better ways of doing things.

The growing sense of muddle leads some powerful voices to argue that it is too confusing, and too chaotic, that central government needs to step in, to slim down, straighten out, simplify governance, to shift power backwards into old systems 'where you knew where you stood'. But it cannot be done. It is precisely because the old ways of doing things can't work now, and can't be made to work, that new ways are opening up.

Not all unintended consequences are bad, however. The very experience of managing across the boundaries, working in the spaces between bureaucratic, market and network cultures, creates space for innovation. People working in these spaces learn extraordinary skills and are beginning to develop the capacity to work in complexity demanded by the future. The constant collision of different assumptions and traditions offers scope to challenge on all sides. The very messiness begins to break down old systems and procedures, which cannot function in chaos. Different people find themselves able to work well in this new environment, and the glass ceiling thins in areas of innovation and creativity.

Public organisations need to change far more radically than they have done thus far, and I explore the ways that organisations can evolve. New skills and capabilities are needed – entrepreneurial skills, the capacity to manage risk and manage legitimacy – not simply at the top but throughout public organisations. But learning is not a simple process. Alongside new learning, there is a need for 'unlearning' – challenging and rethinking the theories that underpin personal and organisational interventions. In exploring the reasons why change is so hard, we need to recognise the importance of emotional stratagems that lock people into patterns of behaviour and safe routines. Matching capabilities are needed within politics and within civil society if new relationships are to be sustained. Here the challenge is greater. I suggest that a combination of learning, exploration, reflection and dialogue is needed. A sustained process of experiential learning needs to include 'citizen-governors' if local governance is to succeed. The rules of engagement between civil society and between local public services are being actively renegotiated, and skills to do that are needed on all sides.

In the final chapters, I sketch out the creative solutions that are emerging, examine examples of successful practice, and indicate a way forward.

The structure of the book

It may help to offer some signposts which will enable readers to choose a path through the chapters that follow. Chapter 2, following, sets out the theoretical perspectives that underpin the rest of the book. It explores the definitions of local governance coined by Gerry Stoker and Rod Rhodes, and the distinctions that have been drawn between local governance and traditional local government. It goes on to examine two further crucial concepts: 'public value' and 'legitimacy'. The shift from government to governance is not merely a response to the fragmentation of service delivery; there are new assumptions about what local governance is for. What are the emerging roles of local governance? And are they political, or managerial? The chapter concludes with an examination of a fourth concept: 'local'. What are the implications of regional and neighbourhood governance arrangements?

Chapter 3 looks at the relationship between public agencies and local communities, and examines the trend towards greater public consultation from both sides. It examines the successes and failures of the booming consultation industry. It suggests that the current dialogue constructs citizens into mere consumers, and by doing so limits the nature of the interaction. I explore a wider range of roles available to members of the public, and draw on some fascinating conversations between ordinary people living on inner-city estates about the nature of identity, belonging and community, illustrating how much people have already thought about these issues. The chapter goes on to explore the usefulness of recent work on 'social capital'. Here the old battle between right and left about the role of the state is quietly being refought. A brief look at the history of community engagement over the past forty years shows that relationships between government and communities have always been problematic; power, inequality and exclusion are inextricably part of governance. Government agencies can play a role in radical change, but there is always a 'drag' in large bureaucracies back to 'systems maintenance' and continuity. As roles and relationships change, it is important to expose both the impact of government agencies on wider society, and the impact of relationships within civil society on attempts to take collective action. What are the rules of engagement for citizens. What responsibilities do they carry to make governance work?

Chapter 4 looks at the ways in which public organisations, particularly local authorities, have changed over the past twenty years. It charts the transition from professionally-based, departmentally-structured bureaucracies, to 'hybrid' organisations with elements of bureaucracy existing alongside contracts and networks. It examines the problems that these changes bring, and suggests that public sector organisations cannot simply be made to work in the ways that private companies do, since their roles and responsibilities are different. Crucially, a public sector organisation has to interact with the public, not simply as customers but as 'citizen-authorisers' and as co-producers. Crucial to a modern public service organisation is the capacity to build and sustain relationships with citizens, and with other agencies. I suggest that what is emerging is a 'relationship organisation' characterized by the capacity of all its members to build and work within reciprocal relationships. A relationship organisation is primarily connected outwards. Within it, individuals are used to thinking about their roles and responsibilities; they can see the big picture, see how things interconnect and make judgements about the best ways to act. They are self-aware about the roles they take, and their expectations of others. Professionals and staff are less territorial, comfortable in teams outside their conventional training, able to learn from other ways of seeing and working, and capable of creating new solutions by fusing different perspectives. Work is interesting, enjoyable and often difficult. Decisions are based on evidence, feedback is constant, and systems respond swiftly. Members of relationship organisations don't act as individuals. A relationship organisation must be capable of translating the experience of many individual relationships into a wide capacity to act on behalf of the whole community. I go on to look at what that might mean for organisational forms, systems, culture and leadership. There are implications for the introduction of new technology and the hard-wiring of organisational relationships.

Chapter 5 examines the emerging role of partnerships. The experience of local networks and partnerships is mixed; there are examples of remarkable success, and practice suggests there is no single model for success.

Most governance partnerships so far have been primarily between public agencies. However, all organisations are experiencing difficulties. Duplication, lack of agreement about outcomes, departmental boundaries, competitiveness – all lead to initiative overload, conflicting and duplicating targets, unrealistic bidding deadlines, complex monitoring systems that require process compliance, and command and control behaviours. I explore the emerging consensus about the conditions for successful partnerships, and set out some key success factors. Local governance involves interactions between a wide range of agencies, and to understand it we must move away from linear models. All the players at local level are trying to pursue their own aims, working within a changing environment and trying to reshape that environment and influence others. The outcomes are the result of the interaction of all these players, and not simply the outcomes intended by the centre. By examining the 'whole system' it is possible for patterns of interaction to be observed and explored so that all players can learn to work with them. I argue that if networks of local agencies are successful in working together, then the legitimacy and accountability of these new partnerships becomes important. Questions about who is inside and outside these networks, and who decides, become important for local democracy.

Chapter 6 explores the implications of a transition from government to governance for local politicians. The impact of new political structures within the UK, including mayors and elected cabinets is not yet clear. The question, as with other structural change, is what political behaviours do they make more or less likely? I discuss change so far, and the concerns that are emerging; we are witnessing a process of transition. In some places the deadly committees and stuffy public meetings of the old world are giving way to more creative interactions. I suggest that, in politics, informal structures and systems may be more important than the formal changes. Without a change to political thinking and ways of working, new governance arrangements are unlikely to succeed. New relationships of governance hold up to the light the culture of politics, and expose to scrutiny the roles that politicians play. The cultures that underpin local politics are reinforced by the media, and by us, the public; the new skills needed are still political – negotiating, bridge-building, visioning, facilitating, empowering, inspiring – but are seldom honoured or rewarded.

The politics of local governance is not limited to the arrangements within which councillors work. Despite a managerial language that smothers the possibilities of conflict, the reality is that local governance is highly political. Local governance is inevitably about power and the use of power.

By engaging citizens in decision-making processes, by bringing business people into task-forces and partnerships, governance makes politicians of us all. If we are not alert to the strengths and weaknesses of political cultures, we may find that we simply replicate the worst of political cultures within 'community representation.'

Chapter 7 looks at why change is so hard. It examines what goes wrong, and looks at some of the familiar patterns when change runs out of steam. There is much that is faddish about organisational change; popular management gurus imply that improved organisational cultures can be designed and controlled by effective managers – and create the image of the hero manager responsible for creating the 'can-do' culture. But culture is not a simple thing to change. We can see it as a system of meanings, depictions and symbols that represent the values and realities of a community. It is a set of rhythms and patterns, myths and stories, deep-seated assumptions and behaviours which cannot easily be manipulated, though they can be attended to until we have a depth of understanding that can lead to change.

Public organisations are not simply poor copies of private sector organisations, they are culturally very distinct. Public organisations include within them the tensions and inequalities of wider society, but carry responsibilities – for community safety, for comprehensive education, for health in which all citizens expect to be treated equally. The chapter examines the sense of personal confusion and dissonance public managers and staff experience between the publicly stated culture and their own lived reality. Managers and staff are learning to manage that dissonance, trying to make sense of the contradictory things they are asked to do in a society that is no longer clear about their roles. Despite the fairy-tale simplicity of management text-books, the world they inhabit is one where power is multi-located, in which change is not simply driven by command and control but command and control systems exist, and in which all individuals bring their own values, beliefs and ideas to work. The reality rather than the illusion of change involves processes that engage with the lived realities of managers and staff rather than the hype of management gurus. They have to build an explanation of their role and purpose that makes sense and enables them to feel safe and useful within changing organisations with moving boundaries.

Chapter 8 looks at how managers, professionals and staff inside public organisations can learn to do this. There is a welcome recognition of the need for public agencies to become learning organisations, and there is some new investment in training and education. But few of the required capabilities can be learnt through formal education; some of the most

educated people turn out to be useless at local governance. And even training is more problematic than may at first appear. Learning is not a straightforward process; much of our real learning is informal as we absorb
assumptions about our role and status, about what is possible, what works,
what makes sense, what it is safe to try. Each professional, organisation,
community or management culture carries assumptions that are learnt
informally. While formal learning teaches us what to do, informal learning
teaches us how to be. I explore many of the current experiments in experiential and interactive learning, and the conditions for successful learning.
The chapter goes on to examine the concept of organisational learning and
the ways that public organisations can share, store and disseminate learning. It examines the impact of networks of governance, and suggests that,
used well, these could accelerate learning.

In Chapter 9 I examine how the lessons about managerial and organisational learning might be translated into learning for councillors, for citizen-
governors on boards or quangos. Time spent in shared exploration is as
important for governors as it is for managers. The questions they face –
'who do we serve', 'in whose interests are we working', 'what's at stake',
'how do we balance accountabilities' – do not require management skills,
but they do require governance skills. I go on to consider how we might
develop learning within civil society about how to do 'governance'. While
there is some investment taking place in lifelong learning, and developing
community capacity, it is usually investment in conventional training.
Where could resources come from to widen the experience of community
learning? We are discovering that many modern consultation techniques
have the interactive and deliberative qualities that can create learning and
build new forms of dialogue within communities. Instead of treating public
engagement as simply consultation, we could begin to see it as a process
of social learning.

In conclusion, I argue that new approaches to change are beginning to
work. They are not easy, and they take time. But the old ways have already
failed. I offer some examples of live projects that seem to be taking the
agenda forward, and warn against attempts to over-control a complex
process of change. I suggest that the engagement, motivation and understanding of the women and men engaged in governance is worth a thousand policy initiatives.

2 Issues in Local Governance

In this chapter I intend to examine the concepts that form the theoretical underpinning for an inquiry into making local governance work. The concepts, 'governance', 'public value', 'legitimacy', 'accountability' and 'local' may be familiar to both academics and practitioners, but they repay investigation. Each encompasses several meanings, and local managers, politicians and community leaders find themselves trapped between these meanings. Their ability to solve day-to-day problems is constrained by the unspoken assumptions behind them.

From government to governance

The first concept is that of governance. Until recently, academics have studied local government, but Gerry Stoker has popularised the argument that the vast shifting map of local agencies makes it impossible to treat local government as a single organisation (Stoker, 1991, 1999). Because of the externalisation of many services, the centralisation of others and the creation of new quangos, local government is only one actor among a network of agencies. Local governance describes the way these agencies interact at local level. Rhodes describes governance as carried out through 'self-organising, inter-organisational networks' (Rhodes, 1997, p. 15). But governance is crucially also about politics, both formal and informal. I will use the word governance to describe emerging new forms of collective decision-making at local level which lead to the development of different relationships, not simply between public agencies but between citizens and public agencies.

While there is always a tendency for theory to outrun lived experience, the reality of governance through a network of agencies is becoming familiar to managers and politicians at local level, and the language of governance has been adopted in the field. Almost all local agencies are now working across organisational boundaries, and some have made it work. There is a small group of local authorities, managers, politicians and community leaders blasting into the future. In many places new projects are run in very different ways from the old, while at the same time there are still inward-looking councils and agencies where few ideas arrive from the outside world, where nothing much has changed. The 'tail' of the change is lengthening, and creating extraordinary varieties of thinking and practice.

Most academics have explained the switch from government to governance as a change in government process, of 'how' local communities are governed. I want to argue that we are not simply witnessing a structural change in the institutions that make up government. After all, the process of negotiation within and between policy communities and the intermediation of powerful interest groups has been a characteristic of government for many years. What has also happened is a shift in the 'project' of governance – of the outcomes expected from processes of intervention. This translates into a change of *purpose* – a new set of ideas about what governance is *for*.

In order to track this change, it helps to recap the recent past in local government history. Change in the purpose of government is not always made explicit in the policy process; it reflects, in part, changes in the balance of power between different interest groups or classes, and sometimes that shift of power is so profound that it also changes the political party or alliance in power. One example was the 1945 government in the UK, which reflected the shift of power towards working people. But changes in a government's role and purpose do not reflect in a simple way the distribution of power in society. Governments in democracies have to win tacit consent from the electorate, and support from a wide group of interests. Government role and purpose is also affected by the prevailing ideological climate, by the values held within a society, by the ways different interest groups within a society create their own identity and perceive their needs and wants, and by the level of their political mobilisation. The Thatcher revolution, which attacked prevailing assumptions underlying the welfare state, was supported by an ideological climate within which a substantial section of the working class aspired to home ownership and the choices and freedoms of the private sector, and felt constrained by the dull uniformity of state provision.

The role and purpose of government is also directly influenced by the ideology and projects of the dominant political parties. The project of the Thatcher and Major governments evolved piecemeal over time; it was described as an attack on a 'centralising, managerial, bureaucratic interventionist style of government' (Thatcher, 1993, p. 6). Services were privatised, competition introduced, managers brought in from the private sector, and public service provision was fragmented through a range of single-purpose agencies and quangos (Weir and Hall, 1994). The idea that government was intended to provide basic service was replaced by the idea of the 'enabling state', in which government merely commissioned provision from a range of providers. While the idea of the 'enabling state' caught on, Nicholas Ridley's powerful vision of the local council that met once a year to let contracts never happened. In practice, direct provision of many services continued uninterrupted. What the Thatcher and Major governments did not do was to 'roll back the state' or even to reduce spending. The size and scale of local government as well as central government spending remained relatively constant.

Ironically, one of the outcomes of the 1980s and 1990s was to centralise decision-making over local spending. The democratic role of councillors went unrecognised during much of this time, and was consistently undermined. As a powerful local Conservative leader said at a confidential meeting of local politicians to his Labour counterparts – 'lets face it, it's not us against you, its all of us against the government'. The effect of stripping local government of power over spending was to diminish the role of Conservative as well as Labour and Liberal democratic-controlled local government.

Government projects are not simply defined at the centre. At local level, also, the political project changed in many cities of the UK, but in the opposite direction. In the late 1970s local government had faced an equally trenchant criticism from the left, 'Local government was regarded by the left as nothing more than the rest home for the geriatric right' (Seyd, 1987). In 1977, Cockburn treated the London borough of Lambeth as an illustration of imposed managerialism oppressing both staff and local people, describing Lambeth as 'a key part of the state in capitalist society' (Cockburn, 1977, p. 41). The Community Development Programmes of the 1970s developed a radical critique of government action, and there were attempts to politicise community action against local councils and represent it as straightforward 'class struggle'. By the early 1980s there was new interest by young Labour activists in local government, and it became fashionable to talk about the 'New Municipal Left' (Lansley, Goss and Wolmar, 1987). Radical Labour councils increased nursery provision, set up training and regeneration projects, decentralised to neighbourhood offices and developed equal opportunities policies for the first time. The new councils took on the Conservative government in a series of confrontations, and local politicians became household names as they fought spending cuts, ratecapping, the abolition of the metropolitan authorities, the abolition of the Greater London Council – and were systematically defeated. Hindsight brought self-criticism. The new councils in the 1980s 'spent more money than ever before but did not succeed in radically improving the nature and delivery of local services'. By 'fervently supporting public enterprise, we then became associated with its incompetence – inefficient and overstaffed, and its frequent indifference towards consumers' (LCC, 1988). Defeat brought a new humility. What John Stewart called 'public service orientation' replaced struggle. Local councils were reminded that 'they must be judged by the quality of service and that those for whom the services are provided should have a key role in assessing them' (Stewart and Stoker, 1988, p. 16). Eyes turned to the radical experiences abroad, particularly in Sweden.

While explicit political differences about the purpose of local governance are fought out between political parties, and between politicians at different levels, the continuities and changes within the systems and structures of government agencies also affect reality. Inertia both in the civil service and local bureaucracies can deflect and absorb much of the energy of powerful but short-lived political masters. Implicit assumptions about the role of government are built into the practice and behaviour of interest groups, and into administrative traditions, while equally powerful assumptions carried by the media condition the public response. Professional practice has been slow to change, and challenged rather than accepted both the shift to private-sector-style managerialism driven from the centre, and local experiments in decentralisation. Changes in the style and activity of government agencies have been relatively modest. The extent to which local people experienced any real difference as a result of the tremors of the 1980s and 1990s has depended as much on local circumstances as on central direction.

By the mid-1990s, UK local government had become quiet. Despite the fact that most of the councils were Labour or Liberal Democrat, relationships with the Conservative government were civilised and low key. It turned out that competition and compulsory competitive tendering (CCT) offered a useful way of tackling inefficiency and restoring managerial control over chaotic industrial relationships. Management systems were overhauled, service quality improved slightly, not simply because of externalisation but because in-house service providers began to introduce better business practices in order to compete. All shades of the political spectrum abandoned a reliance on direct provision and learned to live with a mixed economy. On the other hand, CCT did not produce the wholesale privatisation or the dramatic increase in service quality for which Conservatives had hoped. Spending remained remarkably stable; the costs of service provision reduced slightly, while the costs of service purchasing and monitoring went up. Managers became accepted as having leadership roles within

local government organisations, and local government became less dangerous, and less exciting.

Similar sorts of effects were visible in health and police services, which
have always been more directly controlled from Westminster. Despite radical imposed change – which required massive investments of resources
and energy to implement, the final result was neither as transformative nor
as catastrophic as had been prophesied. Organisations, structures and job
titles came and went with enormous rapidity, while the basic services sur-
vived as best they could. The impact of service reforms and a mixed economy was probably marginally good, while the impact of spending cuts was
translated directly into service cuts for local people. The centre, the bureaucracies and the management systems continued to grow, while front-line
services began to shrink.

The impact of two decades of change at national level has been a 'policy
mess' (Rhodes, 1997, p. 283) and has led to the creation of 'self-steering
networks by accident' (p. 110). At local level the impact has been no less
chaotic and troublesome, although I will argue that this, of itself, creates
opportunities. While no doubt things could have been managed better, the
reality is that the current state of confusion and process overload is the
result of a fundamental change from government to governance that has
not been matched by a change in management systems and behaviours.
Agencies at all levels are often trying to manage in a new world using old
ways; we are experiencing the inevitable collision between old and new.

Changing context – changing expectations

The rapid changes in private sector consumption, greater product differentiation, careful segmentation of markets and customers, individual customi-
sation, less waiting, less queuing – affects consumption in the public sector.
The day-to-day experience of choice in the private sector creates consumer
expectations of similar differentiation and choice within the public sector.
The mixed economy has allowed a limited process of experimentation,
benchmarking and comparison drawing on the skills and knowledge of private and voluntary sector partners, which may be about to accelerate.

For many people, public provision is no longer as important as it was;
there have already been dramatic changes in the prosperity of many working people during the last two decades. While most people still depend on
public provision of health and education, fewer and fewer people depend
on the public sector for housing, leisure and libraries. For a significant

proportion of ordinary working people, public provision has become marginal to their lives. They can, and do, substitute private provision when public services fail. For those who depend entirely on state services this leads to the marginalisation of their needs and a perilous relationship of dependency on services of shrinking social priority.

The way individuals experience government is changing. Access to information, for example, means that there is less and less reliance on the information made available by government agencies. Patients can go onto the Internet to find out information about a surgical intervention before deciding whether or not to trust the doctors. Citizens can check their rights through European as well as domestic law. There is better public understanding of the issues and problems that government attempts to tackle, but the fallibility of government policy is clearer. The limitations of professional knowledge become increasingly apparent in the new age of public risk. We have more rights, more choice, and more anxiety. We increasingly have to make difficult choices and trade-offs about our own lives, with less protection. We have to deal with the risks that confront us, to weigh up options, and to actively negotiate solutions. All this makes us want to negotiate our relationship with government: the public expects less of government, since more and more of most people's lives is lived outside the narrowing zone of state provision and control, but demands more of government in the spheres where private and voluntary action cannot substitute.

Increasing global access to information, greater individual autonomy and the emergence of a more reflexive citizenry means that the democratisation of society is outrunning democratic government (Giddens, 1998, p. 71). The crisis of democracy comes because our society is not democratic enough. Citizens want different things from government, not simply greater administrative efficiency but greater transparency and openness, a capacity for managing new technological risks, and the renewal of civic society. While law-makers assume that local people 'just want their bins emptied on time' local people say they want 'a sense of pride, all people living together in peace … children feeling safe … respect for one another' (see Walsall MBC, 1999). Our societies are also generating increasing levels of self-organisation. Governments are not always required to do things for us, but they are necessary to create the conditions in which we can do things for ourselves. The old communities are burning out, and cities are very different to how they were in the 1960s and 1970s. There may be less sense of 'community' but greater diversity makes it easier to accept different ways of seeing the world, and harder for majority communities to be blind to the existence of other ways of living.

The experience of neo-liberalism for two decades changed much of the context for government. People have become used to a mixed economy of provision, and attention has now shifted from delivery systems to the wider problems experienced by communities. The experiments of CCT and privatisation did not, by and large, fail; but the introduction of the market has not replaced local governance or public provision, simply changed its nature.

The changing purpose of governance

By 1997, the incoming Labour government argued that public services were in desperate need of modernisation, a modernisation that Thatcherism had failed to carry out. Public managers were portrayed as bureaucratic, sluggish and resistant to change. Modernisation was no longer simply about increasing efficiency, but about increasing effectiveness. Under the Blair government the challenge to direct provision of services continues, but with a new emphasis on a mixed economy that includes joint ventures, and partnerships. A new attack has been directed at the 'silo mentality' which leads to isolated services and fragmented intervention. New government initiatives and new government money requires a wide range of partners to work together to contribute to improvements in local education, employment, safety and health. The pressure is not simply to do less with less, but to spend less and do more. The new concern for outcomes – for social goals – represents a profound change of political language; it presages not a return to *status quo ante* but a new insistence that improvements in performance and integration of delivery can better achieve social goals without the need for additional resources. National targets have been set, performance indicators are published, and local performance will be monitored. There is an explosion of national inspectorates, and inspectors.

But there is an equivalent, and contradictory stress on local accountability. Concern about the local democratic deficit continues, but is no longer simply to be tackled by the removal of local power, but by the introduction of a range of other measures to involve and include communities – from surveys and panels to focus groups and citizen juries and referenda. There is considerable interest in learning drawn from the USA and Europe about social capital building. Local communities and local businesses are to be drawn into local decision-making, and local planning, and there is considerable rhetoric about involving local people at the neighbourhood level.

What makes the new 'project' so difficult to pin down is not simply the inherent contradictions and tensions at the centre, but because it is not

simply driven from central government. It had been broadly welcomed at
local level, and is seen by many managers and practitioners on the ground
as 'better than what went before' and as drawing on common-sense learning from the field. While there are many grumbles about the way central
government is imposing change, there is a sense in which the direction of
change is seen to 'fit' reality, as if government has caught up with a trajec-
tory of change which had become increasingly dissonant with the old
mantras of privatisation and efficiency. There has been a shift. There is an
emerging consensus that the purpose of local governance is different from
the old purpose of local government.

Local government was expected to act as the provider of a range of basic
services on which local people depended. Now, the provision of services
is no longer seen as 'good enough' in itself to justify state intervention.
The services provided or commissioned must be seen to 'add value' by
virtue of their being provided through systems of governance, and funded
by citizens. They must offer 'best value', be targeted to the right people,
match people's needs and wants, achieve levels of user-satisfaction, must
be efficient and effective and contribute to the achievement of wider goals –
community sustainability, social inclusion, community safety. Even more
radical, the test of value is no longer necessarily limited to state provision;
the emergence of institutions of governance makes it possible to explore
the contribution that private, voluntary and community provision can be
expected to make to social outcomes.

But in a mixed economy of provision, what is the basis on which choices
are made about services and government interventions? What are the criteria for choosing? What is the role of the public commissioner or purchaser
of services? What are they buying services for? It cannot simply be
assumed that current services are useful or even necessary. It cannot be
assumed that cheapest is best. It cannot be assumed that current providers
are the best providers. So how do we make or discuss judgments about the
relative merits of different activities and services? It is here that the second
concept I want to discuss becomes important, the concept of 'public value'.

Public value

Public value is important if we are to evaluate the success of local governance. The measurement culture of the 1980s and 1990s introduced concepts such as economy, efficiency and effectiveness as measures of local
government performance. Of these, only economy and efficiency could

be taken seriously since effectiveness only becomes meaningful when a previous question – 'what is this service intended to achieve' – has been answered. Since there were often multiple and conflicting answers to the second question, effectiveness has been the source of endless debate and precious little evaluation. Some of the most useful work on effectiveness has been done within the health service, where clinical effectiveness has been examined on an evidence basis. In the case of clinical intervention, there is at least a firm starting point as to what counts as a 'good' result. In other areas of public policy – education, social care, libraries, housing – this is more ambiguous. The movement away from measuring outputs to measuring outcomes refocuses attention on the *intention* of public policy. (Although we must continue to be wary of the elision of intentions and their results. In the absence of meaningful evaluation, we may never learn what the consequences of many interventions really are.)

The transition from identifying good public services as effective, rather than as simply efficient, has focused on the importance of value. Local services are expected to add value, indeed local authorities are under a duty to secure 'best value' on behalf of their residents. But what do we mean by value and how do we know what is best? In classical economics, value is a term translatable directly into the balance sheet; 'added value' is the difference between the sale price of the final product and the cost of all the materials that went into its production, including the cost of labour. The value is either added by entrepreneurial skill in reconfiguring resources (classical), or by the unpaid labour of the workers (Marxist). But public services do not simply operate according to capitalist economics. There is clearly no purpose in a public agency maximising profit, since the profit is gleaned from the taxpayer who is also the owner who receives it. We cannot assume that value is added by the maximum volume of service for the minimum cost, since unless the service is successful in meeting social goals, it may simply be unnecessary.

Value in an ordinary everyday sense is a more complex word. Things are valuable if they have worth, and they can have sentimental value or personal value. Value seems to contain a sense of quality or of importance; for a public service such as education to be described as 'valuable' it implies that it contributes effectively to public goals. These different meanings of value are all in play as local agencies begin to address the conundrum of what counts as best value.

In an important contribution to the debate about public management, Mark Moore argues that the purpose of public services is to add public value (Moore, 1996), which is defined as a measurable improvement in social outcomes. If public value is not added, there is no reason for services to be provided by the public sector, or to use public resources. The concept of public value offers a currency for a debate within and between different outcomes. The evolution of local governance makes it necessary for local communities, citizens, managers and politicians, to discuss *how* to balance progress towards different outcomes. Without a concept of public value, such choices become impossible.

There has been a long-standing economic debate between those (on the right) who argue that the public sector 'spends' the value created in the private sector, and those (on the left) who argue that the public sector contributes to private accumulation through providing the infrastructure, trained workforce and so on that the private sector needs. Mark Moore argues that, in addition, public services add value by drawing on resources that are in the economic sense 'free' – the resources of consent, compliance and public action. Public managers create public value by orchestrating resources in new ways to secure better social outcomes for the public, similar to the processes by which private entrepreneurs add private value. (Public sector workers may or may not also be subject to the extraction of surplus value.) But Moore argues that additional public value is obtained by the winning of consent for a solution, since this directly contributes to the outcome of a fair, well-ordered society which citizens desire. By drawing on the additional resources that are available within democratically legitimated processes, it is possible to achieve more for limited financial resources. In the recent past these resources have been neglected, or downgraded, and a public service was assumed to require public servants in a salaried capacity to run it. They are, however, scarce and precious. As citizens we choose a government that gets the right balance between the things we want to do for ourselves, and the things we want done for us.

Meaningful parallels with the private sector cannot be reduced to the importation of business efficiency into the public sector. That is to entirely misunderstand the relationship between production and value. If the role of public organisations is to create public value, just as the role of the private sector is to create private value, then what is important is the translation of the dynamic processes that lead to innovation and increases in profit in the private sector into dynamic processes that can lead to innovation and increases in public value in the public sphere. These are not the same in the public sphere as they are in the private sphere. One of the vital differences is that they can only function if our processes of democracy and accountability are strong enough to cope with the problems and tensions that innovation creates.

There remains, however, a very difficult problem. We have suggested so far that the emerging project of local governance is to add public value, defined as optimising the achievement of social outcomes. But which social outcomes? And how are we to decide?

The government has chosen to focus on a few relatively uncontentious and popular issues such as 'less crime'. However, even this turns out to be more complicated than it seems and immediately begs a series of questions. Do we mean less crime, or less perceived crime? (since the people who fear crime most are, paradoxically, those least likely to be affected by it). Are we trying to catch more criminals, or to prevent crimes from occurring? Which are the most important crimes to prevent? Are they the most serious ones – assaults, murders (in which case we would concentrate attention on fights between young men) – are they those that cause the most annoyance to the voting public – car theft, burglary – or those that affect the most vulnerable – mugging, domestic violence, racial harassment. For each simple government outcome, there is half a century of policy and social science argument, and a long cycle of unevaluated government interventions. Inevitably, then, as these are unpacked at local level, managers, politicians and citizens are already discovering the difficulty in disentangling the contributory factors to these outcomes. Outcomes often conflict. With limited resources and time we have to choose between, and choose within, intended outcomes; we have to create a balance between competing outcomes. Since different outcomes will seem more or less important depending on who you are, the crucial question is 'who decides?' This is where the third and fourth concepts of legitimacy and accountability become important.

Legitimacy and accountability

If governance decisions are to be made on behalf of the public, in a democracy this requires that the decision-makers be considered to be legitimate – that they have agreed or delegated authority to make those decisions. The creation and use of public value requires public consent. This may be at a relatively low level – through compliance or inertia – or at a high level through commitment and participation. But without consent governance fails. This has traditionally been seen as gained through the democratic process, through elected local councils. The fall in local electoral turnouts, problems in attracting people to be councillors, the reducing power of local authorities, all contribute to a perception of a local democratic deficit. While councillors are elected year after year, their capacity to mobilise consent diminishes.

Central government fares no better, however, and across the world respect and trust in government of all sorts has diminished over the past few decades; voting has dipped sharply. However, in the UK, respect for local services and local politicians holds up well in comparison with national government (Young and Rao, 1997).

Elsewhere in the world, local democracy is flourishing, and worldwide there has been a longer-term trend towards decentralisation – a trend the UK has bucked. 'The most powerful trends legitimising democracy in the mid-1990s are taking place, worldwide, at the local level' (Castells, 1997, p. 350). In the USA, 'reinventing government' has been highly influential on the New Democrats, and there has been a resurgence of interest in state and local governance as federal government has lost credibility. Experiments in Sweden, Norway and Denmark have led to a far greater devolution of power to local level in those countries, and even in countries where the neo-liberal attack on local government was more ferocious than in the UK, such as Australia, citizens and politicians are beginning to have second thoughts. South Africa is experimenting courageously with governance models involving dialogue and compromise, and the assemblies in Scotland, Wales and Ireland offer occasional glimpses of future models of governance.

The struggles between central and local government have always been characterised by appeals to different electorates, but both have a democratic basis. Democratic legitimacy should not be underestimated, since it offers a demonstration of proven consent not only for the decisions taken but also for the individuals taking them. It offers one of the rare opportunities for the public to withdraw consent, by voting. It offers the only direct relationship of accountability since it gives citizens powers of dismissal; and politicians remain fundamentally accountable in ways that other actors are not – for the whole 'shooting match' of balancing outcomes, intended or unintended, with the ultimate sanction of being dismissed if the overall outcomes do not command public support.

If local governance takes place through a shifting partial network of agencies, then the legitimacy of this network become paramount. Until now the conventional assumptions about the old systems of legitimacy have remained intact, offering an umbrella for all sorts of agencies through their accountability to democratically elected government at central and local level. However, as the legitimacy of elected government dips, and the capacity of elected government in any case to control the outcomes of intervention weakens, this becomes less and less satisfactory.

And it is not as if democratic legitimacy is the only kind, there are other reasons why it may be important for people to have a say, and a stake, in decisions. As citizens we are willing to admit a wide range of legitimacies, and one source is knowledge. People have to have the right knowledge to make decisions, and this underpins the legitimacy of both professionals and public managers. But it also increasingly applies to individual service users and local communities, since their 'self-knowledge' makes it important to engage them in governance. The enduring tension between some professionals and users about who knows best is in many ways a battle between the legitimacy of the 'expert' and personal knowledge. There is also the legitimacy that derives from leadership or the capacity to mobilise followers – that of the community leader, the charismatic priest, the campaigner. There is a legitimacy that goes with a function performed on behalf of a wider community – the role of the police officer, the judge, the director of finance, and the auditor. And finally there is a legitimacy that derives from the capacity to build consent, to find a solution with which everyone agrees.

Because all these legitimacies are real, they cannot be simply disregarded or 'trumped' by political legitimacy. Good managers of the political process, whether they are politicians, managers or community leaders, instinctively find ways to negotiate with and between these different legitimacies. Done badly, delicate processes of negotiation come apart – politicians feel trapped by conflicting demands, managers believe their expertise goes unacknowledged, knowledge is wasted, citizens become embittered. There is an ever-present possibility that power struggles become destructive – a failure to negotiate legitimacy may not simply exclude some actors from decision-making, but may weaken the capacity to act of all actors. Seldom do we acknowledge this formally. The emergence of relationships of governance makes it clearer that we are in an era of multiple legitimacies, all of which are relevant and important, and therefore that effective governance requires both that all actors are able to recognise the legitimacy of other actors, and that they are able to negotiate shared legitimacy on a continual basis.

But in a world of complex legitimacies, how are we to solve this puzzle? How are the complex compromises between different sorts of legitimacy themselves to be legitimised? How are the trade-offs to be managed?

In part the answer comes from an exploration of the concept of accountability. Legitimacy is not the same as accountability. As citizens we may recognise the good sense in involving multiple stakeholders in local governance, but be alarmed at the lack of information we have about what they are doing, the absence of decision trails or clear audit arrangements, the opaque nature of the transactions that seem to go on, and the absence of mechanisms to hold these 'governors' to account. Each agency involved in local networks has different systems of accountability, some through ministers, others through local politicians, shareholders, local committees or boards, and the audit and regulation regimes are different in every case. There is work to be done to create modern systems of accountability that can match the reality of local governance. Without transparency of decision-making, and routes for redress, the fears of democracy-watchers such as Stuart Weir seem justified (Weir and Beetham, 1999). We will return to the issue of accountability in Chapter 5.

Emerging roles for governance networks

The roles of government have always been wider than service provision; they have, for example, involved representation, regulation, defense, law-making and policing. In the twentieth century, governments have become expected to 'help protect and safeguard rights', and to ensure social justice (Held, 1997, p. 15), and they play a role in managing and controlling markets (Hutton, 1995, p. 25). There has always been a debate about which roles are best carried out at local level, but several writers suggest new roles in supporting and orchestrating self-government – roles that can only be carried out close to where people are. Held argues that new government roles should be subject to subsidiarity, and should 'involve people in the direct determination of the conditions of their own association' (1997, p. 235). Beck argues that the role of government should not be to substitute for local people's self-organisation, but to support it. The government would facilitate the negotiation of interests within and between groups capable of self-organisation, and would support the finding of a voice by interests that are not organised but could become so. Beck argues that what is emerging is a 'negotiation state' which 'arranges stages and conversations and directs the show' (Beck, 1997, p. 39).

Government agencies no longer assume that theirs are the only voices worth hearing: 'The goal is the constructions of realities in which the constructions of realities of other systems have some freedom of action' (Beck, 1997, quoting Willke, 1992, p. 41). The roles listed in Box 2.1 are no longer translatable into simple organisational tasks. Many of them cannot be carried out within organisational boundaries, and require organisations to reach across to other agencies, or to people within local communities. Many of them will not, necessarily, be carried out within a conventional institution at all. They require not bureaucratic procedures, but the building of working relationships.

Box 2.1 *Emerging roles for local governance*

- Regulation, to prevent abuse of power
- Market management
- Leading negotiations about desired local outcomes
- Creating spaces for civic dialogue
- Providing the resources to make things happen
- Commissioning and providing a range of services
- Positively helping disadvantaged or excluded groups to negotiate inclusion
- Enabling and supporting self-management
- Setting the framework for democratic participation.

Some of these roles seem particularly the reserve of local authorities, which have legal powers, for example, to regulate. Others, however, may involve the local police or the local health authority, voluntary or community groups. In practice, other government agencies feel uncomfortable with the difficult balancing acts required, and have only taken on governance roles sporadically. The role of local authorities in the UK will be strengthened by the new power to act to 'promote social, economic and environmental well-being' in the Local Government Act. Their democratic legitimacy also carries with it a role of community leadership, but community leadership can no longer mean substituting for the views and contributions of the rest of the community. It is a process of orchestration. Successful governance offers the possibility of functioning networks capable of identifying goals, mobilising consent, integrating intervention and reconfiguring resources, but this will not always happen. The alternatives of inertia, duplication, legitimisation crises, conflict or service failure will always be possible.

It is no longer clear which of the roles of local governance are those of politicians or those of managers. The trouble with this distinction reflects a concern about the limits of our categories, since these roles are not either political or managerial in any narrow sense of the word. I will go on to argue that the narrow 'party-political' interpretation of the democratic role is weakening electoral democracy, just as a narrow managerial understanding of organisations underestimates the contribution of leaders and staff within public agencies. In both cases we are impoverishing the range of possibilities that might be created. These could equally be seen as the roles of community leaders, as dutiful citizens, and of informal networks of individuals. The right question may be a different one: what must politicians and managers do to enable these roles to be fulfilled?

What do we mean by local?

In the UK, local government has been subject to a series of reorganisations, reflecting unease about the appropriate size and level for local government. The result is both very much larger authorities than exist in other European countries, and an almost random pattern of authorities across the county. The randomness in itself does not present new problems; indeed diversity may be useful. However, it reflects the reality that democratically elected structures at local level are at the same time too small for strategic decision-making and too large for local engagement. We therefore see the emergence, almost despite the political process, of two additional levels of governance – the regional and the neighbourhood. The boundaries of local governance need not be constrained by those of formal local government, and we might ask to what extent is any site of collective decision-making a site of governance?

The final concept to be explored here is therefore that of 'local'. The Urban Task Force recently defined locality spatially, in terms of the facilities that can be reached easily (see Figure 2.1). But physical proximity does not necessarily create a sense of identity or belonging; urban and rural neighbourhoods may be very different in this respect. What counts as a relatively short distance in an isolated rural area may carry us into alien territory in a city. 'Local' is also about identity, about belonging, connectedness, shared assumptions and shared history. Local identity can become a political construct; created in opposition to people 'not like us' – city versus country dwellers, long standing residents versus newcomers or outsiders. A third element is that of scale; formal organisational boundaries have often been created through a felt need to create economies of scale or to offer scope for strategic decision-making. Arguments for setting local authority boundaries have often been about making sure they represented a large enough cross-section of the population to escape narrow class boundaries. But economies of scale do not necessarily increase efficiency, and there are diseconomies of scale to be considered, particularly in relation to representative democracy. The lowest levels of UK local government are far larger than the lowest level of government in most other European countries. The final element of 'local' is that of power. The local can represent a site of power, and a site of

Figure 2.1 *Different definitions of a locality*

Possible facility – Catchment population	
City facilities	
Stadium	City
Cathedral	City
City hall	City
Theatre	City
District or town	
Sports centre	25 000–40 000
District centre	25 000–40 000
Library	12 000–30 000
Health centre	9 000–12 000
Neighbourhood	
Community offices	7 500
Community centre	7 000–15 000
Pub	5 000–7 000
Post office	5 000–10 000
Local hubs	
Primary school	2 500–4 000
Doctor	2 500–3 000
Corner shop	2 000–5 000

Radius labels: 150–250 m, 400–600 m, 2–6 km, 4–10 km radius

Source: Urban Task Force (1999).
Note: This chart is indicative and is based upon city-scale urban areas. Catchments will vary in specific areas.

opposition to power located at other levels, the region, or the nation state for example. Locality can offer a base from which shared interests can be negotiated with other geographical areas or negotiated with national or regional government. It is important to assemble enough power to be able to negotiate; if a locality is too small it may not be sufficiently powerful to be listened to by others. Figure 2.2 summarises the elements of 'local'.

Figrue 2.2   *The elements that made up 'local'*

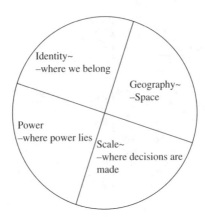

The emergence of the neighbourhood

Some local authorities have been committed to some form of locality governance for decades. More recently, many local authorities have created neighbourhood committees or area forums, and some have supported community self-government through community development trusts or community-led projects. In some cases these represent formal levels of government, in others they are informal. The emergence of the 'neighbourhood' has been accelerated by new government initiatives to tackle urban deprivation that require a neighbourhood or area focus: single regeneration budget (SRB) schemes, Surestart, New Deal for Communities, and so forth. The rural experience is different because of the continuing existence of parish councils.

There is an assumption that neighbourhoods provide a locality for belonging because they are smaller, but this often confuses local geographical space with identity. The influential Social Exclusion Unit, located in the Cabinet Office, has developed a National Strategy for Neighbourhood Renewal and has commended neighbourhood management, particularly in areas of poor public sector housing (Social Exclusion Unit, 2000). There is considerable confusion about the differences between neighbourhood management (which is about service delivery systems and deals with local people as customers), neighbourhood renewal partnership (which involves local people in co-production), and neighbourhood governance (which engages people as citizen-authorisers in governance at neighbourhood level). All are important, but solve different problems and may be appropriate in different circumstances (see Goss and Sharman, 2000).

The neighbourhood is emerging alongside the local town or borough as the focus for governance. This is made easier by the consensus around new roles for governance, since many of the roles we discussed above work best at local level. While this raises exciting possibilities, it transfers to the neighbourhood many of the dilemmas we have discussed above. Neighbourhoods will have to deal with questions of public value, of legitimacy and accountability. How will diverse local communities share goals? How do neighbourhoods relate to other levels of governance? Do they exist with the permission of the local council (so that they would be able to be shut down by the council) or are they developing a different sort of legitimacy of their own? Could they form an alternative to local councils? How representative do neighbourhood forums need to be? How can wider consent be built? How will tensions or inequalities between neighbourhoods be resolved? What happens when one neighbourhood is far poorer than the others (or far richer)? How can we balance strategic imperatives (road-building schemes, house building, mental hospital sites, and factory locations) with the needs and preferences of people in local areas? Should people be able to decide how much self-governance they want – or do they have a civic duty to take part locally?

While practice is still evolving, it is clear that in those areas where community engagement has been part of the local authority landscape for many years, lessons have been quietly learnt from the experiments of the 1970s and 1980s. The role of local authorities will be crucial. Will they support neighbourhood governance and help to resolve these dilemmas, or will they continue to try to control and direct activity at the neighbourhood level? In Boxes 2.2–2.4 I set out three examples of emerging experiments in governance at the neighbourhood level.

Box 2.2   *A fragmented urban community*

Roughly a quarter of a million people live closely together in a London borough which includes fine Georgian houses and cultural amenities, leafy suburbs and areas of intense deprivation. They have very little in common except their residence in one of the most diverse communities in Britain. Over 100 languages are spoken in the borough, and over 30 per cent of the population are from ethnic minorities.   *(continued)*

The council had its problems in the 1970s and 1980s and has
recovered slowly but still felt it had little track record of success, or
image of excellence on which to build a shared identity.

A new administration therefore has an ambitious plan to work
with the community to build a sense of identity based not on the
'borough' but on the five town centres that make sense to local people. Each one will have its own identity based on a vision created
by local people, with different street furniture and a different style –
each 'town' will have a forum with power to influence policy and
£100 000 to spend in capital. The borough intends to dissolve its
identity into each of the five component 'towns', to create a structure of governance that matches the diversity of the community,
and will then work in partnership with the localities as well as with
the private sector both as deliverers and users of services.

Box 2.3   *Making sense of neighbourhood in a large city*

In one metropolitan district council, the history of experiments with
locality governance goes back a long way. The council had several
high-profile experiments in decentralisation over 20 years, which has
given an opportunity to learn from mistakes as well as successes. In
1996, an SRB2 (the second stage of the single regeneration budget
programme) bid was awarded for 'empowering local communities'
and bringing 14.6 million into seven areas of the borough. From
1996, facilitators worked in these seven areas to prepare for local
committees, and following community consultation each area was
divided into constituencies of approximately 100 households. In 1997,
democratic elections were held for each patch with all local residents
aged 16 or over able to stand for election and vote. Young people have
the right to elect two youth representatives onto each local committee.
The committees began meeting in December 1997, elected officers
and developed constitutions and rules; they make decisions over the
projects funded by SRB and can influence all council services. Local
networks of council staff have begun to develop close working relationships with the committees, and partner organisations including the
health authority have identified lead managers to respond to each local
committee. The Health Authority, police, colleges, chamber of com-
merce, Training and Education Councils (TECs) and the voluntary
sector have all signed up to the idea.

Box 2.4   *A community development trust*

A large urban development corporation, its work complete, was due to close down and hand its assets back to the local authority. During its final years, the development corporation began to involve the local community in succession planning. It had established a community team, sponsored local projects through grants and wanted to invite ideas from the local community about how this work could continue. It asked for suggestions. The local vicar and the local head teacher convened a public meeting to discuss the possible successor body and to send back views from the community. At the first meeting, the idea of a community development trust (CDT) was suggested, and a steering group set up. The steering group sent in views to the development corporation, but there was a strong feeling that what was really needed was to make sure that the communities that had put up with all the havoc of regeneration should continue to get funding for local projects. The steering group produced a leaflet to explain the situation to local people, set up the trust as a company, and has been working steadily for several years with the development corporation and the council to gain recognition as a possible successor body to fund local projects. They had imaginative ideas about ways to use revenues to sustain local community activity.

At the time of writing, it is not clear how things will turn out. Changes in governance arrangements mean that the assets have been transferred to the local authority, together with the powers to support local communities. The council decided to reconsider the viability of the community development trust, and suggested setting up a new CDT with new boundaries which coincided better with the local authority strategic plan. It is not clear yet whether there is community support for the proposed CDT, and the community representatives who worked so hard feel that their work may be wasted. We shall see.

Centre, region, local and neighbourhood

Governance inevitably takes place at many levels, and can no longer be seen as simply something carried out by local authorities or government agencies. There are also examples of governance taking place at neighbourhood level outside state agencies – through community development trusts, tenant management organisations and community groups, for example.

One of the most interesting dilemmas for the future of governance is whether and when it is useful to formalise the concept of neighbourhood by creating structures of governance with spatial boundaries – or whether it actually help the process of governance to have overlapping and fuzzy boundaries, with different groups of people coming together for different reasons and with governance structures that can rise and fall depending on the energy levels of participant and the life-cycle of the neighbourhood.

Is government reaching down, or is civil society reaching up? Does neighbourhood governance mean carrying the structures of conventional government down to neighbourhood level (formal meetings, minutes, rules of probity, standing orders, committees)? This may stifle innovation underneath bureaucratic systems. Is there a possibility of working within the looser conventions of the voluntary and social sector (informal structures, practical systems, minimal paperwork)? – in which case problems encountered throughout the voluntary sector of creating effective agency, securing consent, protecting against fraud and so on will reoccur. Or should the rules of the private sector (fast experimentation with rapid death for failed experiments) be followed? – in which case conflicts between commercial and social interests may emerge, and rapid disinvestment could cause dislocation. Is it possible for something new to be negotiated which learns from, but does not replicate, all of these traditions?

While it is almost always the case that government agencies, or quangos, or temporary agencies such as development corporations play a role in the establishment and support of governance networks, there is no necessary reason why governance must always be led by, or even dominated by, government agencies. Stoker and Young (1993) explore the role of 'third force' organisations in leading local initiatives: community development trusts, community boards, community housing associations, consortia and SRB boards all play a role in governance. Local authorities have been given a statutory role in community leadership at the town, borough or county level, but we may wish to think of governance as something broader and more interesting – as something that happens whenever a collectivity of local people and agencies secures popular consent for a course of action.

Governance also takes place at the regional or sub-regional level – and not always through formal structures. Partnerships such as the Thames Gateway in East London, or in the major city regions of the midlands and the north are responsible for much of the thinking and planning around regeneration. The government offices in the regions and the regional development agencies clearly engage in governance; and service provision, market-making and regulation are all happening at a regional level. This has been formalised in Scotland, Wales and Northern Ireland, and while in England there are no directly elected regional structures, informal assemblies, forums and partnerships exist. Councillors and managers are increasingly working across local authority boundaries in a network of overlapping regional and sub-regional meetings.

Inevitably, local governance is not simply concerned with the local, but about the interface *between* levels of government – European, central, regional, local and neighbourhood. The role of the local governance is not simply to work at the local level, but to negotiate relationships with other levels of governance. Whilst it has been a particularly British fixation to separate out the roles of different levels of government, governance in the sense of a network of decision-making takes place not simply at each of these different levels, but is precisely the process of networking between, and in the spaces between, these different levels. When we think about structures, systems and capacities for effective local governance, it will be as important to think about the structures, systems and capabilities at the interface between levels as it is to think about these within individual organisations. Neighbourhood governance structures cannot function without support and legitimacy from local agencies, and local plans depend on regional resource distribution. Local governance cannot simply be analysed by watching public agencies at the local level. Power does not work that way.

3 Local Governance and Communities

Box 3.1 *How communities experience local governance...*

At 7.00 p.m. people began to file into the school hall. It smelt of polish and children. The chairs that had been set out in rows were child-sized, and the adults who squeezed into them experienced a sense of being lower than usual, towered over by the platform at the front of the room. A red cloth with the council's coat of arms covered the platform, water and glasses were laid out for the speakers.

People kept coming in, women with prams and toddlers, an old man with a stick, a noisy group of women pensioners, families, the occasional lone man. The audience swelled to over a hundred, with some standing at the back. The noise of the room rose as chairs scraped, neighbours exchanged pleasantries and sharp comments about the council. One of the pensioners was being nudged to say something about the warden scheme they all lived in. A young woman sat between two fidgeting children, checking through her paperwork. The meeting was due to begin at 7.30. It was a close summer evening, the room was sticky and at 7.45 eyes began to flick to the heavy school clock. At 7.55 a plump young man, perspiring fiercely, strode towards the platform, followed by two managers in grey suits. The young man sat, and the older of the two managers, with an Armani insignia on his shirt, passed him a sheaf of papers. He looked through the papers for a few moments, breathing heavily. The room quieted. Then he stood again.

'Thank-you for coming to this the first of ten public consultation meetings about the Council's strategy.' He spoke for about fifteen minutes, about Modernisation, strategy, the need for partnership, the council's commitment to consultation and the need to regenerate the area. There was much more, but it is hard to remember. 'And now the Director of Corporate Services will give you a presentation about

(continued)

---

the council's community plan;' the younger of the two managers stood up. He switched on the overhead projector. Nothing happened. He leant over and fiddled with it for a few seconds, and then turned to the switch on the floor and an indistinct light was cast on the grey wall behind. The first slide was colourful, but crowded with words and dissolved into illegibility two rows back. The man's voice was level, not always audible... 'a series of fundamental Best Value reviews... new structure for the council's management team... A new executive team and a series of scrutiny committees... a pilot for New Deal for Communities... A Health Action Zone.' Slide followed slide for about 25 minutes. The clock slowly ticked round to 9.00; an hour of listening and still no one from the community had spoken.

The light behind the last diagram was switched off. The chair announced that after a coffee break there would be workshop groups to discuss the council's five key priorities and give feedback. But people were slipping away. When the workshop groups reassembled there were many empty chairs. Among those who had left were the young people, and everyone from the black and ethnic minority communities.

In the final report-back session, some groups had tried to prioritise the five key priorities as asked, but many talked about parking, repairs, pram sheds and crime on the estate. The frustration of the audience was breaking through. The few people who had come as practiced complainers had a readier audience now. 'What's the point of having a high-faluting vision when you can't even get the bleeding windows fixed. The windows in Mandela Court have been broken for a month now.' 'And the street lights', another voice chimed in, 'I've reported the light out at the bottom of James St. and the girl just said it was private now and I had to report it somewhere else. Useless.'

The older manager stood to explain that the meeting was to discuss overall strategy for the whole borough, not just details, and that his department was not responsible for streetlights. 'Bloody typical', said a loud voice, 'You won't actually do anything'. A local youth worker stood up and made a prepared speech about the funding cuts to the local youth project, 'How can we regenerate the area when every time local kids get involved in anything the funding is cut off?'

(continued)

The councillor, sensing the mood, tried to explain that the youth project was funded by a special grant which was time-limited and had been replaced by a new scheme with different criteria. He made an impassioned speech about the constraints facing the council, the need for the community to pull together, the commitment he shared to make the area a better place. There were new opportunities now, new sources of funds, 'But I need your support and commitment'. As the meeting ended, the local participants drifted off onto the estate, or to the pub. 'Why do I bother?', muttered the frustrated parent as she stuffed away her papers, 'Why did I think this would be any different from the last ten times?'

'Why do I bother?' mumbled the councillor, as he struggled into his car at the end of another 18-hour day.

Local governance is not simply something that happens between powerful agencies. The most important relationship in governance is not between levels of government, but between government and people, and this relationship is being redefined in practice and renegotiated on both sides. Ministers are attempting to redefine the role of government – to re-make the contract it has with the people. Squeezed by increasing costs of welfare provision on one hand, and by a belief that there is a ceiling to the tax bill 'middle England' is prepared to meet – national politicians no longer feel able to provide support from cradle to grave. Government agencies provide fewer services directly, and the public is called upon to share responsibility for social goals. The Blair government promises, from their side, greater accountability to the public, more effective performance and value for money and a greater capacity to listen to and respond to public concerns. 'Modernising government is a vital part of our programme of renewal for Britain' (Blair, 1999).

A government announcement of a new relationship between government and people cannot be accepted on its own terms. Contracts cannot be renegotiated unilaterally. Nor can we always assume that government announcements will translate into practice, not least because the announcements are made by ministers who are a long way away from daily contact with ordinary people. The relationship between government and people is experienced, every day, between the social security clerk and the claimant, between the council housing manager and the tenant, between the traffic control officer and the residents' group, between the school inspector and the parent governors. These day-to-day encounters make up the real relationship between state and citizen, but even here there is evidence that the renegotiation is underway.

Ordinary managers and professionals are learning more about the views of service users, beginning to engage ordinary people in making difficult choices, and working alongside communities on a day-to-day basis. Government guidance and legislation will require local authorities to consult their consumers, the Best Value regime includes measures of customer satisfaction, and community planning formalises public consultation. Local councils are beginning to research customer needs as carefully as their private sector competitors, using focus groups, mystery visitors and mystery shoppers to learn about the customer experience, and to train staff in customer care. Public agencies can tailor services to meet different needs, and offer direct payments which allow customers to design their own services. League tables enable local voters to compare their local area to neighbouring areas. Many local authorities also report publicly on achievement of local goals, and select committees and scrutiny committees allow citizens to give evidence or to take part in service reviews.

In some localities the dialogue with the community has been underway for many years. Local authorities, health authorities, police authorities and community groups are learning fast about effective public consultation, and the volume of consultation is increasing rapidly. Traditional methods such as consultation documents or public meetings still dominate, but their use is declining and they are being replaced by new techniques such as interactive web sites and visioning events. The use of surveys and community panels is spreading, as is the increasing use of focus groups, citizen juries, workshops and consensus conferences (see, for example, Stewart, 1995, 1996, 1997; Stoker, 1997; Goss, 1999; Lowndes *et al.*, 1998). Of course there are old-fashioned exceptions, and practice is patchy even in the best localities. But it is national agencies that lag behind, the lead on interaction with the public as citizens has been taken at local level. Figure 3.1 shows the various forms of participation used by authorities.

Many local authorities have established area forums or committees, sometimes with access to a specific 'pot' of capital funding, sometimes able to commission local services or to submit a plan for the locality. Some sort of community consultation or engagement at the neighbourhood level exists in almost every local authority in the country, and is often likely to involve the local health authority, police authority and community groups (see Figure 3.1).

But there is a lot that goes wrong. There is often too much jargon; documents are circulated to community groups only in a final version, with a

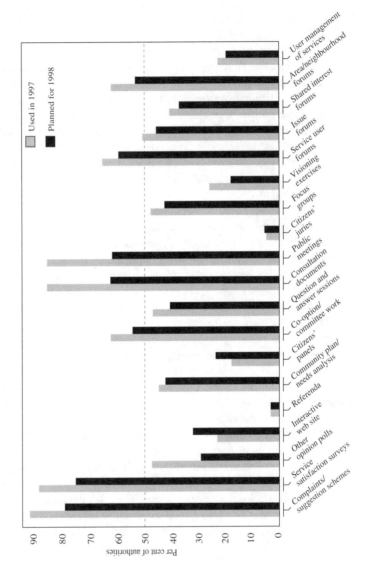

Figure 3.1 *Forms of participation*

Source: Lowndes *et al.* (1998).

tight deadline for comments; public meetings still have much the same format, except now there may be workshop discussions and flipcharts; meetings can be difficult and adversarial, dominated by 'the usual suspects', unrepresentative, vague or pointless. Some of the problems encountered are simply the teething problems to be expected with any new processes, and mistakes may be made by inexperienced council staff or community members that need not be repeated. There is a lot of reinventing the wheel – few managers or community activists read the good-practice guides about consultation that continue to pile up, most learn from their own experience. Over time, therefore, people learn how to structure meetings to make them interesting, how to avoid bad chairing, and how to attract people to come from different sections of the community. Surveys are redesigned to make them more useful, and panels are used more appropriately. There are now many examples of successful, enjoyable consultation.

Fascinatingly, when consultation problems are explored with groups of public managers, one of the responses is often that expectations are too high or that the public doesn't really want to be involved. And yet the research evidence is diametrically opposed to this; a 1999 survey in Islington showed that 30 per cent of those interviewed wanted to be more involved in the work of the council! In workshop after workshop with local people, participants express willingness to come back and continue the work they have begun and to take part in future events. They are able to define the characteristics of 'good consultation' – it must be interesting, relevant and useful. Where it is, there is no problem with sustaining a long-term dialogue, and, despite their bad experiences, members of the public are generally very understanding of the problems faced by public agencies and tolerant of problems they experience in responding.

The more interesting problems are occurring on the inside of local agencies. Organisations that are finding it easy to set up successful consultation are finding it hard to follow through because of confusion about what the consultation is *for*, a confusion about who the consultation is *with*, and about the sort of *relationship* that is being created.

What is consultation for?

There have been many attempts to create an analytical framework for exploring the different dimensions of consultation, beginning with Arnstein's ladder of participation (Arnstein, 1971). They all help to distinguish between situations when public agencies are simply trying to give or

Table 3.1   *Current range of methods for engagement*

Giving information	*Consultation/ listening*	*Exploring/ innovating/ visioning*	*Judging/ deciding together*	*Delegating/ supporting/ decision-making*
Sign-posting	Surveys	Consultative workshops	Deliberative polls	Neighbourhood committees
Leaflets/ newsletters/ reports	Focus groups Priority search	Visioning workshops	Citizen's juries	Town/estate plans
Community profiles	Interactive community profiles	Simulations, open-space events	Negotiation workshops	Tenant management organisations
Feedback on surveys and consultation	Public meetings Forums		Community issue groups	
Annual performanace reports			Community workshops	Community development, trust
Support/advice	Panels	Planning for real community discovery	Consensus conferences	Partnerships/ contracts with communities
Video/internet communication	Video boxes	Use of theatre, arts/media		Referendums/ tele-voting

Source: Goss (1999).

get information to help them to work more effectively, and situations when power is being shared or given away. I have produced a variation that attempts to link the purpose of consultation to the techniques that are used (Goss, 1999, p. 28), and this is shown in Table 3.1.

The reality is, however, that managers and staff are often unclear about why people are being consulted, and the role members of the public are expected to play. Are member of the public being asked to help define the problem, or to suggest solutions? Are they simply being told things, or are their opinions valued? Are they simply invited to express preferences, or will their decision be final? Are people being consulted as representatives, or simply as themselves? Processes are put in place in response to government initiatives or local instructions, without resolving these issues.

The public is asked to rank or choose between strategic priorities that are vague – 'improving the environment' or 'promoting the economy', for example. They are asked to express a view about decisions about which they have insufficient background knowledge. Consultation is often designed around the priorities of powerful agencies instead of the preoccupations of local people, and agencies are not always clear in their own minds about the legitimacy of the consultation process and about the value they will place on public views compared to expert professional knowledge or political choices. Expensive citizen's juries can be ignored if they don't reach a conclusion that fits with councillor or officer assumptions. Hospital closures go ahead against opposition when there is no financial alternative.

Local authorities use public meetings and consultation exercises to explain about new service structures, or new neighbourhood forums. Consultation offers decision support, giving information about public priorities and public opinion. Public agencies need feedback on service quality and customer satisfaction, and service provision. Local people can help with service design, testing new 'products' and giving advice on how services might be used. In regeneration projects, consultation can play a role in creating a community and giving local people some control over their own affairs. These different purposes are often jumbled up, although they are not always compatible. It is not always clear to the public what the consulting organisation wants out of the consultation, nor what they intend to do afterwards.

Who is consultation with?

In the 1980s, public agencies were exhorted to treat the public primarily as customers, but this demonstrated a spectacular failure within government to think seriously about the real relationships between the public and government.

'Customer' implies a range of options (Le Grand, 1990) which do not always exist within the public sector. Some public services are provided universally, in circumstances where there are no alternative providers (Goss, 1989). Some are highly subsidised, and provided to vulnerable groups who cannot afford private sector alternatives. The customer of public services is therefore often one who has little choice, and who lacks the capacity to 'exit'. Not all public services are consumed individually. Many are provided for the benefit of the community collectively and may be of only marginal benefit to us as individuals (environmental health services, trading standards, parks, street cleaning and so on), and are experienced by the public as 'remote beneficiaries' rather than as an individual customers.

Local government also plays a role in regulating and controlling the activities of individuals. Mark Moore argues that there is a distinction between customer as beneficiary and customer as obligatee. He says about the word

obligatee, 'I almost like its ugliness – it makes the point that we foist responsibility onto people' (1999, p. 52). Obligatees are those who are dealt with
by the police forces, prisons, environmental protection agencies or tax-
collecting agencies; they are people against whom regulation or enforcement
action is taken. He suggests the need for relationships of civil reciprocity that strengthen the sense of 'obligation' and prevent hostility to enforcement action.

Members of the public are not customers of public services. All citizens
in a democracy are 'owners' and 'authorisers' of public interventions – as
voters, but also as taxpayers, willing to pay for those purposes we collectively decide (Moore, 1999). The role of an elector is seen as passive, but the
public can also be 'governors' – people who take part in governance activity
through elected office. The scope for acting as governors is widening – governors include councillors, but they also include those who participate in
local boards or community groups, tenants associations in decision-making
forums, in consultation events. The role is becoming more active, and citizens can help to explore and understand social problems, design policy
responses to public problems, choose between alternatives, evaluate success.

A strong voice for citizens as authorisers is essential if action is to be
taken that might challenge the interests of some sections of the community
in the interests of the whole. Acting as governors, rather than as selfish
consumers, citizens can sanction strong government action and radical
intervention, they can support redistribution of income or lifechances, they
can back high public expenditure on public transport, health or education,
and they can empower governments to curtail exploitation or abuse, placing obligations on themselves and others to conform.

Citizens are also capable of being 'activist/providers' – able to provide
services for themselves and for their local communities through voluntary
work, good neighbourliness or running community businesses. Voluntary
sector activity provides a wide range of the services on which local communities depend – from youth clubs, leisure centres and sports clubs, to meals
on wheels and 'lets' schemes. Activity can be very formal through community businesses, or informal through neighbours that pop in to look after
elderly neighbours, or baby-sitting circles. Citizens produce public value
through self-help, sharing knowledge with others and supporting others.
Public value is added through the extent to which citizens reinforce social
norms and rules within civil society, by helping the police with their
enquiries, or through controlling kids on the estate. Without the active consent and participation of citizens, public agencies cannot achieve social
goals. The active engagement of parents is important in improving a child's

Table 3.2 *Roles as citizens*

Consumers	Governors	Activist/producers
Consumers either of public services or of services provided by activist/producers	Citizens as owner-authorisers	Citizens producing public value themselves
Client/beneficiary	Voter	Providers of services
Obligatee	Taxpayer	Co-producers
Remote beneficiary	Community member	Self-helpers
		Obliging others to act

Source: From Moore (1999).

chances of learning; and strenuous efforts of individuals are needed to reduce smoking, drinking and drug abuse. The term co-production has been coined to express the process by which public value is produced through partnership between public agencies and local people. Co-production can be used to describe all the instances where public and private resources combine with the resources of local communities to intervene actively to improve matters.

Where citizens are consumers, they may consume not simply public and private sector services, but also services provided by other 'citizen activists' such as local voluntary organisations, community groups and so forth. Accountability to citizens therefore always embraces the concept that people within civil society could also see themselves to a greater or lesser extent as accountable to *each other* through a range of roles as listed in Table 3.2. Relationships of governance increasingly have to reflect and to recognise these roles, and to create appropriate spaces within which these roles can be exercised.

Throughout this section I have used the term citizen to describe a member of the public as if it is a comprehensive term. But of course it isn't. The concept of rights and responsibilities conveyed by citizenship excludes immigrants and refugees within our communities, and has an impact on how they see themselves and are seen by others as part of civil society. I will explore this further in the section on exclusion below.

Engaging with government

Seen from the standpoint of civil society, the process of engaging with government immediately looks different. The reasons change. Public agencies consult local people in part because they have to, they are measured on the results, they need feedback. Why does the community respond?

Why do people come to consultation meetings? It is clear that they do not simply come as customers, and the reasons people have for engaging with governance are as diverse as the people themselves. In consultation workshops where we have asked the question, people have said they came because they were interested in the subject, because they wanted information about what went on in their area, because they were passionate about a particular issue such as protecting the local school, or because their family had suffered because of poor provision and they wanted to make sure 'it didn't happen to anyone else'. All these different reasons give rise to fruitful exchanges but they often conflict with the reasons for which local agencies began the process.

As soon as one asks the question, it is clear that there is no uniform community involved in dialogue. There is no binary process of agency talking to community. The old class-identities that held communities together and apart are decaying, and there are few of the old tight-knit working-class communities left. A recent consultation process explored with people in Southwark their sense of community. Older people, for example, are often struggling with the loss of a sense of community they remember from their youth – 'Bermondsey was a lovely community thirty years ago ... Where I am now I don't even know my next door neighbours' (Consultation in Consort and Friary wards, OPM, 1999).

For younger people, the concept of community is complex, something they are struggling with. 'Community is people living in the same area', said a white youth, but there was a debate about whether the sense of place was about Peckham, the estate, the Old Kent Road or London. 'It's shared common interest', said someone from a group of owner-occupiers. For the black youths, 'blackness' formed a key basis for their identity. Other people formulated ideas of community based on interest around leisure activities, football clubs and religion. The discussion groups moved on to think about interactions between people: 'Community is knowing people', said someone from the group of white youths. 'A group of people taking an interest in where they live and the upkeep of their community, looking after one another, trying to unite together. If there is a problem, talking about it. Just a warm feeling really.' 'The people round this table are for the moment a community because we are talking to each other which we don't usually do.' All the participants recognised and were ready to talk about the multicultural nature of their local community. 'It's about accepting, nurturing and appreciating cultural differences, rather than trying to become a melting pot.'

Asked what made a community good, people mentioned facilities, but the bottom line was 'positive growth and the interaction of the people within it'. 'People talking to each other rather than just walking past'; 'A good community is an attitude'; A Michael Jackson song was mentioned more than once; 'You start with the man in the mirror,' said one black youth (OPM, 1999). This sort of conversation could be echoed across the country. The complex nature of modern communities and the problems of how you live in them are not just matters for academic research, the discussion is taking place on the streets.

Identities are multiple and overlapping. Our sense of belonging is no longer defined simply through class or race or gender, but through all of these things alongside geography, interests, lifestyles, shared experiences and solidarity. As individuals we struggle to make sense of ourselves as a person we are comfortable with, and with whom the world can deal. Sometimes there are real tensions involved in trying to accomplish this since we are often construed or labelled by the outside world in ways that make little sense from the inside. We may show different faces in different circumstances, and we may experience dissonance between the ways we are treated in different roles. 'Identity marks the conjuncture of our past with the social, cultural and economic relations we live within' (Rutherford, 1990, p. 19). Public agencies are learning to recognise and value difference, and to resist the temptation to paste identities onto people from the outside. Traditional methods of consultation attempt to crush difference and create a single answer – a majority, in a survey or a public meeting – whereas it is often more interesting to listen to different and distinct voices, to understand and recognise their unique circumstances.

Youth councils are beginning to flourish across the country, offering opportunities for young people to shape their own views and hold a dialogue with councils on their own terms. For example, Birmingham's Youth Meetings involved over 500 people and were designed with young people in mind, including graffiti walls and response sheets. A recent consultation with people with disabilities in a London borough was designed and led by people who themselves had disabilities and who designed a process they called conversations, which enabled the people consulted to decide the issues they wanted to talk about as well as responding to the interviewers' questions. The process revealed subtle but all-important failures in local provision to meet the needs of individuals. One example was the meals-on-wheels service, as experienced by Asian women with severe disabilities:

And another thing, the meals on wheels they just say it is ... Asian food, but each culture, the way they make it is different. Probably a Punjabi lady cooked it and it is different ... if it is a Gujerati person they should provide Gujerati food and if it is a Punjabi person, they should provide Punjabi food ... I didn't eat the food. (from an interview with Asian women with disabilities, as part of a best-value review)

Local people are able to identify the limitations that have been created by the roles into which they have been constructed in the past, and to see the possibility of breaking through them; 'We are conditioned not to look after ourselves' (OPM, 1998). They are able to make sensible suggestions about how new roles might be developed, and what safeguards are needed.

The sorts of responses people make to consultation depend, in part, on the roles people have been 'constructed into' and the identities they have been given. If local people are constructed by the processes of engagement as customers, they will respond by identifying needs and wants, and by handing responsibility back to the 'provider'. But as co-producers, people will want to negotiate terms for projects, will want to take part in deciding what is needed and how it is to be supported and funded, and can add their own resources if there is sufficient reciprocity to make this seem worthwhile. And as governor/authorisers local people can begin to balance competing objectives, and to mobilise the consent that will enable a decisive intervention to take place. Local people invited to take part in processes of deliberation about the future of an area learn to stop simply fighting their corner, and look for ways to balance different needs, to negotiate with others, to build consent for compromise. Public managers and politicians are often surprised by the sophistication with which complex judgments can be made by groups of ordinary people. The surprise is as important as the sophistication.

The nature of the relationship

Often people are unclear about what sorts of relationships are being created. There is an assumption within local authorities, health authorities and police authorities that managers and politicians go out to consult the community and then come back and 'do' governance. But of course that misses the point. It is the total set of relationships between public agencies and the public *in action* that makes up governance.

The questions 'what is consultation for?', 'what should it be about', are not simply questions for public agencies, they are important subjects for consultation. The process of consultation has often been one-way, designed by the local authority or a partnership of local agencies who set out the process in advance, specify the length of the meetings, the scope of the remit, the agenda. And yet, given what we all know through personal experience about relationships, this is a strange way to go about things. In a relationship, potential friends or partners find out about each other, make tentative moves, wait for a response, think about it, and respond in turn. They are negotiated, evolutionary, processes of conversation. And in any conversation, while one participant may be so excited about their new plans that they want to talk first and may enjoy being asked questions for quite a while, eventually they also find out what their partner wants to talk about. In most conversations each person brings a very different set of interests and subjects and each attempt to propose a subject will be met with questioning, listening, active engagement or an attempt to change the subject. It is the process of *being heard*, of having an equality of power over what it is considered important to talk about, that makes the relationship work. Of course, if one person has a crisis there will be enough trust to enable their problems to dominate the conversation for many days. But eventually, things will balance.

By contrast, the meeting described in the opening section of this chapter offered no scope for conversation; one side did all the talking and was unwilling to hear the issues the other side found important. This reflects a constant public experience in encountering public institutions. The exchange is seldom two-way. And it is interesting to hear from local people how recurrent is the frustration of not being heard, not being answered, not being able to get through. Members of the public who find their letters are not answered, that their calls only reach voicemail systems, experience the absence of any relationship. 'I listen to Greensleeves so many times and then I become abusive' (OPM, 1999, p. 12). They feel angry, unvalued, slighted. There is none of the sense of interdependence, of mutual regard or of reciprocity necessary to make a relationship work. 'Unless they can keep an appointment why should we trust them to be able to do anything else if they can't even do anything as simple as that' (OPM, 1999, p. 24).

The conversations we are describing are not simply between two partners; there are many voices each of which is trying to be heard, they do not all agree, they do not all have the same way of seeing things. It is more like a noisy dinner party than a tête-à-tête! We do not know yet how to have these sorts of public relationships.

And, of course, things are more complicated because organisations cannot have relationships; only people can. And therefore crucial to the relationship between public agencies and the public is a sense of who are the people who stand for the agency, and what role they play in encounters with the public. Here again, experience varies widely. Some people feel able to participate as themselves, clear about what they bring and contribute, able to build relationships with others, to promise action, to respond directly to problems. Others feel locked into a representative role, or as cogs in a machine unable to respond without reporting back to committees or line managers. This failure to respond prevents relationships from forming – because the reciprocity that is essential to build trust is missing. It is at if, at the end of a successful first date, you look expectantly at your new friend and they say, 'don't know if I can see you again. I'll have to ask my mum'. The power that individuals have to make promises and keep them is as important on the inside of organisations as it is on the outside.

If we simply watch carefully the encounters between staff within public agencies and the public, they can tell us a lot about the nature of the relationship. I watched one such encounter recently. An angry consumer arrived in the local council office and began to make a scene, shouting at the junior officer behind the desk. The officer was polite, and explained that he could not solve the problem but he would take a note and pass it on to the right office. The customer continued to shout – this is the third office he has visited, and each time he has been passed on to someone else. He appealed to other members of the public for support. The member of staff eventually stood up and went into the back room, saying he was going to get his manager. The irate customer swore loudly about the uselessness of the council and stormed out. When the manager returned, he was gone. This encounter is a ritual one, almost scripted – everyone knows what is going to happen next. The relationship is a dysfunctional one, in which every encounter reinforces the assumptions that are already carried about the failures of the other side – and no one acts to break through or to change things. There is none of the sense of shared exploration that would be present if the relationship worked.

Public meetings are another pattern, a predictable form of interaction. They are often called at moments of crisis, and there are roles to be played – the outraged community representative, the saddened dedicated professional, the 'it's not my fault it's government policy' speech by the senior managers, the sympathetic 'but we've all got to be realistic about what is possible' closing remarks by the politician. These are ritual events that are not intended to change anything, but are simply to try and explain official action and act as lighting rods for community anger.

The interesting question is – how could these encounters be different? What could break through these patterns of interaction? Where creative and imaginative staff have changed these relationships, what have they done? How can the prejudices and assumptions that members of the public carry be challenged or changed?

Response fatigue

Seen from the standpoint of public agencies, it looks as if there is very rapid change. Investment in consultation is soaring, and public managers are beginning to look outwards from within their organisational structures. However, they do so with many of their structures, systems and frames of reference intact. The managers and staff who find out about consumer views learn about the failures of their services, and to put right service failure requires new ways of doing things. And yet things are done the way they are because of shoestring budgets, careful compromises, old technology and difficulties in communication. These problems have a long history. The current way of doing things makes sense from the inside of the organisation. The managers who meet the public on a day-to-day basis may not have the authority to put things right. Long hierarchical chains, lengthy decision-making cycles, the competing pressures of operational problems and competing claims for scarce resources all mean that user views may be heard, but not acted upon.

There is often a 'new problem – new structure' mindset that underpins the design of solutions to public sector problems. Public sector organisations are structured in ways that ensure that new problems are dealt with incrementally, leaving the previous deployment of resources and people relatively intact, and creating something new – a unit, a post, a committee, a project. Consultation often takes place in specially arranged meetings, newly-created forums, often using dedicated resources and staff. These are 'added on' with no necessary connectivity with day-to-day practice. The only way that learning from consultation can be translated into the organisation is by being written up into a report, which is then sent to councillors or managers for consideration. But precisely because what may be heard is outside the usual way of doing things, the organisational status quo remains intact and able to marshal reasons as to why change would be unnecessary or undesirable. The few champions of public views are on the outside, or are the junior managers who organised the meetings and wrote the report.

Because the authority or the commitment to use resources differently does not always accompany consultation, solutions can only be found with those resources that exist at the margins. Decision-making is not wired-up

to deliver a rapid response, and there are few places within public organisations for regular conversations about product and service innovation to
take place.

The alternative to designing ever more elaborate mechanisms for consultation is to open up mainstream organisational arrangements to constant
feedback and response. When operational managers work directly with
service users, change is more likely since decision-makers learn to see
things differently. Rather than send officials 'out' – it would be possible to
bring the public 'in'. A different sort of interaction, one which does not
involve local people offloading their problems onto the local agency and
then demanding action, or does not involve a public agency in marshalling
evidence to defend their record – but which involves instead some shared
or negotiated process of planning action – would require very different
behaviours by all concerned.

The romance of civil society

There is a vogue now to bring people from outside government into decision-making. Community planning conferences, regeneration partnerships,
task forces, project groups, the boards of regional development agencies and
community trusts all now involve people who are neither politicians nor public sector managers. There is a romanticism about civil society which implies
that somehow if people are simply from the outside they can 'represent'
community needs and aspirations in an unproblematic way. Business-men
and women and community entrepreneurs are seen to bring new skills and
talents missing from traditional local politics and town-hall bureaucracies.

It is true that outsider eyes are useful in identifying problems and solutions that are invisible to the institutionalised. Their genuine horror at
long-established procedures can shock old hands into thinking again. They
bring new cultures, new assumptions and new ways of thinking. But the
processes of governance are difficult, and there is nothing inherent in the
experience of businesspeople or community representatives that enables
them to carry it out. Many businessmen and women and community representatives flounder in the conflicts between different cultures, find it
impossible to make sense of the job that is asked of them, and get lost
within the complex systems and procedures they are asked to operate.
They have not learnt the skills of 'wading through treacle', of finding
pathways through bureaucracy to make things happen, of building strategic
alliances, of fixing things in the white noise of complexity.

The new spaces for governance that involve community representatives and business people can no longer be governed by the 'rules' of individual member agencies, since they explicitly cross barriers between agencies. There is nothing for it but to negotiate out the tensions between different agency needs, between the different cultures of the private, public and voluntary sectors. These tensions are often experienced as personal, as individuals feel excluded or marginalised, and they can make it almost impossible for work to continue. Tenant representatives put onto boards can find themselves marginalised or ignored; they neither understand the jargon nor the unspoken rules.

There can also be problems of bad behaviour – since there are no institutional rules to contain it. Tenant or community representatives are often aggressive, used to the experience of needing to shout to be heard. There are examples of community managers who fail to treat staff properly, tenant-board bullies, and area committee grandees who accumulate power and exclude others. These problems are not unknown within traditional political and managerial structures but, precisely because of this, rules have emerged.

Community representatives have to negotiate their own legitimacy, come to terms with the roles they play and the extent to which they are authorised to act for others. They inevitably have to explore their own accountabilities and recognise the need to build support for actions they plan. Other local citizens are as conscious as local agencies about the unrepresentative nature of a community planning conference or a focus group. A discussion group of a few dozen people does not substitute for accountable decision-makers. When participants on a citizens' jury, for example, were asked whether or not their decision should stand, they said no, it should be referred to councillors since they recognised the limited legitimacy they carried. But they did want their deliberations to be taken seriously, fully aware of the weight that careful judgement made with full information *ought* to carry (Clarke, 1999). Citizens will not tolerate the handing over of decisions about their lives to a bunch of randomly chosen focus groups. Issues of transparency and accountability are as important within community engagement as they are within conventional governance.

Public sector agencies have been very conscious of their own responsibilities for fairness, equity and financial probity. They are understandably reluctant to hand over control to local groups who may not be competent, or fair. But the arguments have been used to prevent any serious transfer of power, rather than to rethink the ways in which public engagement could incorporate issues of transparency, legitimacy and accountability. Public managers have often also questioned the value of too much consultation, and tried to ensure that resources are not wasted that are needed to provide basic services. The question of waste and duplication is as important for the public as it is for agencies. In my experience no member of the public values 'volume of consultation' as a good thing. Measures of consultation that rely on numbers of meetings or numbers of people attending entirely miss the point. Citizens wish to spend the minimum effort needed to be heard and to be confident that action will follow. 'You managers', said one group of people with physical disabilities in a consultation workshop, 'think the best consultation is when you consult everyone and don't have to change anything. We think the best sort of consultation would be if you talked to one of us and changed everything'.

1960–2000: from community development to social capital

Experiments in community participation are not new; considerable invest-ment in consultation, area committees and neighbourhood councils took place in the 1960s, 1970s and 1980s. The Urban Programme and the Com-munity Development Programme created community-based projects that had considerable local impact for a while. The underpinning theories of a cycle of deprivation led to the conclusion that professional community workers could begin to develop communities, working to build skills, self-confidence and capacity through community-led projects, cooperatives, community centres, youth projects and so on. The projects succeeded in attracting considerable attention at the time, but began to drift, and as eval-uation studies drew from an increasingly strident Marxist frame of refer-ence they were drawn into more central government control and their community focus began to dissolve.

An exploration of the history of relationships between communities and local agencies since the war might help to avoid remaking old mistakes (see Goss, 1989). Councils in the 1960s and 1970s were struggling to improve conditions of life for impoverished communities, but at the same time were dominated by empire-building politicians and by technocratic professionals and could not hear and would not credit what was said to them. The Com-munity Development Programmes and other experiments did establish fas-cinating projects that pointed to the potential of community self-government, but they coexisted with housing clearance and redevelopment that ripped the heart out of old working-class communities, and with economic changes that stamped out the manufacturing base on which they depended. They could not begin to compete. The frustration of local people often bubbled over into community action of varying degrees of creativity – but often the young leftists attempting to stir local people to action had their own agendas no less elitist and excluding than those of the councils they were 'in and against'. The experiments in local management and community-led projects in the 1970s were at the margins. Little power was, in reality, devolved, as new projects were bolted on to the edges of unchanged bureaucracies. Community-led projects were shut down and disbanded when short-term funding ran out. Few people inside the institutions of government could hear what communities were saying, and there was little government will at local or national level to respond.

Community development lost momentum in the 1980s and 1990s, but experiments continued, and authorities such as Walsall, Basildon, Tower Hamlets and Lambeth made attempts to devolve power, learnt from mistakes, and quietly continued to put these lessons into practice. Central government attention switched to City Challenge and a limited number of community-based boards including businesspeople as well as community representatives. Neighbourhood forums and committees became less fashionable, and some devolution attempts were reversed, but the process of engaging communities continued at local level in many places.

By the late 1990s, however, interest in community engagement revived. The answer to Mrs Thatcher's claim that 'there is no such thing as society' has been the rediscovery of social capital. Not only does society exist, but it can also be demonstrated to add economic value. Putnam defines it as the 'features of social organisation, such as trust, norms and networks that can improve the efficiency of society by facilitating coordinated action' (Putnam, 1993). Social capital is derived from human relationships, communication and networks, and adds value – 'like other forms of capital, social capital is productive' (Coleman, 1990). These ideas are not new. Social capital has become popular as an organising idea precisely because it can be claimed by traditional and Keynsian economists, by Durkheimians, Weberians, Marxists and post-Marxists. However, there are dangers of tautology lurking is such a universally useful idea. Portes argues there is a danger of 'explaining major social outcomes by relabelling them with a novel term and then employing the same term to formulate sweeping policy prescriptions' (Portes, 1998, p. 21).

Social relationships inevitably have negative as well as positive consequences. For example, strong family or kinship networks may provide powerful support, access to work and so on, but as everyone who has moved to the big city to escape their family knows, it can also involve heavy obligations and limit possibilities. Social capital may be particularly

strong within an ethnic group that experiences discrimination and prejudice, forcing the community together and closing off other avenues of
social advancement. Communities which are shut out of conventional
career opportunities and support systems do fall back on themselves and
can create powerful networks of mutual obligation. Portes points out that
this can often, however, be at the cost of vulnerability to freeloading from
within the community and an inability to break out of community boundaries. Deprived or isolated communities may develop gang or Mafia networks of protection and identification. Social agencies trying to investigate
harassment or crime on deprived estates often come up against a wall of
silence because of community conventions against 'grassing to the authorities'. This offers some protection, but condemns people to victimisation
by thugs and bullies inside the community.

Several authors suggest that the most important form of social capital
operates beyond immediate family and kin and involves a sense of reciprocity that extends to a wider social group, or to civil society as a whole.
It is this sense of social belonging that leads to 'civility' and that means we
pay debts on time, give money to charity and obey traffic rules (Portes,
1998, p. 7). There is no immediate 'return' – the beneficiaries of the capital
are other members of the community, who can extend loans without fear of
non-payment, benefit from charity or send their kids to play in the street
without concern. Halpern suggests that social trust between strangers, is
the most important dimension of social capital, the 'invisible default action
in our everyday life, ... a silent contract, an unspoken knowledge of "how
to go on" ' (Halpern, 1998, p. 35). But this sense of belonging to society is
not available to everyone. In the past, social obligations have been very
narrow. Societies which pride themselves on high levels of mutual obligation may nevertheless be highly stratified in terms of class, race or gender,
and highly exclusionary of people with mental health problems, street
homeless people or gypsies – and yet expect civility from those groups
without reciprocation. As we shall explore later, the generation of social
mutuality in situations of extreme inequality is problematic. Changing
notions of social obligations are not the same as the decline of social
obligation. Emerging new social expectations among the young, such as
respect for autonomy, tolerance or care for the environment may be as
important as the older values of mutual obligation.

While almost everyone agrees that social capital is a good thing, as soon
as we consider the role that governance plays in sustaining or building
social capital, political differences reemerge. Conservatives argue that
too much government has destroyed social capital and undermined the

self-reliance of civil society. Liberals and socialists argue that on the contrary the state plays a crucial role in nurturing a vibrant civil society. Putnam (1993) suggests that government may actually have little effect – he found considerable societal indifference to government action.

British writers such as Halpern (1998) and Szreter (1999) argue that governance has a specific role to play in building the best sorts of social capital. Through participation in consultation, information-sharing, serving on committees, attending forums or self-government through tenant boards or community trusts, people have opportunities to build contacts outside their own narrow circles and create openings into a wider world. Szreter suggests that it is these weak relationships with comparative strangers that open up access to wider social possibilities, to training, and to information. It is therefore the looser citizenship activities such as attending the school parent–teachers meeting, helping out at a jumble sale, joining the residents association, volunteering or running the local playscheme that optimise social capital. Good governance can create the 'weak' social ties that hold a complex modern society together.

This offers a very strong potential role for local government; it can use its resources to create a network of engagement within civil society. 'An extensive and dense range of relatively weak ties establishing multi-lateral lines of communication between the maximum number of citizens is the key sign of well-developed social capital' (Szreter, 1999, p. 39).

Government agencies could support the creation of conditions which engender social trust and prevent exclusion; consultation processes, for example, offer opportunities to build these 'weak ties', and can be structured in ways that include the 'excluded' – public agencies can offer support, facilities and training, back up and facilitation. Governance networks could create pathways that go beyond the confines of the first role that individuals take on (attending a meeting or focus group), enabling people to move on to act as parent governors, volunteers in a youth project, tenant board members, or to access training. There is clear evidence that experiments in tenant management and control help to build social capital (Gillanders, 1999), but there are few equivalent opportunities for local people to translate their experience in managing other sorts of services.

Local and central government are not outside the processes that break down social capital. The communities that are now labelled as socially excluded did not willfully or stupidly throw their social capital away; they have been subject to a relentless process of economic decline, social dislocation and impoverishment. While there is a greater understanding by local agencies of the needs of local communities, and greater responsiveness, government agencies are bumbling around trying to think of ways of creating new social capital, while wasting existing and potential social capital on a terrifying scale.

One of the simplest forms of waste is simply waste of time. The hours spent queuing for services – waiting for repair men that never come, struggling with computerised phone systems – is a constant irritant for harassed people with few resources to spare. But since these are the problems of mainstream delivery, not of community governance, they are not counted. Public agencies can fail to count the value of social interaction into cost and benefits of service provision. Delivery systems can be efficient, but increase social isolation. Closing local offices, transferring services to the internet or call centres may all speed up obvious service functions, but break down the day-to-day human interactions that used to exist. Public agencies can destroy the creativity and morale of local groups by encouraging local people to spend hundreds of hours on local plans or local initiatives and then changing their minds. This is seldom a deliberate act of sabotage; government guidelines may change, the minister is replaced, new criteria are introduced, funding sources disappear, politicians win or lose power – and suddenly a community group that has put in years of hard work can find itself abandoned by the authorities in which it put its trust.

Newly-elected politicians and recently-appointed managers often approach communities with considerable enthusiasm about new initiatives, new citizen panels or a new partnership. But communities have long memories. Even in areas of high mobility there will be people who took part in initiatives 10, 20 or 30 years ago. There will be a folk memory of previous attempts at community engagement, and an image of local agencies built up over time, so that the relationship between local agencies and local people will have a long history. But often within public organisations we have neither ways to store and exchange learning from past experiments, nor many managers and staff left who remember them.

Relationships between local agencies and local communities throughout the twentieth century have been beset with difficulties, distrust, tensions and dilemmas. Learning about those dilemmas is helpful, since it begins to concede to the community wisdom about things that have gone before, and to recognise the continuity of past failures. New vehicles, such as community development trusts (CDTs), attempt to transfer assets as well as decision-making power. Some CDTs have been very successful, while elsewhere they have faltered because of the failure of real dialogue or shared goals. Problems with funding may make local people feel they are being dumped with responsibility for expensive services, without the means to make them work.

Revisiting theory

The theories used to explain the relationship between state and civil society have their own history. Radical community activists and young professionals in the 1970s, brought up with the theories of Carchedi (1977) and Poulantzas (1975), saw local and central government as inevitably acting to reinforce the interests of business and capital. Others used the arguments of Habermas (1971) and Offe (1984) to suggest that state welfare organisations could exploit their relative autonomy. Post-Marxists broke through the concept of relative autonomy, recognising that there was no necessary correspondence between state action and the interests of any section of the community, that there was no such thing as 'the state' or even as 'the capitalist class'. Government like all other social spaces was 'an arena of struggle, constituted and divided by opposing interests rather than a centralised and unified political actor' (Thompson and McHugh, 1995, p. 93). Pluralist commentators saw the state as composed of different groups within the political elite competing for support, and within the administrative elite as competing to service different interests, within a Weberian framework of multidimensional power. Government plays many different roles, and the professionals and managers within each will have different goals, training, attitudes and beliefs.

In both traditions, the explanatory hold of structural factors has weakened as the complex interaction of many factors is recognised. But this does not mean that all of these influencing factors are equal, nor that it is not important to theorise the conditions influencing change, simply that, as we shall explore in Chapter 5, the impact of interactions cannot be read off in any linear fashion. When governments, locally or nationally, attempt to act they are doing so in the context of an existing (although sometimes changing) balance of power, a prevailing ideological climate and a political project (more or less articulated) within the various government organisations. These conditions can be to an extent localised in time and space, but they are seldom constituted entirely at the local level. The reality, as we shall explore later, is often one of 'complex, and often internally contradictory and inconsistent organisational apparatus' (Clegg *et al.*, 1987, p. 281).

People inside local government and other public agencies have often done their best to meet local needs, but have been imprisoned within ways of looking at and understanding the world that seal them off from the experiences, understandings and perceptions of the people they serve. The impact of government is never neutral. The emerging network of government agencies involves negotiations between powerful players with millions of pounds, and community groups and individuals with very little.

Inequalities within society are reproduced through the inequalities within public organisations, and between communities.

It is not necessary to see this as a conspiracy, or to believe that any specific outcome is the necessary consequence of the current balance of power. Power is always shifting. There is still a powerful degree of 'non-decision making' (Bachrach and Baratz, 1962), and regardless of the good motives and intentions of those in government agencies there is always a simple drag factor created by complex bureaucracies and elaborate systems which pulls back towards continuity. The status quo prevails except at moments of radical upheaval, where strong political pressure is brought to bear. The agencies linked together within local governance never *necessarily* act in any specific interests. As we observed earlier, local governance is a complex system – a 'site of struggle' – and consists of many different people within a complicated set of relationships inside and out. We need to carefully observe the extent to which relationships between citizens and government change.

It is probably true that there is more will and commitment within local agencies than ever before to engage differently with citizens, but this is happening from within organisational systems and structures that can barely cope and without any consistent conceptual framework to guide change. It may be that the creaking systems and processes are the last gasp of old ways of doing things and will soon be shed to make space for radically different relationships. There is the possibility of a new space opening up – of 'outside and for' the state – a civil society able to recognise and value the role of government agencies within relationships of governance, but able to negotiate and limit what that role should be. Or we could go back round the loop again.

An analysis of the relationship between government and people should not be so simplistic that it assumes governments always act effectively and well at promoting civil society, nor should it assume hidden agendas or vested interests. There is the possibility of 'cock-up' as well as conspiracy, and it is possible to recognise both the potential role for government as well as the complex reasons why government so often fails. It is important also to recognise the realities of the tensions and inequalities within civil society to which governance has to respond, but which it cannot simply magic away.

We need a theory and practice of governance that recognises the problematic relationship between public organisations and the citizens they serve, and recognises the roles of citizens and government organisations in maintaining, influencing and recasting the relationships that make up governance.

Exclusion and inequality

One test of any new relationship between government and civil society is the capacity to deal with inequality. It has been addressed obliquely through the language of social exclusions, but exclusion is seen as a noun – a problem to be solved – rather than a verb – an active process. Actions by government and by people within civil society may exclude people; the way relationships of governance are constructed affects the way that individuals and groups can participate. Exclusion challenges the possibilities of community engagement, since it sets some people outside the arrangements by which civil society governs itself. The response to social exclusion must, to an extent, define the rights and responsibilities that go with citizenship and the sorts of relationships that are expected of both state and individuals within civil society (Miller, 1999).

If we recognise that identity and community are now characterised by diversity, this creates problems for governance. Diversity does not simply mean that society is very different; it offers excitement and creativity, but it also locks in extreme deprivation. Different communities are more or less able to help themselves. Inequality endangers the possibility of reflexive dialogue, since the weakest, even if they are heard, may be ignored by the powerful. Poverty, poor health, disability, illiteracy and narrow horizons all make it harder to experience anything in a reflexive way. Conventional democracy offers a set of rules in which every citizen has access to a vote, and every representative has access to information and decision-making. New processes of consultation and engagement run the risk of abandoning this careful structure of 'equality', reintroducing randomness or pre-democratic decision-making by established powerblocs.

Much of the debate about local governance has been blind to the implications of social and economic inequality. It is not clear whether a new and more negotiated democracy can tackle previously intractable social problems, or whether it will simply reveal (and perhaps challenge) the realities of different power and life chances at the local level. The concept of a 'dialogic democracy' does not yet offer a solution to the problems of inequality and the abuse of power.

Serious community engagement cannot take place without an explicit recognition of issues of inequality. One response is to see community consultation as a sham when some people are richer and more influential than others. Alternatively, processes have to be designed which enable all participants to explore ways of dealing with inequality as part of their engagement with governance. This might involve some baseline commitment to engage by all those capable of influencing events, and there would need to be a sufficiently level playing field to make dialogue meaningful. Dialogue can be meaningful between unequal partners, but only if the terms of engagement are actively created as part of the process of dialogue.

Miller has developed a fascinating analysis of possible governance reactions to social exclusion, shown in Figure 3.2. *Required inclusion* is inherent in much of the current Blair government thinking which implies that we all have responsibilities to assume as well as rights to exercise, and it is necessary to compel 'accepted behaviour' from those who fail to comply. Perhaps the clearest example of required inclusion would be action to force street homeless people into hostels. In *Fragmented exclusion*, by contrast, the state plays no role in creating conditions of social cohesion, and individuals and communities act and define themselves as they wish. Such an approach is often advocated by the libertarian right, but can also be preferred by some communities which feel excluded. They have ceased to expect help from society as a whole and want freedom to self-organise to 'look after our own' – as in the black-power movement, or the gay movement in San Francisco in the early years. In between, *voluntary inclusion* offers individuals opportunities for work or for participation in wider society, but if they fail to take these opportunities when they are offered they are assumed to have chosen exclusion and are not entitled to further help. This characterises some of the New Democrat thinking in the United States – 'You had your chance buddy. You blew it.'

Figure 3.2 *A range of possible government responses to social cohesion*

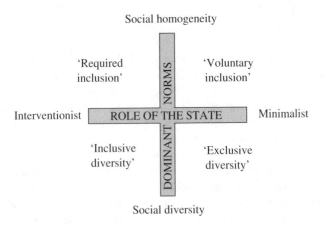

Source: Miller (1999).

Miller's fourth option, *negotiated inclusion*, requires a combination of interventionist action and a recognition of the experience of discrimination and 'active exclusion', and a value of diversity. The state would create opportunities for the negotiation of social responsibilities, for dialogue about the tensions between social obligations and personal freedom, and help to orchestrate the cementing of active social contracts around live relationships of trust. Miller recognises there are limits which each society sets – paedophiles would not be allowed to negotiate engagement on their own terms, for example – and the best reality includes both an element of required inclusion and some tolerance of voluntary exclusion even if there is greater scope for social negotiation. What he identifies, however, is that the role of the state is negotiated also. It is not possible for central or local networks of governance to simply impose contractual social obligations on citizens without itself earning the trust and respect of citizens and negotiating legitimacy to do so. Without consent, the state can do nothing except through threat of violence. We are beginning to see the possibility, therefore, of a local network of governance which does not simply presume the rules of inclusion, or of decision-making, but which enables them to be actively negotiated.

It may not be possible, or even desirable, to recreate a strong sense of belonging between different sections of the community. 'If we can accept otherness, we can at least secure the minimum belonging afforded by a common life under the regime of procedural fairness' (Ignatieff, 1996). Communities can begin to negotiate their own community of governance which may not mean shared interests, or a community of identity, but which represents shared spaces in which people can debate, explore and exchange peacefully.

Rules of engagement

Processes of governance and processes of inclusion are inevitably inter-linked; the way state and government organisations act will always either reinforce the existing inequalities within society or challenge them. I suggested in Chapter 2 that emerging roles for local governance networks could include setting the framework for democratic participation and positively helping disadvantaged groups to negotiate inclusion. It is clear that without positive action on the part of public agencies they are unlikely adequately to listen to, or engage with, the views and needs of disadvantaged and excluded people. There is a considerable literature now about good practice and about ways to 'empower the disempowered' (Martins and Miller, 1999), and there is easily accessible advice about engaging with young people, people from ethnic minorities, women, people with disabilities, people with mental illness or learning difficulties (see for example, Beresford and Croft, 1993; Prasha and Shan, 1986; Dowson, 1991; Hart, 1992; Phillips, 1993; Sills and Desai, 1996; NISW, 1993). But to succeed, public agencies have to want to do so. In addition, the impact that government agencies have on social inclusion should be subject to public debate and scrutiny as well as to academic analysis.

The responsibilities for a process of negotiated inclusion do not, however, rest solely with local authorities or public agencies. As citizens become engaged in governance – or become their own governors, in community groups or tenants associations – what are the governance behaviours expected of them? What assumptions are carried about standards of ethics and behaviour? To whom and by whom are they held to account? When and how are managers and staff able to bring their own ethics and values into their relationships with the public? How do they deal with bullying or prejudice? How do citizens find ways to challenge each other constructively? Are government agencies able to say no? What rights do community agencies have to challenge prejudice or crass behaviour by their local authorities? What rights do the local authorities have to challenge the behaviour of other agencies, or individuals? To whom might they appeal? On what basis? What are the rules that might govern negotiated or consensual problem-solving, to ensure that all voices are heard and to ensure that the balance of power is at least transparent? Who enforces them?

While relationships between government agencies and civil society are becoming healthier, there is still little or no understanding about how to structure and manage them. We do not yet have strong enough social assumptions about the behaviours that should govern civic relationships in the modern world. There is a need to negotiate new rules of engagement, for citizens as well as for politicians and managers.

4 The Relationship Organisation

If I try to picture a local government organisation, I can immediately see a large imposing building. It might be Victorian, redbrick with ornate arches and crenellations and a motto over the front entrance. It might be a vast 1930s neo-classical palace with an imposing set of steps and pillars on either side of the entrance. Inside, depending on organisational priorities and culture, there is either an open reception desk, with three charming women sitting behind it, or a dingy cubbyhole with two security guards. From the entrance lobby there is a wide marble staircase with gloomy committee rooms upstairs. In all directions, endless corridors stretch away, each with hundreds of identical doors. Behind these doors can be found senior managers of a variety of different titles, each with secretaries, and further down the corridors groups of managers, policy staff, researchers, support staff – becoming more and more junior. Somewhere out in the town are the front-line staff, in depots and in district sub-offices, in schools, nurseries, parks or libraries, in vans or cars, or perhaps in local people's homes. They seem a long way away.

The image I carry in my head of a town hall may not really be accurate, but we all carry powerful images of what organisations are, or can be. How far do those images, histories and assumptions limit our capacity to create organisations capable of responding to the challenge of local governance? What are the real limits to organisational change? How far have we travelled already? How much further is there to go?

Organisations are changing. During the twentieth century the world was dominated by large corporations, often national in character, capable of controlling the actions of everyone from the chief executive to the postboy, with complex bureaucratic systems, procedures and rules. For Weber (1984), bureaucracy was part of a universal tendency in response to the great changes of industrialisation. The concept of rational order was vital to the modernisation of society envisaged in the nineteenth century, and organisational authority was made rational by basing it on precise and predictable rules. The separation of office and office holder created rule-governed systems of appointment and reward. Status was accumulated through hierarchy, with a chain of command and division of labour based on definable rights and duties. Calculable rules and written documentation formed the basis of office management, and the bureaucratic organisation was sustained through the motivation of its members by job security and status. Hierarchy built long-term loyalty.

While private organisations share the same characteristics, in the public imagination, the quintessential bureaucracy has always been the state organisation. Nowhere, it has been argued, are rules more necessary than in the organisations of the state, where they guarantee impartiality, freedom from corruption, probity and accountability. The detailed written procedure has been the bulwark against gangsterism for a century.

Emerging organisational forms

In the private sector, the speed of technological change is challenging bureaucracy as the dominant organisational form. The downsides of bureaucracy – poor communication, rigid systems, sluggish feedback and slow response – have become dangerous. There is a powerful element of hype in the world of management textbooks, and while the management gurus talk-up new and emerging organisational forms such as strategic alliances, federal organisations or web-structures – reality lags behind. Nevertheless, communication technology is changing the organisational form. Technological capacity exists to process and communicate information at unimaginable speed, and organisational forms are evolving that rely on the exchange of information in different ways.

Castells argues that we are witnessing the 'crisis of the traditional corporate model of the organization based on vertical integration and hierarchical functional management, the staff and line system of strict technical and social division of labour' (Castells, 1996, p. 156). The competitive edge within the new informational society is created by the ability of organisations to increase their knowledge from all sources as the basis for innovation. The scope of new technology to link up sources of knowledge leads to the evolution of new sorts of organisations, often dominated by small and medium-sized organisations working in networks or alliances, rather than integrated into single huge conglomerates. He traces the growth of strategic alliances: 'the structure of high technology industries in the world is an increasingly complex web of alliances, agreements and joint ventures in which most large corporations are interlinked'. He argues that the shift from vertical bureaucracy to horizontal cooperation means that 'the actual operating unit becomes the business project, enacted by a network'. Information circulates through networks, networks between companies, networks within companies personal networks, computer networks. The horizontal corporation is a 'dynamic and strategically-planned network of self-programmed, self-directed units based on decentralisation, participation and coordination' (Castells, 1996, p. 163).

The power of the big global companies is not challenged, they are simply working differently. But entry becomes easier for innovative small outfits, since networks are open. Since networks are not controlled from the top, the strategy of the network is negotiated – a network enterprise is constituted by the 'intersection of segments of autonomous systems of goals' (*ibid.*, p. 171). The fundamental attributes of networks are their connectedness, and the consistency between network goals and the goals of their components.

If this is true – or even partly true – what does it mean for the public sector? If networks are the fundamental stuff of which new organisations are and will be made, how do public organisations fit in? Do network organisations offer a potential route to innovation to match that within the private sector? Can public organisations develop their own knowledge-based dynamic? Can public organisations break out of bureaucracy?

Abandoning the machine metaphor

One of the most powerful constraining notions around organisations is that an organisation is a sort of machine. Early management theory and practice tried to make the organisation as much like a machine as possible. Taylor (1947) set about removing the autonomy from the work process to ensure that results were replicable thousands and thousands of times without variation. Similarly, organisational structure charts resemble engineering diagrams for the design of a machine.

Gareth Morgan has identified the dangerous strength of the machine metaphor in structuring our thinking about organisations so that we 'expect them to operate as machines, in a routinised, efficient reliable and predictable way' (Morgan, 1986, p. 22). He offers a set of alternative metaphors such as brains, organisms, culture, political systems, psychic prisons, flux and transformation, or instruments of domination, to show how different metaphors enable us to see organisations in different ways. Metaphors are powerful in changing our ways of seeing, but their very strength is also their weakness, since by illuminating the single point of similarity between the two things compared, they blot out the differences. Organisations are no more brains, prisons or organisms than they are machines.

An organisation is a collectivity of people with a capacity for agency. It can be distinguished from other collectivities, such as a mob which 'is a collection of people who may run, shout, and mill about together. But it is a collectivity that cannot make a decision or take an action in its own name, and its boundaries are vague and diffuse' (Argyris and Schon, 1996, p. 8). An organisation, on the other hand, has three distinguishing characteristics. Its members can:

- devise agreed-upon procedures for making decisions in the name of the collectivity;
- delegate to individuals the authority to act for the collectivity; and
- set boundaries between the collectivity and the rest of the world. (*ibid.*, p. 8)

'Before an organisation can be anything else it must be "political" because it is as a political entity that the collectivity can take organisational action' (*ibid.*, p. 9). Indeed, it is the failure to see, study and respond to the politics of organisational interests, conflicts and relationships that slows down the capacity of managers to 'manage into' relationships of governance.

Organisations do not have to live in a single building, or any building; they do not have to have a single unified staff, or a fixed establishment; they do not have to have written rules or managed systems. Nevertheless, many of these things are helpful and, as we will see, survive tenaciously. Some procedures and rules are required by law. For example, most organisations have payrolls, and buildings and structure charts, and they have clear functions and purposes. But organisations can be very small, or loose-knit, can be political parties or social movements, membership organisations, cottage industries, workshops. Organisations can work through networks or webs, they can create virtual organisations with others, they can develop teams that evolve and dissolve when their task is completed. Voluntary and community organisations are often short-lived – they might come together to organise a play event for the summer holidays and then disband. Also, social movements often work through informal networks. There are limits, however, to what it is sensible to call an organisation. To be an organisation it must be possible for its members to agree on the rules of engagement and to agree about what needs to be done and to authorise actions to take place on their behalf.

What counts as an organisation is an empirical question. Some local partnerships function as organisations and some don't, some local communities come together into organisations while others cannot or choose not to. But the reality is that in the sphere of governance individual agencies are still the dominant form of organisation. Local authorities, police authorities, health authorities, and private companies function as powerful and distinct organisations with their own agendas and interests. And the organisational forms within those agencies have not changed radically since the 1970s. The traditional public sector organisation, divided into separate departments managed by senior professionals working in isolated vertical 'silos' cannot cope with the new relationships of governance. It cannot work fast enough or exchange knowledge freely enough to respond to the needs of complex and diverse communities. Current organisational forms are beginning to creak and groan as public managers and politicians try to drive them to accomplish new tasks, or to meet ambitious new outcome targets. In this chapter I want to explore the problems and possibilities of radical organisational reform.

The recent past – evolving local authorities

The traditional British local authority, the sort conjured in the opening paragraph of this chapter, has remained recognisably the same for a century. It has three dominant features: decision-making through a committee system, the structuring of activities through a series of professional departments, and a bureaucratic organisation of the work process. 'Committees have been part of the working of local authorities since the origin of elected local government, and before' (J. Stewart, 2000, p. 43). The committee system 'has an impact on the overall workings of the authority: the cycle set out in members' diaries marks out fixed points throughout the year, the committee cycle sets out the rhythm not merely for the councillors but for senior officers' (*ibid.*, p. 46).

> The workings of local authorities have long been based upon the professional principle. Traditionally each department was dominated by a particular profession ... the professional model expresses continuity. Accepted knowledge can develop but only along professional lines. Professions differ in their culture. Their values differ, as do their ways of working. Each has its own language ... [professionalism] is a force for continuity that can challenge the potential for diversity that lies within local government. (*ibid.*, pp. 46–8)

But as John Stewart points out, departments are an expression not only of professionalism but also of bureaucratic habit,

Professionalism and bureaucracy are structured on different principles. The emphasis of professionalism is on the individual professional whose authority is certified by qualifications. The emphasis of bureaucracy is on the organisation and the rules by which it conducts its business. Professionals working in a bureaucratic organisation resent over-hierarchical or rule-bound control. (*ibid.*, p. 49)

The tension between professional and bureaucratic forms of organisation has existed within public services since their inception.

But this is not the only tension. There has been considerable change in public organisations; in the 1960s and 1970s we saw the introduction of corporate planning and chief executives, the Maud Committee (Maud, 1967) on the management of local government, and the Bains report in the 1970s (Bains, 1972) on local authority management and structure, strengthened the moves towards large corporate bureaucracies and, as John Stewart points out, reinforced tendencies to uniformity. The Thatcher and Major governments drove through a series of structural changes, removing power and funding from local authorities, replacing governmental bodies with quangos such as next-step agencies, introducing market testing and compulsory competitive tendering which brought markets and market values into public services. Under the Conservatives there was a great drive towards efficiency, and the putting in place of the basic management techniques of the private sector – strong managers, performance monitoring, collecting performance information, financial information, unit costing, contract arrangements and so on.

While often opposed at the time, with hindsight these changes have been welcomed rather than otherwise; they at least provide a necessary tool-kit for organisational change. The result has been a strengthening of managerial roles and a growing acceptance of mangerial leadership in the pursuance of effective performance. The changes were achieved not without considerable pain – but, as Stoker (1999) points out, scaring people to death may be a relatively good way of getting change of certain types. There is evidence that local authorities are more popular and seen as more efficient that they were a decade ago (Young and Rao, 1997, p. 127). Nevertheless, the tensions between professional and managerial leadership were not resolved, nor were new tensions between contracting and line-management systems, between direct provision and externalisation, between commissioning and providing, between devolved autonomy and system control, between individual judgement and performance compliance.

Many significant changes in local authorities took place despite, not because of, government policy. In the early years of the Conservative government, local authorities mounted a furious opposition to the privatisation model and tried to create their own alternatives, including cross-departmental initiatives to tackle racism and sexual discrimination, regeneration strategies for run-down inner-city areas, community planning, neighbourhood initiatives and organisational change. Persistent problems of inefficiency discredited these experiments, but they laid important foundations for the initiatives that have subsisted into the 1990s. The new modernisation agenda draws considerably from the experience of radical local authorities in the 1980s. The setting up of women and ethnic minority initiatives did much to create a critical mass for equal opportunities polices that were afterwards followed by the NHS and central government. Community consultation was begun in the 1980s, but built on the community action and community development experience of the 1970s. The creation of neighbourhood initiatives in Walsall, Islington and Tower Hamlets, for example, were developed in the teeth of government insistence on efficiency and service focus, and were part of a process of experimentation. Many of the experiments failed. But despite (or perhaps because of) the mistakes of many local authorities during the 1980s, lessons learnt from crude initiatives have been translated into more successful projects of the 1990s. Many of today's leading councillors and managers came into local government during the early 1980s and have now risen to the top.

As has been well-documented, a large number of local authorities were driven to restructure during the 1990s, often reducing the old eight or nine professional departments to a smaller number of large directorates. These made it possible to achieve greater corporate focus, and to match top directors in other organisations. Most authorities have carried out some sort of purchaser/provider split and externalised some services. The Local Government Review accelerated structural change – new unitaries wanted to introduce modern structures, while the remaining counties and districts felt the need to prove their viability by reorganising. The Local Government Management Board (LGMB) 1995 'Portrait of Change' showed a move towards multifunctional directorates. Many authorities streamlined by reducing the size of the corporate management team and by slimming-down departmental structures. Two-thirds of responding authorities had revised their departmental structures between 1989–92, and a further 40 per cent revised, or revised again their structures between 1992 and 1994 (LGMB, 1995, p. 15). Most local authorities have reorganised and moved away from professionally-based departments to more corporate structures with directorates incorporating several business areas. The process of reorganisation and restructuring is, if anything, accelerating, although the measurable impact of these changes varies widely.

While some authorities have changed a little, a tiny few have changed radically. These experiments have been interesting, partly because they have gone against the grain of direction of government policy, and partly because they may begin to prefigure different organisational forms that are better adapted to the future.

Some authorities have separated out corporate directorates from line management altogether. Kirklees, for example, was one of the first authorities to develop a radical structure. Led by Robert Hughes, a former pop star, a dynamic, iconoclastic inspirational leader impatient for change and frustrated with the traditional departmental bureaucracy, and by John Harman, now Sir John, who created the political space for entrepreneurship and risk-taking, Kirklees abandoned the traditional local authority model, creating spaces for innovation. The department chief officers were replaced by a small corporate executive team, without direct line-management responsibility but charged with addressing strategic issues such as environmental policies, community safety and citizen engagement. Politicians and managers met each week at the policy board, the heart of strategic decision-making; ideas could be put to the policy board from anywhere in the organisation. Each operational service was managed by a head of service with space to innovate, in theory at least. Cross-departmental working has been part of Kirklees culture since the early 1990s – and while theory always outruns practice, there are numerous examples of creative middle and senior managers able to work horizontally, pursue initiatives and change things. The talkback panel, one of the first examples of local authorities working with citizen panels, was the idea of Deborah Wilkinson, then a junior manager. Service innovation, partnership working and joint ventures with the private sector have been characteristics of Kirklees' style for a decade (Leadbeater and Goss, 1998).

South Somerset has innovated in a different direction. A rural district council with a population dispersed through many small villages, the liberal democratic council led at the managerial level by Mel Usher, a radical thinker, embarked upon a dismantling of the traditional structure. The seven departments, chief and deputy officers were replaced with four local areas, each of which was given wide latitude to decide how to deliver local services. The four areas are brought together by a small central executive team which plays the role of convenor and catalyst. The decentralisation, after a false start, was fed by initiatives taken by politicians, senior managers and frontline staff. The first attempt tried to add on a decentralised structure to the previous hierarchy, and the second attempt released the resources and staff that had been bound up in the mainstream hierarchy into the local areas. The diagrams of the organisation have ceased to be linear structure charts – they now have circles joined by feedback loops and arrows (Leadbeater and Goss, 1998).

These early experiments, while more enduring and better-known than others, are now less and less unique. As authorities have begun to innovate, they are developing different models and the result has been that local government is becoming more organisationally diverse than it had been for many years. As John Stewart (2000) documents, there has been a trend towards diversity at local level which must be taken into account if we are to understand the current complexity of local arrangements. His recent book charts the considerable range of organisational and political arrangements by the end of the twentieth century. The powerful unitary constitutional arrangements in the UK make it impossible for local governance to achieve the radical changes possible in federal systems. Organisational roles and boundaries are determined at Westminster, although, as Stewart points out, there are many myths in place which constrain creativity within local government and create greater timidity than necessary in the face of Westminster's power. But there are a few authorities stretching the limits of the space they have.

Changes in other public organisations

All public organisations have been undergoing radical change, and the emergence of new organisational forms depends as much on the changes taking place elsewhere in the public sector as it does on changes in local government. The health service at local level has faced a continual round of structural change, moving from a unified system of hospital management to the purchaser–provider split; the setting-up of hospital and community trusts, district health authorities and regional health authorities; the setting-up of a separate system to manage GPs through Family Health Service Authorities (FHSAs) and then the merger of FHSAs with health authorities; the merger of health authorities to create fewer authorities; the merger of regional health authorities to create fewer smaller regions; the reconfiguration of hospital trusts to create mergers; and the introduction of GP consortia followed by the introduction of Primary Care Groups and Primary Care Trusts. The pace of reorganisation has been such that job titles and the names of health organisations have changed dozens of times in the past decade. The emergence of Primary Care Groups (PCGs) creates new opportunities, however, since in terms of size they make sense at a more local level than the previous Districts, and make it possible to link primary and community care directly to services such as social care and housing. The governance arrangements for the PCGs also offer greater scope for collaboration, since PCG managers seem to be more willing to work across boundaries, and local authority chief executives play a role in PCG boards.

The police have undergone change also. Over the past twenty years they have removed a series of levels of hierarchy, and have transferred much of the administrative and support work away from the police service to staff who are still called 'civilians'. Attempts to introduce a managerial revolution via the Sheehey report and the introduction of performance-related pay were by and large defeated from within the force. The police have also bucked the trend towards centralisation; the regional forces have far greater autonomy than, for example, regional health authorities, and power has been delegated within the regions to the local divisions. A local superintendent running a town police station also has autonomy that few other public managers possess. In addition, senior managers within the police force are increasingly required to work in partnership with local authorities in the development of local crime and disorder strategies and community safety plans. The intention has been a transfer of attention from reaction to crime prevention. Governance has also changed within the police service; during the 1980s police authorities were reconstituted to reduce the proportion of councillors and to introduce board members from business and other sectors, as well as magistrates elected from the magistrates' board.

Voluntary organisations have also changed. The 1980s brought a doubling of funding for the voluntary sector, and in the 1990s voluntary organisations became major providers in some sections of social and community care – particularly in the fields of HIV/AIDs, alcohol abuse and mental illness. The introduction of competition into social care provision has forced local authorities to externalise much of their care provision, often to voluntary sector providers or to partnerships with voluntary sector participation.

The housing association sector has also undergone considerable change, with a move towards larger size as housing associations or Registered Social Landlords (RSLs) have become the major developers of new social housing. Increasingly, they are also taking over current local authority housing through stock transfer. There have been a rapid series of mergers, group structures and consortia developing, and the introduction of joint commissioning has led to the forced, although often welcome development of partnership and contract agreements between RSLs and local authorities.

The parallel changes in all local agencies at once create new opportunities. New spaces for joint working are being created, and it is easier for organisations to come together at regional, locality and neighbourhood levels. Relatively independent police superintendents and PCG managers can operate sensibly in the same geographical territory as new corporate directors within a district or unitary council; whilst local GP practices and local police stations relate to neighbourhoods. But organisational boundaries remain very thick and, as we will explore in Chapter 5, interagency working is only just beginning. The way that organisations are designed constrains and shapes the ways they are used.

The importance of organisational forms

There has been a tendency to simply blame the managers or the professionals for what is wrong with public agencies, but it is important also to understand the structures, systems and cultures they inhabit. The nature of the organisations within which we work have a powerful impact on what is possible, and although organisations are slowly evolving in response to new pressures, it is too slow. Manager and staff often struggle to tackle the problems of governance within dangerously obsolete organisational arrangements. However, these are not fixed, and managers and staff can act to make space for new possibilites within old organisational forms. But public organisations cannot simply be changed by managers and staff without wider consent – since they 'belong' to all of us, and are often created by statute. To change organisations fully will require changes in the thinking of national government, and of the public, as well as changes in the thinking of managers and staff.

It is clear that the design of an organisation – the ways people are physically connected together – can and does impact on the results an organisation can achieve. If people are concentrated in offices or buildings in which they only meet people who think the way they do, or know the things they know, structures can begin to separate and isolate people, close down communication or prevent the exchange of ideas. Strong departmental boundaries or silos (as in missile launch sites where each tunnel is insulated from the others) make it hard for knowledge to be shared. Where support staff are a very long way away from the end-user and have little contact with the public, it is often hard for them to understand how their actions impact on final results. Extensive hierarchies mean that the people who know what needs doing are too junior to have the power to make it happen, and the people who have the power are too 'strategic' to know. Complex structures can make responsibility difficult to assign and accountability vague, but physical connections alone do not create isolation or slow down actions, or encourage vagueness. Structure also represents a shorthand for formal human relationships within an organisation, a drawing of the hierarchy, reporting lines, relative status and relative power of different posts.

The limits to structural change

The most usual change that organisations introduce is structural change – a change illustrated by redrawing the structure chart to illustrate the deleting of posts, changing reporting lines, adding functions or merging depart-ments. The new drawing is symbolic of the change and helps people believe that things will be different in the future.

But since an organisation is not a structure in the engineering sense, the structure chart is always a metaphor – a drawing of how things are sup-posed to be. The structure can often be false in that people do not really behave in the ways that the structure chart suggests they should, and the chart tells us nothing about how these relationships, reporting lines and accountabilities will be used by real people in real time. As a result, when changes are made to the structure, the changes in the drawing are not nec-essarily reflected in real life. Intended structural changes can be bent back into old ways of doing things by the ways that staff and managers behave.

Structural changes such as the closure of local offices and their replace-ment with call-centres often only represent a merging of front-office func-tions, since the actual work of dealing with enquiries is often still dealt with within different departments and using different systems. Departmental mergers into directorates often involves a single director with overall responsibility for, for example, social services and housing, and yet under-neath them the two departments continue to work separately, in different offices, often in different buildings, with different cultures and ways of thinking. It is easy to change the diagram, but harder to change the reality.

Structural barriers to change often seem immense, and yet, somehow, whenever organisations are restructured new barriers replace the old. At the same time, inadequate structure does not seem to present insuperable problems in some places. Problems that have confounded managers in one organisation have been overcome in another. Partnerships that fail in one place succeed in another, and those organisations that seem to be deliver-ing results often have similar structures to many that are not. Structural change has proved on its own to be insufficient. The creation of strategic management teams did not, on its own, ensure that the managers in those teams thought strategically (LGMB, 1995). Some radical experiments work, while others fail. It is clear from the histories of authorities such as Kirklees and South Somerset that the structural changes have not been the only, or even the most important, aspect of change. Over the past decade the effectiveness of structural change has begun to be challenged and public organisations have looked at other factors.

Systems

Perhaps some of the best reforms of the 1980s and 1990s have been systems changes within public sector organisations. The introduction of contracting and competition for the first time introduced the requirement to cost activity, and to develop costing systems which enabled service users (internal and external) to judge value for money. Despite the recurring problems about overheads and central charges, most authorities now know far more about what they get for their money, and are able to compare performance with others. Alongside costing systems public organisations have introduced better performance management systems, and serious business planning. At best, a local authority manager will now be able to assess past performance (using reliable data on costs, outputs and user satisfaction), plan improvements, translate these into clear action plans and measure success. None of this was possible two decades ago.

However, systems are still often focused on the inside of organisations, on reporting lines to government or to senior managers, and not always designed to be convenient to service users. Finance systems often still give information about what happened in the past, rather than what is likely to happen in the future. Financial systems in the future need to be less concerned with accounting for the spending of budgets, and more concerned with resource finding and resource use from different sources, merging and configuring different resource streams and predicting future needs and income streams.

Rigid personnel policies designed to protect and support staff do not necessarily have that outcome. They make it hard to offer secondments or job swaps, to move people around, to create temporary projects, to try things out. Monitoring systems have often collected vast amounts of data, but convert very little of it into knowledge. Without opportunities to reflect on information, to explore what it tells us, there is no change.

Public service systems have to ensure probity, transparency and equity – to ensure clear audit trails and to trace individual departmental accountability for spending or decision-making. They protect staff from blame by political masters, the public or the media, but they may not be helpful in supporting modern organisations. The example of Box 4.1, taken from a real-life consultancy situation, shows how old systems can obstruct effective partnership working:

Box 4.1   *Problems with systems*

A new chief executive of a unitary authority was working alongside a local headteacher in a local partnership to improve performance in schools. He took the opportunity to ask her what she thought of the local authority. 'Ghastly', she said, 'Hopeless'. The chief executive tried to imagine why that might be. The head had just had new investment in her school, was linked into radical new jobs and training initiatives, and was treated with new respect as a valued partner. When he asked why, she told him she had recently submitted a travel claim for a conference that she had attended in London on Education Action Zones. She was not allowed her own budget for such things. After several weeks she had had a letter refusing to pay the claim until she submitted evidence of ownership of the car in which she had travelled. She had borrowed a friend's car and did not bother to submit the claim, convinced it would be fruitless and exhausting. A defensible process to prevent fraud, no doubt dear to the heart of the auditor who invented it, was destroying an important relationship between the authority and the school. No doubt the headteacher should have been less easily defeated, or less quick to dismiss a whole authority because of one instance. But that's how judgements are made.

Innovation depends, crucially, on the 'knowledge in action' developed by staff on the ground. There is neither the time or the necessity for their experiences and judgments to be translated up the hierarchy to decision-makers at the top and then transmitted back down as a new procedure. By the time that process is completed, the world will be different. In the modern organisation systems are primarily needed as conductors: to conduct information and knowledge rapidly around the organisation – information about resources, about service-users' needs, about aggregate problems, about actions taken, about results. Systems need to service the interchange of ideas and knowledge between departments and agencies, and between users and agencies. Rapid feedback systems are needed to design and run modern services.

Systems do not simply support service delivery; they also support the governance relationships within the local community. For example, Norwich has been experimenting with the use of new technology to promote the interface with local communities, and Islington is planning to install interactive booths within local neighbourhoods. If solutions to problems are not simply to be provided by professionals, but negotiated with service users and communities, then systems need to be capable of supporting negotiated decision-making. We are witnessing the beginning of shared information across departments and agencies, the creation of shared databases. New debates about confidentiality, transparency openness and access are beginning. While agencies are beginning to use new technology to interact with the public, access of individual citizens and local communities to data-sharing is still limited.

Change has been steady, but slow. Information and communication technology has transformed the provision of housing management, library and benefit services; leisure cards and smart cards are being introduced; and many authorities are experimenting with call-centres or new delivery systems based on the use of new communications technology. But these experiments have been modest. Lack of money to fund reinvestment in new technology has been a major factor – lack of investment in the time and imagination to rethink delivery systems has been another. The public sector does not have a research and development function aimed at producing new products or delivery systems, and delivery approaches often lag behind the private sector.

Managing change

By the mid-1990s, while restructuring continued, local authorities were also looking at the softer dimensions of organisational change, drawing on organisational theory from the private sector. Most public organisations began to develop mission statements, corporate or strategic plans, and to think and talk about organisational values (LGMB, 1995, p. 20). Books such as *In Search of Excellence* (Peters and Waterman, 1982) and Charles Handy's (1984) *Empty Raincoat* preached the need for different attitudes and behaviours within organisations, and espoused the importance of engaging and empowering staff. Infrastructural organisations such as the Audit Commission, the local government Improvements and Development Agency (IdeA), and the Local Government Association have supported and invested in the management of change. The 1997 Labour Government moved away from simply stressing efficiency, to focusing attention on leadership, skill development and capacity-building. For many local authorities, then, the late 1990s were a time of planned management of change, including management development programmes, awaydays, values workshops and communication strategies (LGMB, 1995, p. 21).

In Chapter 8, I will explore some of the emerging ways of developing the capabilities of managers and staff to fulfil new roles. But it is not simply a matter of finding or growing new managers; it is only possible to work effectively in the right spaces. Motivated people can and do cope with obsolete systems, rigid bureaucracies and stupid rules, but managers and staff often expend enormous effort on work that in the end has no result. Often they give up. Local managers in negotiation with residents cannot promise that windows will be mended or that local projects will be supported if the systems don't function; targets cannot be met if the information technology does not work; and trust cannot be established if social workers have given up trying to allocate cases because the backlog is so great. Nothing will get better if staff are working to 70 'key priorities' and don't know where to start. Systems can get in the way; culture limits ambition. Staff will not use new skills or experiment with new approaches if the organisation makes it dangerous to do so – or fails to recognise or make space for innovation.

The spotlight of organisational change is now focused on culture change, and the culture of public organisations is blamed for many of the bureaucratic and service failures. The culture is seen as bureaucratic, inefficient, arrogant or resistant to change, and problems are blamed on wrong attitudes and behaviours. Managers and staff are disempowered and ill-equipped for change. Many organisations have introduced customer care programmes, business excellence models or quality circles, and have begun to involve staff and managers in exploring obstacles to change and making solutions. By engaging with all the staff, organisations are learning to free-up lines of communication and to spread understanding about why change is needed. Empowering staff and changing the culture have joined the list of buzz-words and the set of change processes that are proving harder in practice than in theory.

It is no easy thing to change attitudes and behaviours. Culture change programmes are often led from the top, involving big presentations and conferences, and vast training programmes that introduce staff to new mission statements and value statements accompanied by glossy production values and confident sounding consultants, slick presentations and opportunities for staff to discuss the 'new culture' and lots of jargon about 'gaining ownership' and 'walking the talk'. But cultures are not simple, and cannot be simply introduced like a new brand of cereal. Values are not so much learnt as absorbed, and there is often a gap between espoused values and experienced values, so that an organisation that says it values honesty may also be finding it very hard to have a dialogue with staff about future redundancies. Cultures can be discovered not by reading mission statements or business plans, but by understanding the traditions, the stories, the gossip.

Jokes can be particularly important, like this one at a nurses' conference:

Question   What do you do when you see a Health Trust manager coming towards you with half their face blown off?
Answer   Don't panic, take aim more carefully, and fire again.

Organisations can have cultures that seem very bizarre from the outside, but seem familiar and make sense to those on the inside. Organisational cultures can also differ profoundly – in some organisations cleverness is valued and rewarded, in others rapid action (even if it is a knee-jerk response with little thought) is seen as good. Some organisations have a cultural tendency to punctuality, others to lateness, some are secret cultures, others are open. Attitudes and behaviour are formed through experience, and cultures themselves determine what we notice as strange or dysfunctional, and what we do not.

Cultures are not an accident; they are affected, but not determined, by organisational leaders. Cultures are reinforced by assumptions learnt through association with colleagues and by professional theories and prejudices about how the world works. Also there are always powerful subcultures within organisations. However, as we shall see in Chapter 7, we need to work hard before we identify culture or individual attitudes and behaviours as the problem, since we need to understand the conditions that reinforce those attitudes. While culture helps to determine how we design structures and systems, culture is also powerfully formed by those structures and systems. External realities constrain the work carried out within public agencies. 'Culture is affected by the systemic pressures that occur within public services' (Tarplett, 1999, p. 159).

Work cultures are often shared responses to the problems and dilemmas that managers and staff face. 'Jobsworth' cultures can be created where there is no interest in listening to staff ideas, heavy penalties for stepping outside the rules, and no reward for innovation. Professional arrogance is reinforced through tight rationing in the face of conflicting and unexamined user needs, which forces professionals to act as 'gatekeepers'. If professions are isolated from each other in working practice, they are unlikely to share ideas or build respect. Staff who work with highly dependent or challenging clients often develop highly self-protective cultures to cope. High levels of sickness and absenteeism often reflect unacknowledged stress, poor management and conflicting demands. In the next chapter we will examine a less simplistic view of organisational culture.

Opportunities and constraints – the inevitability of unintended consequences

Local authorities, like other public sector agencies, have not simply 'done what they are told'; some have tried to avoid change, and others have learnt to test the limits of government policy and find space to follow local goals. During the early 1990s it was clear that a small number of local authorities were unwilling to be straightjacketed into the shrinking role for local authorities, and began to work alongside other like-minded public agencies. They found that a narrow focus on efficiency did not enable them to manage through the complex problems emerging in their localities. Local authorities had already moved into the territory of 'outcomes' before they were invited to do so by government.

The reality has been (at least) two waves of change, the first, driven by central government in the 1980s, introduced basic business practices into public organisations – extended competition, and externalisation. As the LGMB (1995) report shows, there is skepticism among chief executives about the effectiveness of the first generation of changes. Local authorities were able in many ways to absorb or to deflect the intentions behind compulsory competitive tendering (CCT), and the persistence of bureaucratic processes often undermined or neutralised new business processes. Professionals found the paperwork irksome and meaningless, and failed to use it. The crude focus on customers made little sense to managers trying to balance complex accountabilities, and matching business processes to public outcomes did not prove easy. The second wave, in the 1990s, was driven by a new generation of senior managers and chief executives, who saw the public sector as having lost its way under a government that didn't value public agencies, and found it hard to sustain the morale of staff (Goss, 1996). A process of positive engagement with purpose was a way of holding organisations together and making sense of the world they encountered. In some agencies the first wave of change has been the most appropriate and successful, and the impact of the second wave has been slight. In others, the second wave has hit before the first. In any case, the waves have not been separate but crashed into each other, producing currents, eddies and ripples.

What has been the result of these changes? Lowndes suggests that there is no real coherence, that in practice there is 'a complex and differentiated body of ideas and practices. Some "new management" ideas lose currency quickly and are dismissed as fads ... other ideas are rapidly accepted and acquire the status of "common sense"' (Lowndes, 1999, p. 27). Some aspect of the new management are relatively easy to implement, while others require a much longer timeframe. 'New management' has not stayed still but evolved and acquired new dimensions. 'It is dynamic and internally differentiated and, moreover, contains potentially contradictory elements' (*ibid.*, p. 27). She argues that practitioner debates tend to overestimate the discontinuity between old and new management approaches, and see change as something that succeeds or fails rather than something that happens. Gerry Stoker has pointed to the problems of implementation gaps and unintended consequences, and the tensions between the different prescriptions within new management. 'Hierarchical leadership is not easily made compatible with a market-driven system ... competition and formal contracts are not easy bedfellows with the trust and shared ethics of networking' (Stoker, 1999, p. 4).

Organisational performance has clearly improved, and satisfaction rates have increased. Change has clearly been visible. In a recent survey of local authority managers, 94 per cent disagreed with the statement 'nothing has changed' (Lowndes, 1999, p. 33). Nevertheless, managers made an interesting distinction between different levels of change, distinguishing between changes in the 'formal' and the 'real' organisation, at the 'surface' and 'deeper down' and between leaders and laggards among departments (*ibid.*, p. 33). These different levels of change could represent a gap between appearance and reality, or simply different stages in a long-term process reached at different speeds by different players.

Interviews with local government managers indicate that the experience of change has not been a happy one. Managers express worries about breakdown in the ways people treat each other, and there are constant references to 'resistance to change', and a continuing worry about what is being lost. Practitioners and managers have been skeptical about the value of new management, and worried about losing the values of the old 'high professional standards' and the 'clear focus on service delivery'. Messages from politicians at national and local level have also often been mixed. Modernisation is often seen as distracting attention from the real job; new language is often absorbed, but used to describe old practice, and there has been a lot of rebadging. Managers and staff often simply say, 'we did this before', to every new organisational change process. And even when the need for change is understood and often welcomed, the change processes chosen are often seen as short-lived, or faddish.

While all authorities have changed a little, only a very few local authorities have changed a lot. Most, despite restructuring, have kept a pyramid structure with decision-makers at the top and front-line workers at the bottom. The structure charts of the 1980s need to be amended, but are still recognisable. The activities of housing, social services and education are, by and large, carried out in separate departments, and few authorities have co-located their service with other agencies. The systems have seldom been radically overhauled, even when departments have been merged into single directorates. The organisational problems of ten years ago – improving performance, problems with communication, member–officer relationships, and linkages between departments – still seem familiar. In the health service, despite the whirlwind of reconfiguration, the same organisational problems as before still seem to be recognisable. While it is possible to be astonished at the speed of change – it is also striking from the outside that so much has stayed the same.

The creation of hybrids

Lowndes shows vividly in her analysis that the process of local governance is seen as 'managing the mess'. New structures, systems, skills and capabilities to respond to the new environment are pasted onto existing bureaucratic forms. Where neighbourhood forums have been set up, they have not replaced centralised forms of service-delivery and decision-making, they have been added on. Partnerships don't replace the corporate decision-making of each agency, and since top decision-makers don't attend partnership meetings, they don't always know about or reflect partnership priorities. Line-management delivery systems remain intact, but at the same time horizontal network management systems have been created.

Local authorities have produced strategies for educational development, community safety, agenda 21, social exclusion, lifelong learning, healthy living and so forth. They have also set up pilot projects and zones (we will explore some of these cross-boundary partnerships in Chapter 5). In these initiatives, managers and staff often work horizontally on project teams accountable outside their normal line-management arrangements, at the same time as they continue their operational duties. There are a number of internal horizontal 'culture change' project groups on topics such as training, community consultation, communications and motivating staff. And some chief officers have dual responsibilities for a service directorate such as education, and also for a cross-departmental outcome such as community safety. At neighbourhood level, neighbourhood forums and coordinators have been established without any line management responsibility, responsible for coordinating council activities at neighbourhood level.

These arrangements create a matrix structure (often unintended), and can create exciting spaces for innovation. They represent a step forward from the old, but can encourage an inward focus and consume a lot of energy through duplicating and overlapping structures. In talking to local government managers the most important problems are overload, lack of time and exhaustion. They are excited, but exhausted. This is not simply a problem of the absence of will, or effort; managers are experiencing real limits in the capacity to change public agencies given the constraints of accountability and the expectations of the public and of politicians. There are important reasons why public sector organisations are structured as bureaucracies. We, the public, want to see certainty and uniformity of treatment, and want to be able to track decisions. We like firm rules, and competent systems. These mean that we don't have to worry about arbitrary, biased or unfair decision-making. Public agencies are responsible for creating rules of engagement, regulating and setting boundaries, and they need to be transparent and accountable. But if they are to innovate as effectively as in the private sector, then they will need to develop open, creative ways of working. Private networks can move fast, since action can follow new knowledge very quickly, but public networks cannot work at the same speed since they cannot act without gaining legitimacy for change. We will return in a later chapter to issues of network accountability, but unless new organisational forms can be successfully held to account, old forms are likely to persist.

The governance revolution does not affect all of the functions of public agencies equally. John Stewart has always reminded us that there is no need for all the different activities within local government to be managed in the same ways. The fire service requires very different ways of working to teaching, to highways engineering or to bin emptying; and the introduction of a purchaser/provider split requires different organisational arrangements in those areas managed through contracts than in those managed directly. Since there are several very different functions within governance, if form follows function there will also be several different forms. There are no pure forms of organisations; organisational hybrids are emerging which combine the bureaucratic, market and network modes of operation. The strain being experienced now is created because, despite the experimental projects at the margins, the dominant 'wiring' in public organisations is still bureaucratic. It can't cope.

The relationship organisation

When managers, staff and politicians are asked to invent the sorts of organisations they want to work in, they create something very different. They cover white boards and flip-charts with post-its and sticky paper, with drawings and cartoons that try to illustrate the ways they want to work in the future. They talk about better communication, about people being 'less territorial', about a willingness to be challenged, about taking responsibility for their own actions and having the power to put things right. They argue that more services could be user-focused, and people could be comfortable working in teams outside their conventional training or job. Work could be fun!

We suggested in Chapter 3 that networks of governance are based on the relationships between people inside organisations and in the communities they serve. It follows that it is the quality of relationships that will fundamentally determine the effectiveness of governance. If public organisations have to develop a capacity to establish relationships, then organisational forms must be developed that enable managers and staff to listen and respond, to make and keep promises. A relationship organisation will be one where staff are capable of reciprocity.

A relationship organisation is primarily connected outwards; individuals throughout the organisation are used to thinking about their roles and their responsibilities to the wider community. They can see the big picture – how things interconnect – and make judgements about the best ways to sustain the relationships necessary to achieve local goals. We know in our personal lives that relationships are not straightforward. They involve power, both power identified through status and position, and the power individuals are able to organise for themselves through their own personality, contacts, knowledge and skill. They can be more or less constrained by external rules and systems; and can involve greater or lesser degrees of trust, affection or shared understanding. Relationships with family members may involve affection without trust; relationships with GPs or teachers may involve trust without any real mutual understanding.

The relationship organisation is not just a service-delivery organisation. Managers and staff must be capable of recognising and responding to governance as well as service-delivery functions, and of relating to the public not simply as customers or clients but as authoriser-governors and as co-producers. People within a relationship organisation recognise the range of roles they may play. Relationships between front-line staff and managers and citizens are reflexive, in that the partners in the relationship are able to reflect on its value and effectiveness, and on the way they individually contribute to its effectiveness by what they do or say. That entails a self-consciousness and explicitness about the roles that managers and staff are taking, and their expectations, and about the roles that members of the public are taking, and their expectations in return. Managers or staff may address an individual as a customer, but it is always open to the customer to take on another role, as a citizen with rights, as a potential authoriser or a co-producer.

The roles undertaken in response by public managers become crucial. In the past they have often found themselves in situations where they represent a larger organisation but cannot speak on its behalf. They are forced to refer decisions back, to find out, and to 'see what I can do'. The constraints that prevent public managers from being able to speak as they find and to make and keep promises, harms the possibility of real relationships with local communities. Public managers and staff have to 'stand for' their organisations. But if they are to be able to build relationships, they also have to be fully human, and to carry responsibilities and accountabilities as themselves.

Managers and staff within public organisations are not simply freed to create effective human relationships at the individual level – they cannot, for example, simply authorise levels of spending which both they and the customer agree are necessary – since individual members of staff do not simply act out of their own values and judgement but on behalf of a wider community. There must be systems and rules, accountabilities and decision trails. The requirements of equity, equality and probity do not allow individual solutions to be found without regard to the impact they have on others. A relationship organisation must be capable of translating the experience derived from many individual exchanges into negotiated changes of policy and practice to serve the whole community.

This is not simply a plea for empowerment. That has a place, but it is not simply the individual user or the front-line worker who must be empowered. The objective is to empower a wider interlocking set of communities to plan their own destiny. If we consider the roles sketched out in Chapters 2 and 3 for politicians, managers and citizens, then organisations must be designed in ways that support those roles.

A relationship organisation requires rapid action and feedback. Without good delivery systems, organisations are unable to reciprocate – to respond to what they hear, to do what they say they are going to do. Delivery systems form a crucial connection between the organisation and the public, and must be fast, accurate and responsive. Not only must managers and staff within the organisation always know what is happening to services and be able to guarantee action, but the feedback systems should also reach the citizen, so that they also can judge the effectiveness of service delivery and intervention. Accurate information is essential for a truthful relationship. Systems have to underpin appropriate relationships, although these do not necessarily always involve any significant degree of human interaction. The charming women and men at First Direct bank greet us like long-lost friends, but we know their responses are carefully scripted and controlled. This is not usually a problem, since the system is designed to be responsive to customer needs. But if the system were not user-friendly, if it was impossible to get the system to respond or to find the right person to talk to, the absence of human contact outside the system would be infuriating. We are driven to distraction by a voice-mail system which only offers numbered choices that don't fit our needs. Systems in relationship organisations have to enable us to define for ourselves what we need. They have to enable us to reach someone who can step outside the system response if the system is failing. Public organisations do not yet have a good track record in seamless system interchange. Too many things still go wrong. The capacity to complain, to reach someone on the outside, the accountabilities and transparency of decision-making are all dimensions of reciprocity, of a relationship between organisation and local people.

If organisations are to respond to people outside, they will need fast and effective communication on the inside. Within a conventional bureaucracy those who are junior enough to hear the citizens cannot always themselves be heard. Often organisations are hard-wired so that while consultation can take place, nothing can easily be changed in response. A relationship organisation has constant feedback loops so that changes can be made easily in response to fresh insights – so that learning can be transmitted easily. Strong contractual relationships within the organisation which recognise mutual obligations enable external promises to be made and kept; and shared responsibility makes people work hard to keep their colleagues' promises.

The challenge of information technology

The challenge is not whether agencies involved in local governance embrace new technology, they have no option. Within five years the majority of public services will be on-line, and e-governance will be a reality. This will happen despite the practical difficulties, since local government is famous for achieving almost impossible tasks with almost impossible deadlines. The challenge is to use information technology in ways that support effective relationships. Implemented hastily, by IT anoraks with little understanding of organisational strategy, new technology could be used to hard-wire old provider–customer relationships and to reinforce departmentalism and secrecy. After all, public agencies are likely to be heavily reliant on private sector expertise which has no experience of the wider relationships of governance. Used creatively, on the other hand, information technology could create pathways for sharing knowledge not only between agencies, but also between government and citizens – and offer scope for community or consumer-designed interventions. The way new technology is used will be a crucial dimension of relationship organisations.

New forms for public organisations?

In design terms, a relationship organisation needs the maximum interaction between its constituent parts, and the maximum surface area exposed to the outside. It is tempting to suggest simply tearing away the vertical columns of the conventional organisation, but they make some sense for some functions, and experienced chief executives argue that radical structural change is not possible all at once. They say that staff need structure, that they cling to old structures and ways of working when they feel uncertain. In any case there is no point designing a structure that is beyond the experience and capacity of those who will work in it. The answer is to let new structures evolve; changing the organisation organically, by bending the walls of traditional structures to enable people to work together on a day-to-day basis, sharing buildings and offices and databases. It is possible to make holes in the walls of conventional structures so that it is easier to see out, and easier for new information to get in, to use secondments and job swaps to break through conventional demarcations. Old structures can be bent and folded until they work effectively, and can be wired together in ways that enable energy and knowledge to flow freely.

It helps if managers and staff from different professional backgrounds work together, have desks next to each other, and work in project groups. In relationship organisations, project groups are part of the mainstream and are managed as tightly and held as effectively to account as any vertical line-management structure. Projects are not squeezed in on top of the 'day job' they replace the old working day. In Redbridge, the permanent housing strategy team includes a town planner, a regeneration expert, and a social services manager alongside housing colleagues – all able to share the expertise they need for joined-up working. Relationship boundaries inevitably spill over organisational boundaries, so systems of communication, networking and practice exchange have to involve people from the outside. Increasingly we are seeing the creation of virtual organisations – working spaces created between organisations, rather than within them. In Lewisham, the benefits agency and the housing benefits department share a building; and in many local authority areas, health and local authority managers jointly commission health and social care – in shared buildings, side by side, sharing databases. Some authorities are linking book clubs and reading groups to GP surgeries. In one housing association, the local caretaker is teaching single parents computer skills in the evening.

It is possible to start small: building new ways of working into the mainstream, beginning with small horizontal projects but allowing them more space as they grow, slowly removing old structures as they are outgrown by the new. The process of change has less similarity with engineering and more with horticulture. For example, we might think of propagation by layering – partially breaking the old stem and creating space for a new plant to grow, only severing the link when the new roots are strong. It is possible to build links and to exchange learning between projects, creating 'attractors' so that other managers and staff learn from success.

The emerging relationship organisations will require very different leadership. There is less and less likely to be a 'top' from which instructions and orders can descend. There will still be a centre, but a centre that is moving, circling around the cells, making sure that they are useful and necessary, providing support, redesigning the wiring and capillary systems, and keeping the organisation in constant contact with the outside world. There is still a need for strong direction, but that comes when everyone within the organisation understands what they are trying to achieve and why. A shared sense of 'who we are' and what the organisation is trying to do is essential to shape the relationships that front-line staff make every day. Without a clear framework for making choices, all staff can do is follow procedures. Strong leaders do not try and do everything themselves, but focus the attention of others on the problems that need to be solved. The job of leadership in a relationship organisation is to set direction, to tell the story, to explain the reasons and to then design the spaces in which other people make things happen.

Public agencies are already beginning to discard the old structure charts that used to describe how they worked. Some organisations have tried to turn them upside down, others have replaced the boxes and lines with circles. Relationship organisations are easier to access than old bureaucracies, but harder to draw.

The task is not to try and create a perfect structure, but to find ways that people within organisations can outperform the structural constraints they face. The metaphors needed to help think about such organisations are not mechanical or engineering metaphors, but are more often drawn from the world of physics and biology – for example metaphors about processes for conducting and transforming energy so that it can be put to use. We need to understand the wiring – or the capillary systems – of governance in order to move energy around efficiently. We need to take account of what happens when the power is running, when energy is racing between connections, when the organisation comes alive.

Alternative models for local governance?

Our public service 'hybrid' organisations may evolve, over time, into other models. One possibility would be a clearer cell structure, able to combine and recombine roles and functions at different levels. If the organisation's communication and feedback systems were strong enough, new cells could be created and 'dead' cells discarded with relative ease as needs changed. Service providers might become 'capsule' organisations, with considerable autonomy, but held directly accountable for service failure.

Alternatively, organisational arrangements might follow power to the local neighbourhood. New 'decentred' authorities could emerge. There might be a strategic organisational core slimmed down to the bare minimum at city or locality level, with service delivery organised through contracts negotiated at the neighbourhood level. Neighbourhood governance could be linked to the local council, but might not be. The strategic core might cease to be simply the local authority, and become a 'city board' including politicians and managers from the local council, and board members from the health authority, police service, housing associations, local skills and training councils, voluntary organisations and local businesses. The board could operate as a clearing house for sorting out local strategy and problems, and it would be able to pool the resources of the different local agencies, share support systems and data, and manage interventions through mixed teams.

Elected mayors could emerge at the centre of a web of local governance, working directly with city leaders from other agencies. Although an elected mayor is likely to be preoccupied with popular and media issues, this may focus attention on the outcomes that matter to voters. A higher media profile and a powerful personal office will increase focus on the place rather than any single organisation. If we watch a spider, it spends most of its day patiently maintaining the web. Similarly, the job of the leader at the centre of a web is relationship maintenance. This sort of role has begun to be adopted by mayors in some US cities and towns, who see themselves as coordinators, working across the city or town, moving outside the specific organisation of the local authority, as skilled orchestrators of events.

These models are not ideal types; they are simply illustrations of different organisational forms. Some are already emerging in practice, others exist in other countries but legal and financial constraints prevent their emergence in the UK – yet. They all have weaknesses as well as strengths. The 'web' organisation will be prone to the short-termism and media focus of the mayor, and may disempower others, slowing down delivery. The city board is dependent on the capacity of key leaders to share power and develop a jointly-owned agenda; but with poor leadership it could become paralyzed. The decentred authority could lead to chaos if there are conflicting and overlapping boundaries between the neighbourhoods set up by the local authority and the boundaries of other agencies or zones. There are important dilemmas of legitimacy and accountability to be managed, and dangers of strategic failure. New organisational forms will have their own design faults, different from but probably as difficult to manage as the familiar design faults of traditional structures.

A range of experiments is essential since the answer is not obvious, and there may be several different possible designs, each better adapted to the challenges of local governance than current models. Instead of seeing these problems as evidence of failure, we could understand them as the growing pains of radically different organisational forms.

5 Networks and Partnerships

Different organisational designs for local governance may be emerging, and we are seeing the beginnings of networks or virtual organisations. But the reality is that local organisations are not going to be able to change their form radically in the short term. Whatever, therefore, the long-term possibilities, networks of governance will for the foreseeable future involve cross-boundary working within and between separate organisations with no 'designed-in' linkages or shared systems. In this chapter I want to ask – how well is this working?

Pressures towards cross-boundary working

The pressures driving public sector organisations to work together are threefold: pressures created by the fragmentation of delivery systems, pressures created by government incentives and penalties, and pressures generated locally because of a focus on outcomes. These three are very different: the first reflects a change in the external environment; the second a change in government policy; while the third reflects a change in locally determined purposes and objectives. And they are not experienced or responded to in the same way in all localities.

The introduction of selective externalisation – through CCT, and changes within social services, education, health and housing – means that many public bodies now purchase services from other public, voluntary or private organisations. There are a range of new contract or semi-contract relationships between purchasers and providers, strategic planning is often carried out jointly between commissioner or purchaser organisations, and provision is often made through consortia or collaborative arrangements between providers. Throughout the 1980s and 1990s, public organisations have had to develop skills in commissioning, purchasing, contract management and partnership working. This has not always been easy, and in many cases shared delivery systems still do not work smoothly.

Cross-boundary working has also been driven by government policy. This began under the Conservatives, but the Blair government has been determined to achieve more effective partnership working. The *Modernising Government* White Paper promised 'joined up government in action' (Cabinet Office, 1999, p. 6) and pledged action to 'establish partnerships in delivering services ... to establish common targets, financial frameworks, IT links, management controls and accountability mechanisms' (p. 12). The government has also offered incentives for partnership working, but the drive towards it has not simply come from central government. A third set of pressures comes from a growing focus on community needs at a local level. This is partly because commissioner organisations are free to ask themselves new questions about 'why do we need this' or 'is this the right service', rather than being preoccupied by the day-to-day problems of service delivery. It is also a result of a growing strategic management capacity at the top of many public bodies, and a better understanding of the aspirations of local people. A focus on social outcomes inevitably leads to cross-boundary working, since social problems such as unemployment, community disintegration and rural isolation fall across the core statutory activities of most local agencies. In the 1990s, partnerships in Birmingham, Manchester, Newcastle and Leeds began to transform the urban environment and the local economy. A local partnership in Basildon chose to concentrate on attracting inward investment and has achieved a startling economic transformation. Kensington and Chelsea and Hammersmith and Fulham at the heart of the Aids epidemic in the UK created ground-breaking partnerships between hospitals, health authorities, social services and the voluntary sector that revolutionised care for a new patient group. Change has been driven as much from within local agencies themselves as it has by government or public pressure.

In most local authority areas there is now, typically, a community planning or regeneration partnership, crime and disorder partnership, joint care planning between health and social services, a partnership arrangement between the local housing authority and the housing associations in the area, an Agenda 21 partnership, and a range of lesser partnerships, including drugs action teams, education and training partnerships, and so forth. The scrabble to attract new funding has led to a myriad of overlapping schemes within the deprived areas of the country, all attracting funding on different bases, with different monitoring regimes and different partners involved in each scheme.

Shared working is most often horizontal (that is between different government organisations at the local or neighbourhood level) with less evidence of vertical or diagonal connectivity. Many such schemes are in the early stages of formation. Inevitably, of course, partnerships are built between the hybrid organisations discussed in the last chapter. This means that the people who are sent out to work across agency boundaries are often from the new parts of public organisations, from the chief executives' office or the strategy team, new corporate managers or the most creative of the policy or project managers. They will tend to meet like-minded people who have been sent from other agencies, and they will quickly be able to draft shared strategy and agree objectives. But they do so without always having the operational authority or the practical day-to-day responsibility to make things change within their own organisations. When they go back to their home organisations, they may find it hard to persuade others to carry into action the ideas and suggestions that come from the partners. The hybridisation of public agencies can create a virtual partnership which is no longer connected to mainstream delivery or to the mass of middle managers who make things happen on the ground.

Public agencies are keen to demonstrate their partnership credentials, and afraid to talk about partnership failures. This makes it difficult, except from very close in, to distinguish between a cosmetic partnership and a real one, between effective cross-boundary working and a hopeless mess.

Experience elsewhere

This explicit set of cross-boundary partnership arrangements is more advanced in the UK than in the rest of Europe, but since the fragmentation of government agencies has been greater here than in other countries, there are stronger imperatives to work together across boundaries. The UK has a longer experience of urban initiatives that sit outside the traditional policy departments and agencies than most of Europe. 'Britain is in the lead, rather than lagging, in terms of designing area-based initiatives' (Parkinson, 1998, p. 5). In the UK we are more preoccupied with 'formal partnership' working, but this may be in part a side-effect of a more systematic separation of central, local and regional government, and the absence of less-formal power-sharing traditions such as in France, Spain or Italy. The French 'Contrat de Ville' on which the Local Government Association (LGA) New Commitment to Regeneration is closely modelled represents a 'local application of the old state/department/commune network which has served France well for centuries' (M. Stewart, 2000, p. 43). Traditions in different countries are coloured by very different histories and experiences, thus in

Denmark the problems addressed by targeted initiatives are very small in scale, in the Netherlands a history of rational planning makes consensus building between centre and locality more easily reached, and in areas which have experimented with devolution of power to local authorities there is far greater diversity of approach at local level (for example Norway and Sweden).

The UK may be ahead on the formalisation of joint arrangements through partnership (Burton *et al.*, 1987; Ball, 1994; Geddes, 1998), but this may be as much to do with the failure of evolved relationships as to do with a superiority of structural arrangements. The arrangements emerging in Britain have a more transatlantic origin, where the exchange of practice has been more systematic (see Hambledon and Taylor, 1994; Judd and Parkinson, 1990). Stewart points to the exchange of experiments in both directions, urban development action grants, enterprise zones, and so on (M. Stewart, 2000, p. 44). Messages include the need for strong community involvement and ownership, the need for flexibility of resource use and the importance of social capital and community asset building. However, US states and cities have local power and resources that no UK locality has ever possessed. In Miami, for example, a community vision of the economic positioning of the state led to a change in the local school curriculum to encourage the skills needed for new industries.

Are partnerships or networks working?

It may be too early to tell. Whitehall has commissioned a series of evaluation studies to understand how partnership can be made more effective. Each study adopts a different approach, but the conclusions are dramatically consistent (Stewart, Goss *et al.*, 1999; Richards *et al.*, 1999; M. Stewart, 2000). Almost all participants see partnership working as positive, even essential, but are finding it far harder than expected. The research consensus is that while progress is being made, the obstacles are still formidable. Some things are helping: a focus on outcomes, innovation at local level, unitary status, corporate focus and flatter structures, better consultation, cultural change, investment in training and leadership development. Where professional silos have been broken up, partnership working seems to accelerate. There have been parallel breakthroughs in some areas of the civil service; particularly those involved in 'joined-up' implementation.

But it seems to take a very long time before shared objectives are established and measurable results follow. The processes of getting to know each other, sharing data, identifying problems, identifying resources and planning action can take years, not months. Partnerships are often shaky at first, and while experienced partnerships have been able to solve their early problems, others have deteriorated rapidly. In some cases partnerships set up to bid for funding don't survive long enough to spend it. The 1998 evaluation of single regeneration budget (SRB) partnerships found that between 11 and 30 per cent were performing poorly (in the terms set by government). The consensus among researchers is that partnership arrangements consume a huge amount of time, energy and resources to create relatively limited outcomes and outputs. They are probably still consumers of value, not producers of value. While the potential is considerable, results have so far been small-scale. While partnerships and networks seem to be good at strategy, planning, document writing, research, data-gathering and so on, delivery is harder. Few partnerships have made the transition to pooled resources or joint programmes. Processes seem, in general, to be cumbersome, and practitioners at all levels talk about too many partnerships and about partnership fatigue. Partnerships are often unwieldy, with lots of partners, and there is often a rapid sense of drift and a lack of clarity about purpose.

While structure is not the most important problem, there are structural difficulties created by non-coterminosity, by the layers and different roles of agencies at the regional and national level, by the departmental divisions at national level and within local organisations. 'Zonitis' reinforces territorial jealousies, and partners often lack sufficiently powerful shared interests to overcome the pull back to professional and departmental concerns.

Partnerships are often successful at bidding for and spending additional government funding, but fail to change mainstream services or to bend or reallocate mainstream resources. Partnerships based around city-wide or locality problems are seen as tangential to the activity of the major spending departments. Overstretched operational managers are thus reluctant to lose staff and resources to activities outside 'core business'. Crosscutting issues are driven to the margins by strong departmental interests and traditional silo mentalities, reinforced by professional alliances across central/local boundaries and by powerful incentives to concentrate on national service targets. When messages are contradictory, middle managers often retreat into bureaucratic practice and resist risk-taking. Staff, who experience change as threatening in any case, are unlikely to invest too much energy in difficult cross-agency arrangements if it seems likely that these are not serious compared with mainstream organisational activities.

There is excessive attention to procedural systems and this is made worse by heavy requirements for vertical audit trails. Each government initiative

Figure 5.1 *Whole systems thinking – Negative feedback – 1*

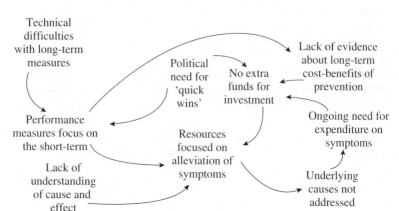

Source: Stewart, M. and Goss, S. *et al.* (1999) *Cross-Cutting Issues in Local Government* (London: DETR, 1999).

Figure 5.2 *Whole systems thinking – Negative feedback – 2*

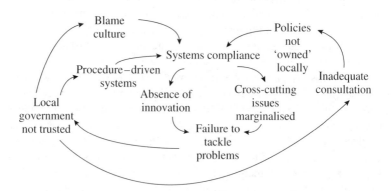

Source: Stewart, M. and Goss, S. *et al.* (1999) *Cross-Cutting Issues in Local Government* (London: DETR, 1999).

has its own funding stream, its own detailed processes for bidding, appraisal, monitoring and delivery, its own 'bells to be rung'. The generation of leverage and matching funding is time consuming and tiresome, and particularly onerous where projects are funded from different sources each requiring information in a different format. Partner organisations are dragged into bureaucracy and board members are forced into detailed administration. With practice, a successful partnership can manage the bureaucracy quite easily, developing a local strategy and then bidding for government resources opportunistically when they fit the strategy rather than being entirely responsive. Some authorities have set up bidding units to make the process more efficient and concentrate knowledge. Nevertheless, there are opportunity costs at all levels. The cost of system compliance, monitoring and reporting eats into the funds available for local projects, and the tyranny of annual funding threatens project continuity. Bidding can also poison local relationships and encourage competition between communities; and fragmented funding makes everything short-term.

Partnerships are often very instrumental. Their main purpose is to bid for funds or to match government requirements, or to win competitions for additional funds. Creative managers within public agencies, always on the look out for new sources to fund overstretched services, will often try to put together schemes and deals, but not necessarily have the leadership authority or capability to make the partnerships or networks function. Linkages are often partial, with good relationships at one level between different organisations but no consistency of linkage at all levels. Frequent changes of personnel mean that links between agencies are constantly broken, and have to be constantly renewed. Relationships of trust are hard to build up between organisations which often have a history of conflict, or which fail to understand the differences in organisational goals and culture. Often the people who go to partnership meetings don't understand what else is happening inside their own organisations, so that they cannot promise on behalf of their organisation, or ensure that their organisation's promises are delivered. These problems reinforce each other, leading to reinforcing cycles of partnership failure. Two examples of negative feedprovided back loops are in Figures 5.1 and 5.2.

Practical solutions at the local level

Much can be done to strengthen positive drivers and to tackle the problems identified above. There is considerable consensus, from research, from the accumulating set of good practice guides and from experience, about the practical steps that can be done to tackle the problems identified at local level:

- In the first place, partner organisations can work together to explore and agree the objectives of cross-boundary working. Without clear shared outcome objectives, action will not follow. These have to be negotiated locally, to make sense to all the local participants. Without hard work to define local problems and to define concepts such as social exclusion or regeneration or diversity in ways that make sense of a local situation, objectives are likely to remain too vague to be actioned.

- Second, partner organisations need to share an understanding of what the partnership/network is *for* – is it primarily for information exchange, for strategic planning, for some limited joint activities, or a wider process of integrated delivery systems, resource pooling and so on. A model developed by the Kings Fund distinguished between competition, cooperation, coordination and coevolution behaviours needed in different circumstances. Is what is being created a loose network, a partnership or a virtual organisation? The different forms have different design and system requirements. A loose network that is merely an idea or information exchange does not necessarily carry the requirements for shared objectives or action plans – but will require shared systems for exchanging information, and some basic network rules. A partnership implies a level of mutuality, a contractual arrangement, and will require work to define roles, expectations, responsibilities and means of redress. A virtual organisation will require attention to its design, agreement about management arrangements, project management, resource flows and systems.

- Third, the organisations need to develop an appropriate shared strategy. Complex government initiatives must simply be treated as the operating context, and local players have to calmly and quietly choose the most important local problems to solve. There is likely to be a critical mass of key actions that will begin to achieve many goals simultaneously. Instead of inventing long lists of actions to match the long list of targets, partnerships can look for synergy and identify the few important ways in which resources could be deployed differently. There should be a realistic expectation that all planned actions will be taken, and that they are sufficient to achieve shared goals.

- Fourth, it is important to clarify roles, expectations and responsibilities for all the players. These will differ depending on the sort of cross-boundary working developed, and will be 'light' in a network and 'heavy' in a virtual organisation. But without explicit agreement about who attends meetings, at what level of seniority, whether or not substitutes are allowed, whether actions can be authorised outside meetings by bilaterals, what happens if organisations cannot or do not deliver and so on – there will be no basis for making the partnership work. It helps to create some sort of contract between participants based on what is expected of everyone. Partners may not all play the same roles within the partnership, but unless this is made explicit, problems may emerge. The partnership or network must fulfil the minimum expectations of all the partners, although it may not be able to live up to the expectations of the most ambitious.

- Fifth, partners will need to work at creating a culture in which cross-boundary working is likely to succeed. This may include sharing understanding of each other's problems and priorities, valuing diversity of perspective and different expertise, and finding processes which can build solutions rather than simply arguing.
- Sixth, partners have to create appropriate shared delivery systems. If partnerships are going to take action, they need to devise decision-making structures, delegate authority to act to carry out those decisions and to set boundaries. There may be a need to link service-delivery systems, perhaps through one-stop shops or call-centres, perhaps through linkages and signposting. Even if only a loose network is intended, holes will have to be drilled through organisational structures that make it possible for people to meet and talk easily. Some partnerships have pooled or swapped staff, or have introduced shadowing or buddying arrangements. Networks and partnerships need information-sharing systems (using email, internet, shared databases, video-conferencing and so on, and may need to create financial systems, audit and decision trails to match their objectives or to develop shared risk-management or option-appraisal systems. Shared training may become essential if organisations are to understand each other.
- Finally, any network or partnership has to have a clear idea of what success would look like, and the evidence that would indicate problems or failure. Agreeing a set of criteria and a process for reflection and review will offer a way to put the partnership back on course when things go wrong.

Box 5.1 *Basildon: a partnership for regeneration*

Basildon set up a partnership to tackle the problems of regeneration. As an old, 'first generation' new town, it had gained a reputation for being down-at-heel and a centre of poverty in wealthy Essex. The partnership brought together several services within the local council,

(continued)

the town police superintendent, the chief executives of the two new local primary care groups, the health authority, the probation service, the employment service, the voluntary sector and key local businesses. The partnership worked together to build shared terms of engagement and to explore what each agency needed and could contribute. As they began to hammer out priorities, it became clear that the long list of partnership objectives was not realistic. Hard negotiation about what each agency could contribute in terms of time, money and energy led to an agreement to concentrate on one shared project which could be achieved, to prepare for a second, and to run an information-exchange network alongside the practical work. The single project was to change the image of the town – in reality and perception – since hard evidence showed that recruitment and retention of good staff depended on a belief that the town was a good place to live. The agencies began to pool resources, share learning and link key staff together in a time-limited but pragmatic set of steps with measurable objectives. Since 1999, progress has been made on a number of other fronts as well as the town image.

We've heard all this before ...

If we know so much about the problems facing cross-boundary initiatives – and about workable solutions – why does nothing seem to change? The same conclusions are drawn in report after report; and yet while more research is commissioned into the problems of joined-up working, more guidance sought, more best-practice examples hunted down, little is done to tackle the underlying forces that mean old patterns are repeated. Murray Stewart, in a recent review of regeneration initiatives argues that the whole of the government community has known these things for many years, 'The absence of integrated working is long-standing, culturally embedded, historically impervious, obvious to all concerned and deeply entrenched in central and local government' (M. Stewart, 2000, p. 56).

For example, at the local level cross-boundary initiatives were set up in the 1960s under the Urban Programme, in the 1970s in the Community Development Programmes, in the 1980s through City Challenge, and now again through a series of initiatives and zones. Several writers remind us that zones are not new (Higgins, 1998; Higgins *et al.*, 1983) and there is a danger that 1990s initiatives mirror the thinking of the 1970s. There are patterns in the history of area-based programmes, from Education Priority Areas, Housing Action Areas and the Urban Programme in the 1960s, to the Inner City Partnerships and City Action Teams in the 1970s and 1980s to City Challenge, New Deal for Communities and Estate Action in the 1990s. The government's Social Exclusion Unit quoted a regeneration specialist: 'One of the most depressing aspects of the study of urban regeneration is the incidence of wheel reinvention and the failure properly to absorb the lessons of experience' (Fordham, 1995, p. 20).

There has never been any systematic learning from the past; what makes us think we can succeed now, when the progress made by these initiatives faded away in the past? Are the current trends towards cross-boundary working different from those that have gone before? Is power still located in the same places, or do the new partnerships represent a different distribution of power? Are new players involved? Do new partnerships involve working in different ways, so that decisions are not only taken by different people but are taken differently?

Making sense of cross-boundary working

Despite the multiplicity of models in development, there is not, as yet, any clarity to the language or any agreed definitional precision. 'Theoretical concepts about partnerships remain vague' (M. Stewart, 2000, p. 20), and the empirical evidence remains ambiguous (see Skelcher and Lowndes, 1998; Roberts *et al.*, 1995; Russell *et al.*, 1996; Brennan *et al.*, 1998). Stewart argues that existing partnerships are highly contextually-specific and come in all shapes, sizes and structures. There are no unique models of successful partnerships, nor is there an easy route to the design of the successful partnership. Indeed, he argues the term is becoming discredited 'since whilst almost all initiatives seem to occur within a partnership of some kind or another (often demanded by central government) at the local level the key players are beginning to become suspicious of new partnerships' (M. Stewart, 2000, p. 48).

It is possible to call anything a partnership or a network, but by doing so it doesn't mean that any particular set of relationships or characteristics is present. The word 'partnership' is commonly used, but whereas within the private sector partnering is well-defined, in the public sector it seems simply to describe any situation when a group of people from different agencies come together regularly.

Rhodes' account of the interrelationships between government agencies, interest groups, professional and producer interests in policy formation offers the most developed theoretical model. Drawing on theories of interest group intermediation (Rhodes, 1997), he suggests that policy networks are characterised by interdependence between organisations; continual interaction between network members in order to exchange resources and negotiate shared purposes; game-like interactions rooted in trust and regulated by rules of the game negotiated and agreed by network partners; and a significant degree of autonomy from the state. He describes a 'game' in which participants manoeuvre for advantage, each 'deploys its resources whether constitutional legal, organisational, financial, political or informational, to maximise influence over outcomes, while trying to avoid becoming dependent on the other "players"' (1997, p. 37). Not only do different organisations have different interests – but within organisations there are different interests and they may work together separately and for different ends across organisational boundaries. For example, health and social care managers may have a shared interest in combining provision to achieve savings in both organisations, while doctors and social workers may have a common interest in sustaining professional distinctions. Rhodes tells us that we cannot assume that any of this flurry of activity does, or is even intended to, achieve results. The 'game' might simply be to move resources around to enhance the status of key players and ensure the production of lots of paperwork, without achieving any measurable results on the ground.

Policy formation is only one dimension of the work that is increasingly carried out within partnerships or networks, and the people engaged in policy formation are different from those engaged in implementation. Since these activities go on at different levels within organisations, partnerships or networks require not simply effective horizontal working at the level of policy, but a multiplicity of vertical, horizontal and diagonal linkages. The power of key players differs between policy formation and implementation. For example, the civil service has predominant power at the stage of national policy formation, and can override the knowledge-from-experience of people from the locality level. Implementation, however, requires coalitions of operational managers (such as GPs, policemen and women, local community members) and their 'reality' may not be reflected in the policy. The power of ministers and civil servants to insist on certain policies and procedures does not and cannot ensure that they succeed on the ground.

The image of a complex 'game' with negotiated rules is helpful, but the level of stability it implies does not exist at local level. The relative power and influence of different actors is the subject of serious contestation, with each agency having different interests and priorities. Their successful functioning is contingent on the actions of politicians, managers and staff within each of the participating organisations. Collaboration will be successful if the forces that drive partners together are more powerful than those that prise them apart. However, the accountabilities of each potential partner are different, which means that central–local relationships are uneven within partnerships.

There is no balancing or policing function capable of ensuring that partnerships or networks work effectively. Outside the framework of the simple organisation, the levers that control performance directly, and the chains of command that can require certain actions and behaviours, break down. In a network, while power may be unequal, the only way that accountability can be established or performance managed is through effective relationships.

Government agencies are part of the wider networks of governance, and there is no single government player, either at central or local level. Even within central government there are many government departments; and within each department civil servants work differently at national, regional and local levels. Each professional group may have different loyalties, and insofar as government is held together and can be seen to act coherently, it does so through the coordinating capacity of the political leadership. A powerful political project is capable of driving the alignment of different parts of government. Without such a project, different parts of government tend to act in contradictory ways. It is not only politicians who are involved in making and changing relationships of power.

Systems thinking

The map of local players is complex, but the 'true' map of players is more complex still, since ministers, civil service departments, government offices of the regions, professional bodies, training colleges and universities are all part of the wider context within which local initiatives take place. A single intervention, such as a government initiative, or an organisational action, does not work in isolation from the actions and reactions of a wide range of other social actors. Systems thinking attempts to build an understanding of the way that the actions of each individual or organisation impact on the whole system.

Systems analysis has been used within organisational theory to explore the way an organisation interacts with its environment, using organic metaphors to describe an organisational system as inherently adaptive. Early functionalist social theory based on closed systems (Parsons, 1951) gave way to thinking based on open systems in which organisations transacted with their environment, and to 'contingency theory' with an emphasis on 'designing organisations rationally so that their internal coherence and external match to their environment are both maximised (Tsoukas, 1994, p. 44).

Senge moves away from seeing organisations as adaptive systems to stressing 'systems thinking' in which strategists understand the systems effects within a wider set of interactions. Systems thinking is a discipline for seeing the structure that underlies complex situations, and for recognising the effects of reinforcing, balancing or interruptive feedback loops within a complex set of interactions. Senge argues that it involves seeing wholes rather than parts, it is 'a framework for seeing interactions rather than things, for seeing patterns of change, rather than static snapshots', (1990, p. 68). The system cannot be limited to a single organisation or set of organisations, 'Systems thinking shows that there is no outside; that you and the cause of your problems are part of a single system' (p. 67).

Kooiman uses analogies from socio-cybernetic systems to register the contingency of systems responses. We are looking at 'the pattern or structure that emerges in a socio-political system as a "common result" or outcome of the interacting intervention efforts of all involved actors. The pattern cannot be reduced to one actor or group of actors in particular' (Kooiman, 1993, p. 258). We cannot predict behaviours and actions from formal relationships and rules, since any actual event will involve the actions and reaction of a number of active players attempting to shape their own environment. But this does not mean that complex interactions are unknown, or unknowable.

Governance can therefore be seen as a systemic series of interactions which cannot simply be examined from the standpoint of any single organisation, treating the rest as 'environment'. Nor can we see the world of governance as a closed system or one that is necessarily or inevitably adaptive. There are no automatic systems effects and the system is not necessarily in balance, since the outcomes are the results of many thousands of actors following their own interests. Individuals and organisations always respond actively to the surroundings and circumstances in which they find themselves. They do not simply follow the rules – but they are never able to act freely, since they are always also constrained or acted upon by other powerful actors.

Government policy does not always achieve the intended impact. As powerful players react they change the conditions within which a policy can be implemented. The implementation of CCT is a good example. The government intention was to drive the externalisation of many council services to the private sector, but the reality was that unless this was also a local intention, it did not happen. In some localities it led to the adoption of more efficient delivery systems by in-house teams that benchmarked themselves more carefully against the private sector; in others it led to 'pretend' competitive procedures and the shuffling of money and systems to comply with the letter of the law; in yet others it led to radical rethinking of provision and the creation of joint ventures or partnership arrangements; and in some it had the unforeseen consequence of bureaucratising service provision by driving tight and over-detailed service specifications that constrain innovation and strangle efficient delivery.

The way to understand a system is to watch it in motion, and we shall explore in Chapter 8 some of the ways to do this. One of the useful lessons for understanding partnerships is that there are no neutral observers of the policy implementation process; the actions of ministers, civil servants, academic commentators and evaluators will all impact on the likely outcome. It is not possible for civil servants to study the effectiveness of partnership working and issue guidance to improve it, without recognising that the very process of 'arms length observation and issuing guidance' itself impacts on the capacity of local agencies to respond appropriately. Powerful system effects can be caused by factors often assumed to be outside the system.

Underlying forces in partnership working

If we look carefully at the evidence of what has led cross-boundary working to fail in the past, we can gather clues about how things might change in the future. There seem to be four sets of forces that have undermined effective cross-boundary working for several decades, which go to the heart of our social policy and government systems. It will not be easy to change them.

The professions

The first problem is the professional isolationism that underlies many social interventions. Professional services have become increasingly specialised and delivered from large separate departments, and they are often matched by equivalent separate departments within central government. This narrows the scope of intervention and well-meaning professional actions can be undermined or cancelled by failures to communicate across boundaries. The Audit Commission evaluation of the youth justice system illustrated this dramatically. As Perri 6 (1997, p. 5) concluded:

> far from solving problems of exclusion, the ways in which government is organised all too often exacerbate them. Dozens of different agencies may deal with the same client. Problems that are in practice rounded ones are sliced into separate segments for treatment by social services, police, probation, the benefits agency and job centres. Problems that require long-term efforts to help repair fractured families, to help people out of drug abuse, to regain confidence and self esteem, are dealt with within the confines of annual spending rounds and by professions, the vast majority of whose efforts go to dealing with the damage of social exclusion after it has happened rather than preventing it.

Andrew Foster (1999) of the Audit Commission argued at a recent conference that 'the challenge is to join up education officers, teachers, social workers, youth workers, the voluntary sector, the police into something that looks like an army for the good rather than loads of shambling armies who just criss-cross peoples' lives'.

While there are magnificent examples that have overcome professional isolationism, there are ever-present tendencies to professionalise the new cross-boundary areas of work. Agenda 21, neighbourhood management, regeneration, social exclusion – are all areas where existing professional bodies and academic institutions will try to create new qualifications and barriers to entry. At worst, new professional groupings will crop up claiming exclusive knowledge to deal with cross-boundary working. To prevent this would require the rethinking of professional training, professional qualifications and the heavy glass ceilings that exist within many professions. Indeed, it will require 'joined-up thinking' from professional institutions so that they develop radically different ways to educate the next generation of public professionals. Like all the other agencies responsible for partnership working, they need the incentives, and the freedom to do so.

Public organisations

The next problem can perhaps be seen as the perverse result of the changes in the 1980s aimed at improving organisational efficiency. By borrowing from private sector practice, we have created for the first time 'the public organisation' separate from a particular service or profession. It has, in some ways, offered an escape route from the dominance of professional thinking, but has replaced a professional focus not with an outcome focus but with an organisational focus. The creation of a Health Trust out of what was before a huge National Health Service has created procedures, loyalties, finance and business systems that relate to an organisation rather than to a linked set of interventions in the public's health. This strengthens the capacity to manage the performance of those activities which are bounded within the organisation, but weakens the capacity to manage performance where activities cross boundaries. The NHS's greatest problems are created at the points of entry and exit from the key organisations – referral systems, waiting lists, GP gatekeeping and discharge policies, for example.

The introduction of new contracts and quasi-commercial arrangements works well within each contract, but difficulties emerge where different contract arrangements begin to collide. Social services care packages, for example, are so complex because of the different contracting strategies of many different players. The creation of a performance culture within these organisational structures has reinforced departmental and organisational boundaries, so that individual departments or business units have business plans, performance management systems and service targets which make it impossible to contribute easily to crosscutting goals. The use of heavily enforced but relatively poor measures of performance add to the problem, since it intensifies the danger of perverse incentives. Measures that assess process rather than outputs, activity rather than results, or organisationally-based populations rather than total populations – all distort intervention. By measuring educational performance within each school, rather than for a local population, an incentive was created for schools to exclude disruptive pupils – which raised their target performance but left disturbed children vandalising the streets. An early housing benefit measure counted the proportion of claims processed within 14 weeks – leading at least one provider to heap up all the claims that passed the due date in a drawer, since once they had failed the deadline there was no incentive to process them at all! These measures have both been abandoned, and at both civil service and local level good work is underway to develop newer and better measures. But any focus on performance within a single department or agency blocks lateral thinking about new delivery systems that might cross boundaries.

The focus on a single organisation does not reflect the motivation and priorities of public managers. Recent research into the motivation of public managers shows that 'for public and voluntary sector managers the outcomes of their work for users and the community provide the most powerful driving force, and the context in which they work towards other

goals', whilst by contrast, the 'prosperity of their organisations is the uni-
fying theme for private sector managers' (Steele, 1999, p. 13). It may be
that the stress on the public sector organisation is a 1980s import from the
private sector rather than an intrinsic feature of public provision.

Central government

The actions of national government contribute to the success or failure of
joined-up working on the ground. Departmental separation at central government level is as serious a boundary as departmental separatism at local
level. 'The structure of central government in the UK is informal and
unsystematic – a historical patchwork continuously adapted and re-adapted
to meet new political fashions and expediencies' (Weir and Beetham,
1999, p. 158). It can be hard even within a department as large as the
Department of the Environment, Transport and the Regions (DETR) for
the civil servants responsible for planning or transport to know what the
civil servants responsible for housing are doing. And yet Whitehall continues to keep a tight grip over local partnerships. For twenty years, local initiatives aimed at tackling cross-boundary problems have been funded and
controlled from the civil service, which leaves them vulnerable not only to
the problems that emerge at local level, but to the problems within the civil
service. These have been well-documented over the years:

> We glimpse in operation a system which is extremely centralised with-
> out, however, being decisive; and procedures which are extraordinarily
> time-consuming, yet leave one with no confidence that the evidence
> has been systematically and objectively explored ... [It] is a process of
> decision-making that is ponderous, ritualised, secretive and highly unre-
> liable in its results. (Professor David Henderson, 1977, in Hennessey,
> 1989, p. 730)

Peter Hennessey quotes Stephen Taylor ten years later, saying the UK
civil service is 'not corrupt, it's not politicised, it's not grossly inefficient
and it's not stupid and those are not things you can say about the civil
service in most other countries' (1989, pp. 692–3), but adds:

> Whitehall is closed, secretive, defensive, over-concerned with tradition
> and precedent, still insufficiently seized of the crucial importance of
> managing people and nothing like as good as it should be ... at con-
> fronting hard long-term problems by thinking forward systematically
> and strategically. (p. 693)

It would be wrong to allow impressions from ten years ago to remain untested, however; the civil service has been changing over the past decade. The introduction of market-testing and private sector personnel has created more performance-conscious, output-focused organisations. Civil servants have begun to work more closely with public servants from local and regional government, to listen more to lay advisers, and to visit the field. The pressures towards partnership working have been felt at all levels of the civil service, and there are now cross-departmental working parties, seminars and networks on a number of themes. Initiatives such as the Social Exclusion Unit, the Urban Task Force and a range of other task-forces have moved beyond old boundaries, and begun to at least 'join up' ideas. The Cabinet Office is exploring issues such as cultural change, leadership and motivation, and the civil service is paying considerable attention to public management rather than simply public policy. Relationships between different parts of the centre, and between the centre and the periphery seem to be improving.

The question must be how deeply are the changes penetrating, and how strongly rooted are the traditions which they are attempting to displace. The political process does not help. Inevitably, the extent to which the civil service has seen itself as serving the incumbent minister reinforces short-termism and what Dunleavy calls 'hyperactivism' (Dunleavy, 1995, p. 6). Ministers are competing for public and party attention, and the quickest way to make an impression is to launch an initiative. But from a ministerial or civil service perspective the 'hit' comes with the publicity around the launch, and there is no further publicity value to be gained as it lumbers through to implementation. So the temptation is to launch something else – close to party conference perhaps – even if, down on the front line, everyone's time is still absorbed implementing the last idea. So initiatives tend to undermine each other, to weaken the impact of the ones that went before. The tradition of policy amateurs, clever people who can 'master a brief' quickly, means that learning about solutions that were tried and failed is lost when the senior civil servants or the ministers who administered them move on.

There is not yet a general recognition that the mechanisms on which central government traditionally relies don't work in the new context of local governance. Old levers are obsolete; they work only in the remaining places where lines of direct and single accountability still exist – for example within the NHS, where NHS direct could be set up by government directive; or in education, where schools were required to introduce a literacy hour. But they don't work, and can't work where accountabilities are complex and cross departmental boundaries.

Policy guidance is still primarily passed down through departmental systems to managers within different agencies and different departments. This disrupts the capacity to deliver through networks on the ground, since it undermines scope for local negotiation and compromise. Education departments within local authorities often feel unable to take a corporate role in local government since they are under such powerful pressure from the Department for Education and Employment (DFEE) to achieve educational targets. The result is a multiplicity of targets, all important in their own right but without priorities. Civil servants monitor compliance, but almost always in process or output terms. When these targets and outcomes conflict, organisational energy cannot be diverted to them all in sufficient quantities to make an impact. A sensible local network would decide locally which of these outcomes was important and ignore the others – but this carries dangers. The penalties for non-compliance may be severe, and it is not always clear in advance where power at Westminster is, and whom it is most important to please.

Local agencies have developed impressive image-management responses to central government initiatives. Managers and staff in public agencies often respond to new government initiatives through a process of 'initiative compliance'. Meetings are set up, documents written, strategies prepared and forms filled in (often by individual policy officers or researchers) to demonstrate conformity to procedural requirements, but without the engagement of the powerful decision-makers necessary to achieve change. The most common result of 'process compliance' is that past activities are simply rebadged to fit the new jargon, and described within new strategy documents. Thus the paperwork is completed, the strategy written, the partnerships set up. The minister can announce success. But none of this means that creative thinking has necessarily taken place.

The complexity of local problems – of geography, history, social institutions, economic circumstances and local personalities – means that solutions depend on the capabilities, strategic thinking and negotiation powers of local players. Successful local action can require the working-out in practice of the mass of interlocking problems faced by local people; and that complexity can only be managed on the ground. The solutions that make sense locally have to emerge from local thinking and action.

Civil servants remain largely outside these networks and it is therefore harder for them to learn about emerging innovation or to behave in the ways that make sense in reciprocal and self-managing networks. Attempts at the centre to learn from good practice lead to a continuation of centralised, paper-based systems – trying to distill the essence of a good local solution, and to standardise its use through good practice guides and manuals. But practice is not usefully transposed in this way. Where innovation works, it is usually because of a shared process of learning and experimentation about what works in a particular environment. It is not the 'solution' that can be transplanted elsewhere, but the process of local exploration and discovery. The application of good practice is like other sorts of learning, a matter not just of supply, but of demand. The emergence of joined-up thinking requires modern levers for change, including venture capital funds, learning laboratories, spaces for practice exchange and open-access knowledge-exchange systems (Leadbeater and Goss, 1998).

Marginal funding

The most depressing dimension of the structuring of cross-boundary initiatives on the margins of public service departments is the absence of proper funding for innovation. Cross-boundary projects have almost all been dependent on small quantities of 'new money', either allocated through pilots or projects (urban programme or community action projects, for example) or through competition and bidding systems (City Challenge, SRB, Education Action Zones, and so on). Partnerships are focused on attracting and spending new money, rather than the bending or using of mainstream resources to achieve change.

A recent study into cross-boundary working challenges the way government defines pilots:

> unlike pilots which are intended to precipitate wholesale change, they are often used as experiments to see if something works, funded by 'new' money and discontinued after the money has run out whether they work or not. This is unhelpful, as it means that learning about initiatives is lost (as evaluations are not done or considered redundant) ... and a growing cynicism breeds amongst professional. (Richards *et al.*, 1999, p. 77)

Despite thirty years of experience in cross-boundary working, the translation of successful lessons into mainstream practice remains slow. Innovative projects constantly have to grub around for new additional funding, despite their proven success in comparison with traditional alternatives. When cuts have to be made, it is often the innovatory projects that are cut. Evaluation studies are carried out over and over again into successful experiments which are never translated into mainstream practice.

And yet, until the invention of 'best value', there was no mechanism to drive the evaluation of mainstream practice. Studies that break through departmental boundaries to analyse results have been damning about the failures of mainstream agencies to learn from innovative projects. The Audit Commission found that agencies managing youth justice failed to implement the policies known to reduce reoffending most effectively (Audit Commission, 1996). And yet, the learning from successful projects could, if replicated, revolutionise the mainstream. The depressing reality is that outside the tiny carefully negotiated space of an individual project, conflicts between competing departmental goals, professional interpretations, financial systems and service targets breaks out. When radical service innovation is forced because of government policy or financial stringency, lessons learnt from cross-boundary projects are seldom applied. It is hard simply to carry on seeing this as accidental after so many years. Surely we must see the continual setting-up of marginal projects, the endless evaluation studies from which no-one ever learns, as a form of displacement activity, whether conscious or unconscious, to avoid disturbance to the status quo.

Are we experiencing a paradigm shift?

Are we trembling on the brink of a Kuhnian paradigm shift? It is possible to envisage the last years of the twentieth century as a moment of transition, a time when structures, systems, culture and capacity are slowly being redesigned across government agencies in ways that make up a fundamental shift. But it would also be possible to see the current changes as simply a new round of marginal projects that will fade away, with most of government policy implemented through traditional organisational structures. If it is the latter, the problems are very serious, since for the reasons explored in the last chapter the old structures and systems of government cannot function successfully within the fragmented network of agencies that now exist. A failure to make networks and partnerships function effectively will necessarily be a failure of governance.

Richards argues that the 1980s have led to the 'unsettling' of the post-war settlement, but a new settlement has not yet been established. She argues that attempts to solve new problems using the old paradigm cannot work, and offers a warning about the 'capacity of the system to handle a highly centralised approach'. She identifies signs of the beginnings of 'outcomes based policy', but argues that these require a new way of configuring the relationship between the central and local levels of government, a 'tight–loose relationship', rather than the 'tight–tight structures of the recent past' (Richards *et al.*, 1999, p. 121).

What would be the criteria for evaluating the extent of change? It seems likely that if a paradigm shift is taking place we should see the rapid development of a number of factors:

- Multiprofessional teams delivering mainstream services.
- Innovations in teaching/learning 'professional' skills and qualifications.
- A loosening of organisational boundaries, pooled resources, cross-agency systems.
- Outcome and population based targets shared by a number of agencies.
- A looser government strategy – concentrating on measuring outcomes and creating freedom to innovate.
- Rolling out and mainstreaming learning from pilots.
- Mainstream funding adapted to reconfigure services and change patterns of investment.

Rules of engagement for partnerships

The chapter so far has summarised current research and evidence about the problems of partnerships. However, even where they succeed, new dilemmas have to be faced. Where partnerships and networks do work effectively, they become a new sort of organisation, with the capacity for agency. There are few of these in existence so far, but we must assume that as the problems detailed in the rest of the chapter are solved, more fully-working networks and partnerships will evolve in the public sector.

The elements that make up a successful relationship organisation also need to be in place in successful partnerships. Outward focus, seeing the big picture, reflexivity, self-consciousness about roles and responsibilities, the capacity to share learning, effective communication, reciprocity – the ability to make and keep promises, and ability to make things happen fast – these are all as important in partnerships as in organisations. The assumption is often made that partnership working is about developing win–win situations in which every agency can achieve its objectives. But that is to be trapped within an organisational perspective. Win–win assumes that the objectives of each organisation are equally important, and Mark Moore (1999) talks about the need to break out of this assumption so that partners offer help to achieve shared goals without any guarantee of an organisational return. If partnerships and networks can move towards defining goals that are genuinely held by and for a community, that ceases to be so difficult to achieve.

What may be necessary is a sort of 'organisational social capital' so that networks of relationships between agencies engender sufficient trust that organisations will help each other in the recognition of long-term reciprocity or status in the organisational community rather than immediate return. There has long been a recognition that partnerships offer the prospect of spending other people's money to achieve organisational goals, but a more sophisticated version would enable organisations to contribute their staff and resources to other people's projects or create pathways to other people's initiatives as the fastest way to achieve social goals.

But how are these goals to be chosen? Networks and partnerships have to find ways to tackle the issues of legitimacy and accountability that we discussed in Chapter 2. Legitimacy is often seen as bound up with leadership. Local authorities, for example often take the lead within partnerships since they have a firm democratic legitimacy for locality-wide issues. But real power within partnerships depends on the issues at stake, and on a combination of resources, commitment, knowledge, influencing power and personalities. It is often assumed that leadership must come from within statutory agencies, but this is also being contested:

> Statutory agencies have the power, they can say yes or no and that has to be challenged. Partnerships can't be about being approved of by the statutory sector. This [the health centre at Bromley by Bow] is a voluntary sector led initiative, and we have struggled really hard to maintain the lead role ... if we hadn't we would never have got past the health authority and the local authority bureaucracy and ideological convictions which would have stopped us from taking a new approach. If you want a radical approach you have to be sure that the partnerships are being led by other people and OK they [the statutory agencies] can be part of the partnerships but they shouldn't have to approve of them. (Alison Trimble, Bromley by Bow centre, quoted in Holman, 1999)

In the process of effective partnership formation, objectives are negotiated, cultures are explored, mutual understanding evolves and compromises are made. One organisation – say, a health authority – might agree that the partnership objective of reducing crime is more important to a small town than the objective with which they began, which was that of reducing heart disease in the area. Or the police authority might agree that since tackling problems of social exclusion were important, then they would give priority to issues such as domestic violence, street homelessness and addiction support rather than burglary. I have argued that clear priorities are vital if local partners are to escape from the 'hamster wheel' of trying to do everything. Public resources are limited (even if they are sometimes wasted), and without clarity of focus and a critical mass of integrated action it is unlikely that local goals can be achieved. Outcomes always have to be traded off against each other; they cannot all be achieved. On the other hand, it is not clear what legitimacy partnerships have for the decisions they make. Any new partnership has to decide how it will balance the requirements of financial probity and efficiency, the requirements of central government politicians, the choice of customers and the views of local citizens, and win consent from the wider community for the balance it has set. Parston and Timmins (1998) call this a 'license to operate'. The process of managing legitimacy is as important for a partnership as it is for any single organisation.

If partnerships must win consent for their plans, they must also be held to account for their actions. And yet a partnership or network is made up of several organisations each of which has its own specific forms of accountability. Individual partners are accountable through the local ballot box or through accountability to ministers – but each has the excuse that partnership failure was not their responsibility. Some of the partners are quangos, and are not directly held to public account, and some may be private sector companies with no public accountability at all. While some partners may have their success at joint working included in the way their performance is monitored, others may not. How are members of partnerships to be held to account for their success or failure – either by each other, or by local people?

There are important issues of equity to be addressed. Who decides who is involved in the partnership and who is excluded? Who decides whom to ask? What system of appeal is there if your organisation is excluded? A partnership of key agencies in a town or city can wield considerable power, and while this is clearly advantageous when setting out to achieve difficult social goals, it also contains scope for abuse. If one private company is included, and a competitor excluded, does it give unfair strategic advantage to the company with the right contacts? If churches are allowed to participate but mosques and temples are not, is that racism? If all religious groups are excluded, does this fail to represent civil society accurately? If young entrepreneurs are excluded but older traditional rotary club members included, is that fair? If there are rival voluntary sector organisations, who decides who is in and who is out? Several commentators have voiced suspicions about 'who is invited to the party' and concerns that 'only a select group of party goers will be chosen' (Baker, 1999, p. 38). Partnerships must be held to account for the decisions they make, and for who they include.

But if partnerships are to be accountable, then their decisions must be transparent and open to scrutiny. The 'wiring' of a partnership – the forms of communication, of information sharing, the expectations of each participant – will have an important impact on the extent to which the partnership working is seen as transparent by local press and public.

Partnerships are rightly struggling with these issues, which are not easy. Relationships need to be sufficiently robust to allow accountability and legitimacy, for example, to be talked about and challenged. Partners or network members have to negotiate about expectations, and to confront difficulties. They need to develop agreement about who is entitled to attend, about who has a veto, about sanctions. They will need to recognise inequalities of power and wealth within the partnership, and develop a response. Transparency and clear decision trails may be more important for partnerships than they are for ordinary organisations which have default systems of accountability. There is a need to evolve rules of engagement for partnerships in governance just as there needs to be rules of engagement for public organisations and for collective activity within civil society.

6　Politics and Politicians

So far, we have examined the impact of a shift from government to governance from an organisational perspective. But the shift has profound implications for local politicians. Does it extend local democracy or threaten it? What sorts of roles emerge for local politicians? And who will become politicians in the future? Can the present structures, systems, attitudes and behaviours within local politics offer the right political framework for the emerging governance agenda?

Governance, as we have argued, inevitably involves the negotiation of power. The dilemmas faced are very political in their nature, and what is fascinating is that as the *politics* of local governance becomes more complex, local *politicians* feel under attack.

Many local councillors have felt threatened by the sorts of changes we have explored so far. They, after all, have carried the responsibility for local decision-making since local democracy was patched together at the end of the last century. The administration of local affairs has been legitimated through the existence of democratically elected ward councillors meeting together in committees and as a full council. Through most of the twentieth century, councillors were powerful decision-makers – able to tear down town centres, plan roads, care for the old and the vulnerable, rebuild slums, change school systems, and build leisure centres and shopping malls. All that is changing. From being the centre of decision-making within a big city, the hub of control in a small town or a rural area, councillors can feel marginalized as only partial players in a different set of political and managerial relationships. Their partners in local governance include local quangos, businesses and community groups – none of which carry the democratic legitimacy of elected councillors. It is easy to sympathise with local councillors who have seen their power eroded by Whitehall over three decades, and now see the prospect of decision-making returned not to the council chamber, but to local networks and partnerships. In the intervening years senior managers have become more powerful, leaders of police authorities and health authorities have become serious strategic players, and community groups have become more self-confident. The role of business is encouraged, but without any resulting insistence on corporate citizenship or accountability from the private sector. The fear of many politicians and observers has been that we are seeing the emergence of a 'new magistracy' of managers and leaders who are no longer elected by local people and therefore are no longer accountable in the way that counts most – capable of being dismissed by local people.

The insistence by elected councillors that they, uniquely, have a democratic mandate and must have a role in leading community governance makes sense. But the question is not whether or not elected councillors are entitled to a community leadership role – but whether or not, in practice, they fulfill it. Is the shift to governance a threat to local democracy? I want to argue that the reality is more complex, more interesting, although in many ways no less dangerous. In this chapter I want to suggest that there have been important failures of local democracy that make a continuation of traditional politics impossible, but the structural changes introducing cabinets or mayors may not address them. Without a change in political culture, both among politicians and within civil society, we are unlikely to develop good governance.

The democratic deficit

Local politics has been losing legitimacy and status in the UK since the 1970s. Voting has decreased overall, and has decreased locally; fewer people vote in British local elections that almost anywhere else in Europe. In 1995, the turn-out for elections in the UK at 40 per cent was the lowest for any European democracy (although the USA can have turnouts as low as 25 per cent for municipal elections). The average turn-out in local elections is over 60 per cent in Portugal, Ireland and Spain, around 70 per cent in France and Germany, and around 80 per cent in Italy, Sweden, Denmark and Belgium (Commission for Local Democracy, 1995). Since then, UK local election turn-out has continued to drop; it was 32 per cent in 1999. This undermines democratic legitimacy. Does a councillor with the support of 20 per cent of the population carry more legitimacy than the democratically elected leader of a large tenant's organisation, or a trade unionist representing a thousand local workers? The local democratic deficit in the UK is not echoed across the rest of Europe. Nor is the tendency towards centralisation and quangos. It would not seem unreasonable to assume that as local democracy has lost power in the UK, so it has lost public interest; local politicians no longer have the high profile they once had. The collapse of local newspapers also means that there is less and less local reporting of political news, and less media scrutiny of local events.

Local politicians are not representative of the wider community. Recent research found that more than half of all councillors were over 45, and none were under 24. A third were retired, and only a third were in full-time work (Rao, 1993). The trend is positive, however, and it would be a mistake to look back to any sort of 'golden age'. When the Maud Committee reported in 1967, only 12 per cent of councillors were women, only 20 per cent of male councillors were under 45, and more than half were over 55. Employers, farmers and managers were overrepresented and manual workers seriously underrepresented (Brown, Jones and McKay, 1999, p. 3). By 1993, 30 per cent of councillors were women, a massive improvement (Rao, 1993), and more councillors (although not many) were from ethnic minorities, and councillors were younger (but not by much).

In the early half of the twentieth century, powerful local loyalties were reflected in political representation. In old docklands and manual-working communities such as Bermondsey and Southwark, representation in the 1930s or 1950s was a process of 'speaking for' neighbours and friends: 'I could represent the people because I was one of them. I worked in the docks, and lived in tenements, same as everyone else. I knew what they wanted. It was what I wanted' (unpublished research notes). The party defined where you belonged: 'If you thought the same as them you were working class, and if you didn't you were middle class' (Goss, 1989, p. 93).

While the close-knit communities of the past are a source of much nostalgia, there were always people left out by such a strongly imagined sense of homogeneity. As the new Londoners arriving from the Caribbean and East Africa discovered, it was lonely on the outside of politically reinforced solidarities. Representation has always been mediated through a powerful mixture of political loyalties, personal interests and cultural identity. The changes in the patterns of social and economic life make diversity more apparent, and continuing social fragmentation makes it harder and harder to 'stand for' a community. It is perhaps more obvious than before that a councillor who thinks they are speaking for everyone may only really speak for themselves. However, that may not present insuperable problems. Rao argues that the assumptions we carry about representation are changing. In a world of increasing diversity, the idea of representation understood as 'resemblance' is misplaced (see Rao, 1998). The public increasingly looks for evidence that councillors are listening and responsive, rather than 'like them'.

Local councils over the past two decades have lost power, money and status. The job has become more managerial, with less scope for making things happen. And at the same time it has become more organisationally demanding, more time-consuming as councillors spend more and more time in long committee meetings. The very taxing nature of the current role of local councillors is off-putting to many people who could not cope with the pressure on their personal life. The formal, relatively dry processes tend to turn off many younger people, and fewer and fewer people want to be councillors; furthermore, more and more people stand down after a short time. A Local Government Management Board (LGMB) survey in 1998 showed that of those councillors leaving politics, 74 per cent had stood down of their own accord. Councillors with degrees are 50 per cent more likely to choose to stand down that those without, and councillors who are school governors or who are involved in other forms of community activity are more likely to stand down than others. Inevitably, therefore, those who choose to become active in politics are those for whom the current structures and systems still 'work' enough for them to gain fulfilment.

Within local politics, the political party has become dominant and the political group, with its own internal party rules and discipline, controls the behaviour of its members. There are fewer independents, and while there are increasing numbers of councils with no single party in overall control, there are still councils in which one party has dominated the council for decades. Young and Rao have drawn together research showing that the public generally feels that councillors should represent local people rather than their political party (1997, p. 138).

All this adds up to a democratic deficit, a failure in the mechanisms of legitimacy and accountability. There is a gap. It is important, however, to remember that none of this cancels the even greater concern that local people feel about over-centralisation or about unaccountable quangos. There is no evidence that local people are willing to relinquish their local councils. Also, the loss of support for politicians is not simply a local phenomenon; while national voting is higher than local voting, it is still falling, and opinion poll research shows that national politicians are trusted less than local ones (British Social Attitudes, 1994, in Rao and Young, 1997).

Old town hall structures

The dominant structures of local politics in the UK have lasted from the nineteenth century to the end of the twentieth. The traditional council was divided into a series of committees, each of which consisted of a chair and a group of councillors from across the political spectrum. The committee was the ultimate invention of the Victorians, an effective process by which a large number of volunteers could transact complex business. Each committee related to a different department or directorate within the council; and each had a 'chief officer', a senior professional, who reported to the committee. Behind him (usually him) were an army of council officers, each of which reported upwards, through the chief. The committee agenda set out a rhythm, not merely for councillors, but for the whole organisation. The committee and council meetings became formal, highly ritualised events. For the most important occasions councillors might be robed and gowned, and the mayor or lord mayor would enter preceded by the mace, a symbol of municipal power.

Relationships between councillors and senior managers were often highly formalised; and while, over time, the town clerk became the chief executive, and titles such as chief architect and borough solicitor gave way to titles such as 'director of environmental services', the chief officers retained certain powers to challenge councillor decisions, and to determine what was lawful and appropriate. The chief officer usually commanded respect as a leader in his or her field, whose professional judgement carried considerable respect, and who often came from a different class and have greater formal education than many of the councillors. Yet councillors were always treated with old-fashioned courtesy:

> The tradition in local government is for officers to treat councillors with equal respectfulness however inept and stupid they may be and irrespective of their activity or somnolence. The councillor is always sir to the officer; even though the former may be an ignorant shopkeeper and the latter a brilliant expert in his profession. Courtesy costs nothing and no profession is more respectful towards its employer than the local government service. (Hasluck, 1930, pp. 90–1, quoted in J. Stewart, 2000)

> Officer roles are defined by tradition. They are there to advise the committee, rather than take part in decisions. Officers present reports and answer questions, but the committee belongs to the members. Officer behaviour is therefore controlled behaviour. They will laugh politely at a member's joke, but it would be out of place to laugh at serious points. (J. Stewart, 2000, p. 239)

Of course, along with the courtesy came condescension. Councillors were not always treated to the honesty and forthright advice that would be expected by a company board. Surface respect sometimes barely concealed contempt for the struggles of older or less well-educated people to understand the issues they faced. The formality of meetings made real exploration and discovery impossible and led to endless delays and bureaucratic obsession.

Much has changed. In many councils the old committee systems are almost unrecognisable. Many councils already have an inner executive that works like a Cabinet. Officers and councillors call each other by forenames, work together in informal discussion groups, and generally act as co-managers of a large corporation. In many councils, perhaps most, there are modern senior managers and modern councillors. But the old traditions remain in some places, and their ghosts are everywhere. Stewart's fascinating book sums up the inward-looking, claustrophobic and old-fashioned formality of old local government, but also manages to highlight the civility, the sense of service and fair play and the calm ordered hierarchy that enabled local government to function smoothly for a hundred years. But it cannot survive; the pressures of change have been eating away at the load-bearing beams of the old structures.

The structures of politics have always coexisted uneasily with the structures of the town hall. The committee system has been hollowed out by a growing weight of group meetings, pre-committee briefings, chair's call-overs and committee group meetings. John Stewart highlights the importance of the political group structures (2000, p. 145) and the wide range of different political arrangements depending on the balance of power. What works in a highly politicised urban authority makes no sense in a rural district where independents hold the balance of power. Political urgency jostles against the departmental system. Politics also overflows the boundaries of a local council; within a party political system, decision-making spaces include the local political party, the guidance from central office, the ministerial phone call, the formulation of regional and national policy.

The collision between the old council structures and the impatience of modern politics has become inevitable. Wainwright (1994) describes the old structure as an enclosed system of government. As governance has taken over from government, decision-making spaces are no longer limited to the panelled rooms and engraved tables of the town hall. As society has changed, decisions are now far more complex and involve partners from other agencies, the chief executives of health authorities, police authorities, local business, regional government offices, neighbourhood projects and zones. 'The task of local authorities can be seen as having moved from the government of perceived certainty to the government of acknowledged uncertainty' (J. Stewart, 2000, p. 109), and 'gradually it came to be realised that an enclosed system of government would require to change or be changed' (*ibid.*, p. 113).

Changing the structures of local politics

In the new government rhetoric about modernisation, councils have been seen as falling behind. The council committee system with its lumbering procedures, nineteenth-century formality and capacity for endless procrastination was seen as the problem. Councillors were secretive, and acted behind closed doors. Local politics were stuck in a time warp. They needed shaking up.

Academics have been arguing forcefully for several years that the system of local politics in the UK is flawed and old-fashioned. Unless council leaders have greater responsibility and greater accountability, it is hard for the public to hold politicians to account, and hard for politicians to deliver. Commentators such as Gerry Stoker and Robin Hambledon argue that a mayoral system similar to that in the USA and in much of continental Europe would make local councils more accountable. Convinced of these arguments, the Blair government has included local government reform within its wider programme to modernise Britain. The White Paper *Modern Local Government: In Touch with the People* sets this out:

> Councils need to break free of old fashioned practices and attitudes. There is a long and proud tradition of councils serving their communities. But the world and how we live today is very different from when our current systems of local government were established. There is no future in the old model of councils trying to plan and run most services. It does not provide the services which people want, and cannot do so in today's world. Equally there is no future for councils which are inward looking – more concerned to maintain their structures and protect their vested interests than listening to their local people and leading their communities. (DETR, 1998)

The government's response to the democratic deficit has been to insist on structural change at local level. Councils are to 'adopt new political structures better suited to their role of community leader' (DETR, 1998). The prospectus for change set out in the government's White Paper included improvements to local democracy including opportunities to experiment with innovative arrangements for local elections, greater consultation, a new ethical framework, a new duty to promote the economic, social and environmental well-being of the area, a raft of even more powerful controls over performance, through Best Value, and changes in the structure of political decision-making. Local authorities are required to separate executive and scrutiny roles, and are offered a choice of models – a directly elected Mayor, a directly elected cabinet or an indirectly elected cabinet – although the scope for variety within these models seems to be infinite. The intention has been to introduce direct accountability. 'People will know who is responsible for decisions and communities will have a clear focus for leadership. Decisions will be scrutinised in public, and those who take them and implement them will be called publicly to account for their performance' (DETR, March 1999).

At the time of writing, these changes are underway. Council responses have been muted and most have gone for the indirectly elected executive model, rather than elected Mayors, but this may be a matter of time. It is always difficult to draw conclusions from work in progress, but since there seem to be emerging patterns it is helpful at least to make observations which may help in the analysis of unfolding events. The clearest role set out for councillors in the new UK system of local government is that of an executive – a role reserved for only a few leading local politicians. The preferred solution of many of the academics urging the change was an executive mayor, a highly visible single politician with clear accountability and powers to act. Most UK local authorities have opted instead for an executive cabinet, maintaining collective decision-making and the old links to political groups. These new executive roles, whether carried out by an individual or a team, are still fuzzy and confusing, and will be clarified over time. In the first place it is not clear how full-time, how well-remunerated, how 'executive' the roles will be.

There are still powerful chief executives within local authorities and the future roles of officers and members are still being negotiated. It is not clear whether the managers within a new local authority will lose their roles of organisational and community leadership and return to being simply clerks, or whether a way can be found for political and managerial leadership to coexist. In the second place, the political systems and relationships will have to adapt to the new systems and there is a formidable political management task to win the support of councillors and parties to a new system that seems to concentrate power in fewer hands. The constitutions and standing orders being developed up and down the country are constructing the role in ways that are often narrow. A focus simply on structural change often means that communication is poor, decision trails weak, transparency faulty and accountability vague.

Already, commentators are beginning to raise concerns about the failure of the reforms to achieve the desired objectives. Critics argue that the new cabinets have been set up, but that nothing has happened to change the ways that councils work. Some cabinets remain secretive, excluding, inward-looking even after the changes, and have failed to take on a wider leadership role. Backbenchers feel excluded from decision-making, and bitter about being second-class councillors.

Early attempts to develop a scrutiny role have also been troublesome. The Westminster model does not translate easily into a local government context. Carried out by the backbenchers of the majority party in power it strains untested relationships, ruptures the loyalties of close political groups and is undermined by powerful group loyalty. Carried out by the opposition, it strengthens adversarial political behaviours and raises the spectre of 'punishment bouts', where the scrutiny committee simply challenges all executive decisions. A third possible alternative is that it becomes a focus of councillor suspicion of managers, and becomes a ritual of blaming and finger-pointing, rather than one of constructive review.

New roles are being created alongside those of executive and scrutiny. Over 40 per cent of local authorities, for example, plan to include some sort of neighbourhood or area committee or forum in their new structures. This is in some ways a more radical change than the renaming of policy committees as executives, but new structures alone will not create effective neighbourhood governance. The design of local decision-making processes will be crucial. There is always a danger that old-fashioned committee rules and protocols will be carried forward into neighbourhood structures, and with chairs and formal council-driven agendas they will begin to resemble mini-committees and act as a rest home for disgruntled backbenchers who feel they have lost power in the council proper and can recreate old roles at neighbourhood level.

Since the new structures are being implemented ahead of legislation, and since many councils have not redesigned political structures for years, we should expect change to be uneven. But it is interesting how quickly the new structures have been bent back into old ways, and become inhabited by the old behaviours. This should not be surprising. The government proposals simply require a change in structure, and as we have seen in the organisational context, structure determines very little. Unless the systems, culture, ways of working, assumptions, attitudes and behaviours of politicians change – it would be strange to expect the simple setting up of new boards and committees to have much impact. If we want to see change, we must look elsewhere. The variety of response to the structural change depends on the evolution of cultural change at local level. Change is most successful in those councils that have been innovating for years, where the new structures simplify things. The political process is in transition, and the new structures do at least symbolically force a jolt in the system – a moment when things are thrown into the air and could, theoretically, be done differently. But will they be? No amount of structural change on its own will work unless there are powerful drivers to change the other dimensions of the political process.

Real and imaginary structures

The organisational form of formal local politics is very different from the bureaucratic hybrid within the local government organisation described in the last chapter. While politicians play a role in the organisational structures – the political processes are organised very differently. Until now, local politicians have been volunteers working in their own time, with responsibilities outside as well as inside the town hall. They meet in formal settings with formal rules, but these are not the only decision-making spaces they inhabit. The architectural metaphor implied in the word 'structure' is relatively weak, since we are referring not to buildings or enforceable hierarchies of authority, but to a frame of rules about relationships and roles, decision-making spaces, titles, job descriptions. The formal political structures – the cabinet, the scrutiny panels, the committees, the partnership boards and the emergency sub-committees – describe the ways that things are supposed to happen. But just as in organisations there can be a gap between theory and practice, between how things are supposed to work and how they really work, so there can be a gap in political structures – a false bottom or a secret compartment. Politics is by its nature informal, and consists of late-night telephone calls and conversations, of soundings and instincts, of 'what ifs' and careful exploration, of checking out and testing the water, of consulting and then moving fast to closure – and the processes that are formalised are always only part of the story.

In political decision-making, then, the relationship between the formal and the informal processes of decision-making are very important. Much of practical politics is inevitably invisible and does not take place in the formal settings. And while committee meetings often seem deadly, there has often been much fascinating flying behind the scenes, squaring the opposition, negotiating, building bridges – to achieve the studied low-key dullness on the night of the committee meeting! Abolishing committees will achieve little, since the committee meetings have always been formalised processes of interaction. They might offer space for backbenchers to perform, or for a ritual display of antagonism between the parties, an opportunity for the public to present a petition, or heckle disconsolately when the chair announces their item. Committee meetings played an important symbolic role in making decisions public, formalising them, recording them and creating a basis on which councillors could be held to account.

But the real centre of political decision making at the local level has been for many years the political group. This is often more formalised within the Labour Party than within the others, but the grouping of councillors from the dominant political party has been the centre of decision-making. The group is also linked to the local political party, and decisions are often taken within the local political party rather than just within the group of councillors. The structural change to executive and scrutiny committees does not simply replace committees with a more modern and logical structure, it also breaks up the relationships between back and frontbench councillors, cuts across the roles of political groups and breaks into the links with local political parties. For some politicians, the new space and opportunities can be used and are very exciting. There are opportunities to create new decision-making structures such as those explored in Chapter 4 – city boards and partnerships. New sorts of deliberative forums are also being created, engaging local people, and there are opportunities to use scrutiny committees as the basis for Socratic investigation and to explore current practice in profound ways.

But, in a highly politicised process it is unrealistic to assume that somehow the political imperatives and loyalties that governed the old system will disappear because of a shift from executive to scrutiny roles. There is still a political party, still a political group, and still powerful ties between the executive and backbench scrutineers. Some of the interim structures set up ahead of the legislation may turn out to be transitional, but the difficulties that are being experienced expose real dilemmas at the heart of politics – since political parties want to continue to hold their executives to account via the group and party, while the government intention has been that the executive should be directly accountable to the public. The public want decisions to be made publicly, but politicians need time for reflection, discussion and deals away from the glare of the public eye. The public wants clear lines of accountability, but the complexities of governance networks and the range of stakeholders to be consulted makes that harder to establish. What has yet to emerge from the new design is a satisfactory solution of the problems of accountability, transparency and legitimacy that the new structures were intended to tackle.

Changing the structures of politics does not necessarily affect the way that politicians behave, just as changing the structures of organisations does not necessarily change attitudes or behaviours or managers. Indeed, politics is even less amenable to structurally-driven change since so much of it is informal. To understand why politics works the way it does, we have to look at other dimensions – at political systems, for example, and at political culture.

Political systems

The committee 'system' has created a powerful rhythm, a metronome that beats time in the town hall. The silencing of the committee rhythm creates both opportunities and dangers, since the annual timetable is disrupted, conventional forms of communication break down, knowledge about how decisions are taken dies out. Old monitoring systems, accountability systems, financial systems become obsolete. Everything has to be recreated, reasons for meeting, deadlines, forms of communications, pathways. My colleague Paul Corrigan has suggested that there is a need for 'air traffic control' in the early weeks of post-committee systems, helping issues and decisions to take off and land where there are no agreed routes. The constitutions and procedures and protocols designed by policy officers are no more likely to prove 'real' than the old rules. New political systems will emerge.

Formal systems are accompanied by powerful informal ones. Councillors spend a lot of time gathering informal information through the media, checking out with the national party and colleagues, checking with neighbours and friends. Formal meetings often have informal aspects, such as information exchange, which are not always recognised, so that committees often act as a conduit for general knowledge about the area and the council which may need to be replaced by other more formal systems if communication is not to break down.

The accountability systems of local politicians are not straightforward. Politicians are formally accountable to their electorates, but the strength of that accountability depends on the marginality of their seat, and the marginality of their party's grip on the council as a whole. How likely is it that if they fail to listen to their local communities they will lose votes? Councillors soon also feel a sense of accountability to the council as an organisation, accountability to the rest of the machine, adhering to the rules and fulfilling obligations to colleagues, carrying out their legal and fiduciary duty. Councillors have to work hard to understand the rules and learn the rituals.

Then there are the other spaces of civil society that councillors often occupy – tenants' meetings, school governors, the community groups in which they might take part, parish councils and voluntary organisations. The fact that councillors are often 'joiners' and activists means that they are often part of many other organisations. Some councillors also feel a sense of accountability to the geographical space they represent; informal systems connect them into their localities, the local pub, the supermarket and the local estate. They see themselves as accountable to their neighbours and friends, deriving pride from their status in the community but also needing to explain and defend themselves at home. A sense of responsibility connects them into their surroundings. But for other councillors the role is almost entirely political; they may not know their neighbours, or feel very connected with their communities. In big cities there is not always a sense of belonging, and local communities have very different views which have to be balanced off against each other.

There is a powerful accountability also to the political party and to the group. The political party is responsible for selecting local candidates, and while it is possible to stand as an independent, most councillors depend on the party ticket to mobilise public support. Councillors can be subsequently deselected regardless of the will of the electorate. The tie is not simply a formal one, since for councillors who are politically active there is a tie of shared political beliefs and shared assumptions. The penalties for failing to represent constituents, or not listening, or neglecting casework are negligible. The penalties for betraying the party or for challenging colleagues, have always been obvious. For many politicians, the personal moment of separation from their colleagues because of a disagreement about principle or political strategy is one of the most painful possible. It affects career, life-chances and friendships. Politicians seldom forgive and never forget.

The political group on the council represents the most powerful set of accountabilities, since this is where positions are distributed and decisions made. The difficulties experienced in trying to implement the policies local politicians believe in, the sense of being embattled – obstructed by central government, by managers, by other powerful agencies, often by local communities – reinforces the extent to which the group is 'home ground' – a place to retreat to from the onslaught of the outside world. There are considerable rewards to be won from adversarial politics, and points to be scored at the expense of the opposition. A good politician is one who can humiliate the opposition in ritual encounters at committee or full council, who can get good knocking press copy in the local paper, who can fire off letters to discomfit the leadership. Being 'in opposition' is often a process of trying to frustrate actions by the leading group, to prevent them from gaining credit with the electorate for policies carried out. Being 'in power' is both a process of trying to respond to community needs, and ensuring that credit for that response can be fully claimed by the majority political party, ideally with a sideswipe at the short-sighted opposition by other parties.

Political culture

Political cultures are as powerful as organisational cultures, although councillors live in the overlapping space between the two. If we try to excavate the culture of politicians it immediately becomes clear that we are dealing with many layers of culture, each overlaid on others. In the first place there is something akin to a town hall culture, which exists regardless of political affiliation. There is a sense of belonging to the council as a whole, a special place with its own rituals and traditions. Each local authority is unique, with a different sense of itself, some with a strong sense of history, others with a pride in forward thinking, some with a powerful sense of place in a historic town or powerful city; others far more defined by the organisational boundaries and preoccupations.

The members' room is at the heart of council life, the locus of power, gossip and knowledge. There are elements of club culture within local councils, a sense of shared interests and preoccupations seldom understood by others, with the town hall as the clubhouse. People look to find their place within the 'club' rather than going outside. The demands of the job are such that most councillors are retired or out of work, and the council club offers many of the things that help to make life meaningful – a sense of purpose, a set of colleagues, useful work to do, intrigue, news – even scandal. And yet there is no recognition given to the power of the 'club', since it has no formal place in the structures that have been designed. Indeed, some of the changes seem to be trying to break up the clubbishness of politics. Perhaps councillors should spend more time listening to and representing the wider community, but the rewards from that are hard to identify. It is cold knocking on doors, frustrating doing case-work, depressing sitting in tenants' meetings and getting shouted at. Where is the honour and reward that would make people want to do more of it? Are there other, more fruitful things to do? If we are to think about change, we have to think also about the accountability and reward systems that might encourage change.

On top, or underneath this is a political culture. Political cultures vary considerably at local level, depending on the distribution of power between the political parties and the local geography and history. Political cultures are often, although not always, antagonistic; and they vary hugely – between city and village, between north and south, even between neighbouring authorities. The atmosphere can be calm, friendly or courteous, with jokes shared between members of different political parties, or they can be conflictual, tense or exciting, driven by powerful political beliefs and strong values. These are seldom phoney. Politicians, by definition, believe in the power of politics to change things. They are passionate about the possibility of life being different. Politicians are far less likely than their managerial equivalents to be satisfied with the status quo.

Political cultures are 'talk' cultures, the currency is of debate, and therefore talk of a particular kind. The facts are often attached to a story, the rational to the emotional. Councillors can make speeches rather than simply conversation; the talk itself has the purpose of solidifying support for one's own position and undermining support for an opponent. The level of debate is often high, the extent of reflection and deliberation considerable, but the tradition of debate carries an assumption that minds are changed through being out-argued, an assumption that is seldom tested.

'Management' in political terms is very different from the conventions followed by salaried managers; the power that goes with political position is not always clear, and seldom unambiguous. And for the more senior politicians, political management has been a long-underestimated skill, since it is seldom seen in public. The role of a political leader is crucial in building an effective team, but it is more difficult than that of a top manager. Local politicians are not employees, nor are they rewarded for performance, the leader has no line-management responsibility and no power to give orders. Worse, political leaders are elected by their colleagues, so any attempt to pull rank or override minority interests can lead to the harbouring of dangerous grudges. These are not always groups of individuals who like each other or who work hard to build bridges; success in politics, after all, is about defining difference, planning advancement, overtaking colleagues, winning.

While in any political group there are creative, supportive, conciliatory and facilitative people – there are always also highly prickly space-seekers. Political leaders have a complicated job to do; they have to work with a group of often very different individuals who have often chosen to be politicians for very different reasons. They have limited sanctions to prevent maverick behaviour; they need to listen and placate and involve a critical mass of colleagues to build a consensus to operate, taking account of the interests, prejudices, ambitions and preferences of each individual. There are often strong rituals and clashing ambitions. Since power is distributed according to shifting political alliances, there can always be challenges to current leaders – however successful they are. Success in the party is more important, ultimately, than success with the public. Managers should perhaps reflect on the differences they would experience if the chief executive was elected by the top 20 managers, none of whom s/he had chosen, and none of whom could be sacked.

And then there are party political cultures, a long history of very different ways of seeing the world, of organising affairs, and of behaving to each other. Political cultures almost always have a strong sense of history, a long memory of past defeats and victories, and a highly symbolic set of reference points. Since councillors are older than the rest of the population, they carry memories on behalf of communities and local parties. The memories of local politicians go back a long way.

Party-political cultures are passionate cultures. Political ideas are derived from our most deep-seated beliefs and value systems, which once formed are very hard to change. Strong political beliefs are formed early in our adult lives, and while for many individuals politics is relatively unimportant, and our political choices may change readily, the fundamental beliefs that underpin those choices change far more slowly. The beliefs of active politicians are constantly reinforced by contact with like-minded people.

Councillors choose to be councillors for all sorts of reasons. And the dismissive public and media assumptions about self-interest are not borne out by the many hours of unpaid labour put in by local politicians. Some become councillors from social conscience, from a sense of duty. Some become councillors because of a fascination with politics itself, from ambition, the wish to build a political career. Some wish to serve or represent local communities or to pursue a particular campaign. Some are interested in local government activities – and discover that it is possible to be involved in high-level decisions without the education or qualifications required of a manager. The glass ceiling is not as solid in politics as it is in management, and it is possible for clever councillors who are working-class, or lack university education, or are women or from ethnic minorities, to achieve leadership positions that they would be unlikely to reach in management. Some councillors are frankly there by accident, because of a freak election victory or because they were talked into it by friends. But whatever the original motivation, the absence of honour, recognition or reward for many of the activities of the council impacts, over time, on the way councillors spend their effort and concentrate their attention. The rewards in the form of promotion, recognition and power come disproportionately to those who exhibit good party or club behaviours. There are only intrinsic rewards for the rest.

New roles and relationships

In Chapter 4 we explored the possible dimensions of a new sort of public sector organisation – a relationship organisation. If this is the model for the future, what are the implications for politicians and for politics? Enough has been said to indicate that structures on their own achieve little. Unless councillors undertake different roles and build different relationships, not much will change. These new roles include, but are not limited to, the roles of executive and scrutiny.

For mayors or members of the 'cabinet', the role is not executive in any simple sense. Much of the crucial decision-making within a locality exists at the interface between public and private agencies. Leading politicians will need to be negotiators and relationship-builders. In some localities, decision-making partnerships already exist on a multi-agency basis. The mayor or leader is still not 'the boss' but one powerful player among many. The executive councillor will need to be a strategist, but will also need to be a skilled orchestrator, looking outwards rather than inwards, linking aspirations and needs across the communities, and bringing together resources from across the locality to respond. We suggested in Chapter 4 that web-like networks or city boards may form the real executive in a locality. There is a difference between decision-making, a process which may involve many participants and take place in many settings, and decision-taking, the formal process with clear lines of accountability. The leadership of the cabinet or mayor can be leadership through orchestration, setting direction, matching resources to priorities, and building the alliances necessary to support good ideas. It need not be the old-fashioned leadership which draws all decisions to the centre.

The role of scrutiny as it was originally conceived is too narrow to match the needs of a relationship organisation. It is not simply the decisions and actions of the local council that need to be subject to scrutiny, nor simply councillors who can legitimately expect to play a role in scrutinising them. But there are signs that as the role evolves, councils are beginning to include members of the public, or local neighbourhood representatives, or call expert witnesses. Scrutiny offers an opportunity not simply for interrogating council officers but for exploring alternatives, thinking creatively or building cross-agency solutions to intractable problems. It then become possible, even obvious, to extend the scrutiny role past the local councillors out into the community, perhaps integrating scrutiny roles with community representation through area forums or neighbourhood panels, perhaps inviting community leaders or respected local people such as bishops or judges to act as scrutineers, or involving local people on a 'jury' basis to serve on a single scrutiny body for a year or so, rather than taking on the full weight of councillor activities. It might be possible for councillors to serve for only a year, or only in a narrow area of activity, to act as a link between council and local people

The scrutiny role can also be rethought, to reconnect councillors to their wider communities. Instead of the limited role of scrutinising decisions, some authorities are setting up 'scrutiny and review groups' which initiate the policy process by investigating important issues or problems. These groups of councillors operate as a mini-research and development group, exploring issues, sometimes inviting partners to work with them, taking evidence, going to see good practice elsewhere, and formulating policy proposals which can then go to the executive

The expectations local people have of their representatives are changing. A recent community panel on issues of governance concluded that while they wanted local councillors to act as regulators and protectors, they also expected local people to inform themselves about local issues and to make their views heard. They wanted local councils 'to listen more and impose less', and expected greater self-governance in the future. Representation might involve taking part in local forums or committees, being on governing bodies of schools or other partnership bodies, attending tenants associations and so forth. It might involve visiting local youth clubs, church groups, mosques or businesses to understand people's experiences and needs. But it is not simply a process of attending meetings in order to defend and explain the council's record, but one of actively building an understanding of the different views and perspectives within the community, feeding them back into the decision-making processes. A true representative seeks out the different and conflicting experiences with his or her patch, taking care to ensure all the relevant voices have been heard – and making efforts to redress the balance and fill gaps – since only when all the voices have been taken into account can a decision be made which offers the best balance for the community

New technology makes new forms of interaction possible. It is probable that at least some councils will have cable-TV stations, able to broadcast local information and transact council business with local people. It would be a relatively small step to run consultation or referenda through local television.

In a world in which direct and participatory democracy coexists with representative democracy the role of a representative changes, and becomes one of ringholder, advocate, broker – listening to and bringing together the views of different communities. The job of the representative becomes that of integrating different sorts of democracy and different sources of democratic legitimacy. The role of individual representation, caseworker or problem-solver is often downplayed as boring, but it is a lynchpin of a democratic process. Effective accountability requires that individuals have access to advice, advocacy and redress. The councillor is able to act as advocate for the least powerful individuals in society; but whether they do so or not, of course, is a matter of politics.

If a local council is to be a true relationship organisation, then the role of the councillor is not simply to learn from and to decide for local people, but to create the networks and relationships within which local people can learn from each other and decide for themselves. Members of the community can play a role not simply in voting, but in actively working to identify problems, and to design and deliver solutions. There are many active players who have a role to play in implementing as well as approving decisions. There is a political role involved not simply in deciding or in scrutinising decisions, but in helping to broker the process of decision-making. Rather than simply hearing the different voices within a community, the broker will attempt to help the different groups to understand each other, and to negotiate with other agencies and other powerful community players to generate solutions that meet local needs.

Where interests are not powerful and well-organised, where there is a relatively fragmented community, perhaps in a rural area or in a deprived area where there are not strong traditions of community representation, there may be a need for a facilitator to help to bring people together and to find ways to solve local problems. One elderly councillor I met recently represented 16 villages in a rural community; he spent much of his time trying to build working networks that enabled these communities to function. In one village, the local post office had closed and the local bus service had disappeared. For the handful of pensioners in their eighties and nineties, without use of cars, this spelt disaster. The councillor thought hard and then went to see the remaining sub-postmaster in a village ten miles away. The result is 'pensions morning' in the local village hall – once a week, the sub-postmaster drives over from the post office, brings the pensions, takes orders for deliveries, and local volunteers organise tea and cakes. Councillors are not only there to talk. Real community leaders act.

Councillors can act to empower and support local decision-makers – perhaps tenants on a local estate making their own decision about whether or not to set up a housing company, or residents in an area earmarked for regeneration deciding how best to spend the available funds. The role here is one of orchestrating the support that the community needs to make decisions well – helping to build capacity by ensuring the right training, information and resources, and finding advocates or 'friends' who can support them in navigating through bureaucracy, and creating the right conditions in external agencies to enable their decisions to be carried through into implementation.

As the roles of formal government organisations change it will become more and more important to be able to identify responsibility and hold people to account. Elected representatives play a vital governance role at local level since they carry on behalf of the wider community a responsibility to ensure that the workings of public agencies are fair, efficient and effective, and meet local needs. There remains a crucial 'dismissability' in elected representatives, which makes it possible to hold them to account for the outcomes of their orchestration and ringholding. Councillors offer the citizen the only obvious focus for discontent or anger. Councillors are, or should be, responsible on our behalf for the overall balance of outcomes, for the pattern of public action and the effectiveness of local intervention. Managers, communities and private organisations will play a part in all this, but someone must be held accountable to the public for success. Without such a clear relationship of accountability the public loses a crucial route for action as citizen-authorisers or as co-producers and become reduced to the role of customers.

We have explored the cultural and systemic reasons for the historic weakness of the governance role. Councillors often have only a hazy sense of their accountability to the public, since the reward systems are so much more powerfully hooked to their service to the political party and to the organisation. Change will therefore require a fundamental rethink not only of local politics, but also of the reward systems that drive local politics.

Real and imaginary community leaders

We should not be too quick to dismiss local politicians as backwoodsmen and women – easily dispensed with in a new modern and managerial local reality. Two important trajectories are about to cross. While councillors are moved sideways and attacked for their lack of skill and training, for their closed clubbish behaviours and for being out of touch, government is at the same time encouraging community participation, tenant control, community self-government and community entrepreneurship. But many community entrepreneurs have in the past been brave enough to join the council. Councillors often started off as parish councillors and community activists, and were often asked to stand because they were effective community leaders. Councillors are often active and vocal members of the community.

Simply replacing them with 'community representatives' misses the point. The problems they face are replicated in community associations and club houses and community trusts across the country. Issues of governance, accountability and corruption affect community organisations just as much as councils. Closed cultures, family-dominated cliques and inward focus are familiar aspects of many tenants' associations and community groups. These are the inevitable traditions of closed communities, of lack of civic dialogue, of tension between different sections of the community. Building open, responsive behaviours is not simply an issue either for managers or for politicians, it is an issue for civil society.

7   Why is Change so Hard?

Box 7.1   A local authority case study

X is a busy city council, recognised by government as a successful local authority. There is a strong and visionary chief executive who in his two years has introduced a new top team, broken up departmental boundaries creating new multi-department directorates. The authority has become a Best Value pilot, has a Surestart scheme, an Education Action Zone, a Regeneration Partnership. It produces glossy strategy documents that are the envy of its neighbours. It can point to a user-consultation strategy, a recent citizens' jury and a large citizens panel. Service performance, however, is variable. In one or two areas (social services, education) it is judged to be poor; most of the other services hover at the bottom end of average, although there are some areas of excellence. Councillors are dissatisfied since user-satisfaction ratings are worryingly low – and are demanding immediate results, or heads will roll. The majority group faces election within two years. The chief executive confides that despite the glossy new systems and structures, very little change seems to be evident on the ground. Recent meetings with local people have been bitter, and the support of the local authority for recent hospital closures by their partner agencies in health was treated by the press as 'betrayal'. The implementation of Best Value and the servicing of partnerships seems to be eating up huge amounts of time – time needed to manage basic performance. The authority has recently embarked upon a major culture change programme – 'to ensure ownership of the values and goals of the organisation by all staff'.

Further discussions with the chief executive are revealing. He describes tension and rivalry between top managers, who still seem to be focused on their departments. He is worried that the recent changes do not run deep, and that the organisation will fall back into old ways; he is conscious the world is changing very fast and is

(continued)

---

worried that they will be left behind. He is hopeful of winning 'Beacon' status, but concerned that the authority might lose its reputation if there is too much bad publicity.

Interviews with individual officers and members help to build up the picture. Service chiefs feel personally under huge pressure to deliver to government agendas – the Director of Education said privately he 'couldn't give a stuff about the corporate agenda, he had to improve the schools or get his legs cut off by the DFEE'. Partnerships were often experienced as a dangerous distraction at a time of limited resources. Members of staff are constantly called to project meetings for vague initiatives with other bodies that seem to do nothing.

The chief executive has identified an energetic group of middle managers that leads much of the project work and the new thinking. They feel committed but exhausted; they were chosen because they were good, but they are now overstretched. Worse, they face jealousy within their departments. They are disproportionately women and black managers and feel overexposed – outside the culture of their departments; their career hangs on the whim of the chief exec. – what if he leaves? And they are frustrated by the length of time taken to make things happen.

In focus groups, with the more junior staff, there are endless worries about job insecurity and about dislocation. One or two older women, a care worker and a secretary say 'it's about time something changed around here – it's like living in the dark ages'. But many of the older men, particularly from the professional groups such as engineers, architects, trading standards managers and housing managers, talk about how all this 'airy fairy' nonsense is stopping people having pride in their job. They feel undervalued and anxious, although there are plenty of jokes. Questions like 'What are your personal objectives' bring responses like 'early retirement' or 'going to the pub' and lots of laughs. I know it would be a mistake to assume that this means these managers are lazy or do not work effectively in their jobs. I make a mental note to check. 'Running a good service isn't valued any more'. There is displacement activity by professional staff – many are active in their professions, or work in their spare time on demanding hobbies such as running youth clubs, gardening or sailing.

(*continued*)

It turns out that the chief executive's favourite middle managers are well-known as the 'praetorian guard'. 'It helps if you wear a skirt', one manager muttered, but he is frowned at by his colleagues. Several people suggest that all this customer consultation was wasting resources. 'It simply raises expectations. We know what they want and we can't afford to give it to them. What's the point of wasting more money asking them again?'

Some groups of staff, especially social services and housing, are worried about their inability to help local people because of cuts. 'We used to run council housing', said one, 'and now we simply "commission" from housing associations. I came into this service because I believed council housing was a right'. Social workers also worry about the privatisation of their service. 'No-one believes in anything any more', and there are mutterings about the government.

The focus group of senior managers talks about lack of strategy, vague goals and lack of leadership. They seem lively and friendly, but don't see strategy as their job. They blame members and the chief officers. When pushed about the problems of poor performance, they talk about their frustration at their limited scope for action. Councillors are seen as punishing, but as simultaneously limiting the scope for action. Managers confide that they cannot get support for sacking anyone, or for externalising services. Drastic action is always ruled out. 'We're told to be the best, but only to use in-house providers who cost 25 per cent above the cheapest competition'. They see the culture change programme as a new fad and expect the chief executive to lose interest when the next fashionable initiative arrives. They tell stories about all the other new management initiatives they have lived through – restructuring, business process reengineering, team building, leadership programmes. 'Not one of them ever reached a conclusion,' said one manager, 'before the next thing started'.

What will happen to this initiative I ask. There is laughter. 'The usual suspects will be enthusiastic'... 'It will take up loads of time and we'll be told to set up lots of new project groups and then slowly people will stop turning up because of day to day crises' ... 'the chief will lose interest and nothing will come of it.'

'What will that teach you?', I ask. 'That it's all a bloody waste of time', says the head of housing maintenance.

I have made this case study up from a range of different authorities and experiences to ensure anonymity. It is no use trying to guess the characters! But while each experience is unique, the patterns repeat over and over again.

Changing organisations

Whenever I work with groups of public managers to define the new capabilities they need for the future, one of the most frequently mentioned is 'management of change'. Public managers are charged with the responsibility for creating new sorts of organisations, the sorts of organisations that will achieve local governance. This is a new responsibility. For many managers, when they entered public service twenty or thirty years ago, change was not seen as a 'management' problem. Changes in direction would emerge from the domains of politics and policy – new political masters would bring new goals and new policy solutions, and the role of the public organisation was to administer these new solutions. Teachers, social workers, doctors, architects, planners and engineers worked within public organisations within predominantly self-managed and autonomous departments, which responded to political pressure but not to managerial control. At the top of public organisations could be found competent administrators, who managed political sensitivities, implemented policy and calmed down the professionals.

It is only with the new public management revolution that we see problems of organisational strategy and direction, of performance and capability, as management problems requiring management solutions. The rise of the public manager has been the rise of a new figure, exercising leadership in large organisations, required to formulate strategy, to orchestrate human resources, make savings, increase efficiency and improve performance. Failures in public policy used to lead to the resignation of the politician; now, more often than not, they lead to the sacking of the manager. If society is not getting better – it can be defined as a managerial failure.

The 1980s management revolution introduced general management into public services, and with it a theory about how organisations work, drawn from the private sector. The introduction of 'managerialism' has changed how people in public agencies think about themselves.

The manager as hero

The starting point of managerialism is that we are invited to see the world through the perspective of the manager. As a reader of management textbooks we are always invited to share the manager's problems and dilemmas, and applaud the manager's success. The manager as hero becomes a new character.

From the perspective of the manager, the organisation has goals – and it is their job to achieve them. In many management textbooks these goals are presented as self-evident, to improve profitability, to win new market share, to develop new products. And managers have power, the power that enables them to hire and fire, to direct the actions of others, to make things happen. The power inherent in management is non-negotiable; it is necessary to get the job done. Power inherent elsewhere 'gets in the way'. Other people are resources to be deployed; the organisation is a 'resource space' in which to deploy them.

The powerful machine metaphors reinforce this view. It is the manager's job to make the machine function smoothly, to generate the right outputs with the right inputs. The manager is outside the machine, pulling the levers, operating the controls. The manager does not have to justify the power he or she wields, or the role they play, it is a necessary part of the functioning of the machine. 'Just doing my job'.

The reality, however, is that managers, even in the private sector, have encountered insuperable problems in trying to see the world that way. The metaphor of the machine breaks down when confronted with the awkward human realities of the workers. Handling the workers has been the most difficult problem in management since the creation of the capitalist firm. Many of the industrial struggles in the nineteenth century were attempts by workers to challenge their treatment as 'part of a machine'; and the concept of alienation in the nineteenth century precisely described the process whereby an inherent part of ourselves, the part that works the machine is alienated from us.

Organisational theory rapidly evolved, therefore, to dealing with problems of human relationships and people management. Benign managers as early as the nineteenth century placed emphasis on caring for their workers, and achieved considerable success in comparison with their less-farsighted competitors. Paternalism led to the building of model villages for workers, complete with housing, parks, schools and medical centres. However, the paternalistic tradition required a powerful religious, moral or altruistic sense, which few managers could muster. A milder form of welfarism in the form of personnel departments, pension plans, health care, stress-counselling and leisure clubs survives.

An alternative approach led to a management science of human relationships. Organisational theory attempted to respond to human problems by introducing a range of approaches drawn from social psychology about how people act and interact. 'Social man' became an inevitable part of management – the Hawthorne studies in the mid 1920s carried out in the Hawthorne Plant of American Telegraph & Telephone (AT&T) led to 'human relationships theory' recognising the value of responding to human needs for social relationships, with stress on cooperation. Team development became a vital element of good management, and managers had to learn how to build teams, how to encourage cooperation and to reward team spirit.

In bureaucracies, however, the experiences of workers have always been slightly different to the experience on the factory floor. Impersonal procedures dominate, and even managers have their own managers in turn, within a complex hierarchy. Bureaucracies are clerical workplaces, inside warm buildings. In the early years of the century, a clerical job, particularly a job in the relative safety of the public sector, offered respectability, security and status. One's place in the hierarchy meant that promotion and reward depended on loyalty and compliance. While we have many cultural references to the deadly mind-numbing dullness of the clerical job, it was at least secure. The nineteenth century and twentieth century experience of work for bureaucrats was different to that of danger, physical exhaustion, noise – it was to do with the ever-present danger of meaninglessness. Bureaucratic work was broken down into narrow procedures, driven by unintelligible logic. Recreation, friendships, skiving, game-playing – even light sabotage – offered alternative ways to create meaning in the working day. In public service bureaucracies, while many staff were diligent and hard-working, they because disconnected with the outcomes they were trying to achieve.

The attack on public services, when it came in the 1970s, came as an attack on bureaucracy – public organisations were seen as flabby, self-serving, producer-driven, unresponsive and inefficient. In the UK, in the USA, in Australia – more slowly in Europe – a neo-liberal critique was developed as if these problems derived from the 'public' nature of public organisations, and as if the private sector was somehow inherently different, and better. At the same time, of course, a similar set of criticisms was being made of the vast private corporation. Managers, particularly middle managers were slow, unimaginative, dull bureaucrats. The world was changing so fast that a revolution was needed. The private sector needed to become light, responsive, customer focused, innovative and creative. Organisations needed to be different. They needed to change their style, their values, their entire personalities. They needed to change their culture.

Well-known books such as Peters and Waterman's (1982) *In Search of Excellence* concentrate on the role of managers in creating the right culture. Managers became no longer simply responsible for controlling the machine or for managing resources; within the cultural revolution they are expected to organise the culture of the organisation. Their job is to exercise leadership in the sphere of values and culture as well as the spheres of performance and financial control. The 'hero manager' is responsible for creating a 'can-do' culture.

Managers were/are expected to mobilise combinations of values, language, ritual and myth to 'unlock the commitment and enthusiasm of employees' (Thompson and McHugh, 1995, p. 198). Managers are expected to develop cultural strategies to share values. The job is now to change attitudes and behaviours, to motivate staff, to create ownership of a shared vision. Textbooks encourage methods of positively reinforcing new behaviours – using celebrations, parties, competitions and prizes. Successful private companies are expected to share their values and their mission with staff, and to engage staff in the celebration of organisational success. Corporate culture has become a key factor in corporate success. Critics on the left have seen the stress on culture as an insidious form of control, far more dangerous than conventional hierarchy (Deetz, 1992; Willmott, 1994), although, as Thompson and McHugh demonstrate in the private sector, and as we shall see in the public sector, this control has never been as all-embracing or as successful as these fears suggest.

More important, the 'manager as hero' perspective takes no account of what goes on in the outside world, or of the other forces and drivers that are outside the domain of management. It creates an unreal expectation of power because in reality managers cannot control everything. At the same time, it leads to an exaggerated sense of incapacity – the idea that since you cannot control everything, nothing can be expected of you. Both are disabling in the organisational context. In the public domain, managers struggle to follow their mythical private sector counterparts.

The problem with culture

The problem is that culture is more complicated than the evangelical outpourings of Peters and Waterman (1982) and others lead us to believe. It helps to hold onto the origins of the word culture, and to draw on its various meanings. It may be more useful, for example, to approach culture through archaeology and anthropology, through theatre and dance, rather than through management science. Culture is the system of meanings, depictions and symbols that express the values and reality of a community. It is as much about rhythms and patterns, myths and stories as it is about 'values' or 'vision'. It is often through understanding the stories and myths of an organisation that one can come to see how tensions and dilemmas are lived within a particular organisational context. Culture cannot be manufactured by managerial effort, although it can be excavated, studied, watched and experienced – in ways that begin to create the sort of understanding that can lead to change. An organisation is not an empty space into which cultures can be grown; cultures are created bottom up, they are brought in from the outside and built through interaction.

Nor can culture be conceptualised in a social and political vacuum; it is not possible to insulate an organisation from society. It may be possible to create 'exceptional space' in which some elements of a wider social culture are exaggerated or suppressed, but it cannot be too far away from the culture of society at large. We can recognise the importance of subcultures, and the powerful informal group norms that are the bedrock of organisational life. But workgroups are just one of the competing claims on the commitment and loyalty of staff – family, religion, trades unions, political parties, professions may also have claims.

The individual is always inside society as well as inside the organisation. Organisations contain all of the tensions and dilemmas that exist in wider society – power differences based on race, gender, education and class – as well as the power relationships structured through the formal hierarchy of the organisation. The organisation is a place where social and organisational cultures interact. It is a 'site of struggle' a place where different interests meet – although some may be more powerful than others. Within an organisation there are many people, as individuals or interest groups, negotiating to try and secure their own goals (directors, trades unions, middle managers, professionals), but an organisation is also part of a wider system of interactions – global, national, regional and local. Organisations reproduce and are a site for the inequalities of power in wider society, and these are likely to impact on what goes on inside the organisation and how it impacts on the wider world.

Organisational culture cannot therefore be thought of as a 'tool' to be mobilised by management. It is a way of describing the patterns, the stories, the ways of seeing and ways of working that emerge through constant interactions within and outside the organisation. Since in each organisation these are different, we can identify an organisational culture, although it is never closed. But it is seldom the 'culture' that is espoused in the glossy brochures. Indeed the real culture is what is created when individual managers and staff confront, and respond to, the 'espoused' culture. The real culture is powerful, but rarely spoken about.

Paul Thomson and David McHugh (1995) argue that the scale of the cultural revolution in the private sector has been hugely exaggerated by its practitioners. While welfarism is not new, most organisations pay very little attention to the well-being of their staff, and rely primarily on hierarchical structures and systems to control behaviour. Staff compliance is still secured through good old-fashioned fear. They argue that there is no real evidence that cultures can be managed in these ways to produce results. Much of the culture stuff is hype – staff told by their boss to take part in a team-building exercise or an 'ownership awayday' will turn up and join in regardless of what they think or feel. Any attempt to challenge the process, or question the rationale carries the risks that are always taken when you criticise the boss.

Staff often see an awayday, or a culture change project as hype, but participate because either other systems of control are in place or because promotion depends on 'demonstrating ownership'. I once went to facilitate an event for top managers within a local authority to develop some shared thinking about strategy. After initial interviews with participants in the session, the head of personnel walked me to the stairs, 'You won't make us sing', he asked anxiously. I laughed thinking it was a random joke. But a week later, in a planning session, another manager said the same thing. It turned out that a year or so before, a consultant had been brought in by the then chief executive (who had now left) to work with managers on a 'vision'. The event had carried the full authority of the chief executive, but the chief had not attended. Authority rested, or seemed to rest, with the consultant. As part of a process of 'gaining ownership', the consultant insisted in the final session that working groups report back by writing, and then singing, a song which espoused their vision. The predominantly middle-aged, male, professional management team had done what they were told. And hated it. The level of embarrassment they had felt still made them emotional two years later. The words 'vision' and 'humiliation' were still tied up in their minds.

Staff have other reasons for engaging with change regardless of the competence or motivational capacity of their managers. In public organisations, many members of staff believe themselves to be dedicated to their clients 'despite the system'. Their own values and understanding may lead them to support change.

Attitudes, behaviour and identity

A key element in 'culture change' is often described as the need to 'change attitudes and behaviour'. We suggested in Chapter 4 that managers need to become creative, risk-managers and empowerers. But achieving this is not simple. Crude assumptions about motivation fail to understand the complexity of the reasons individuals use to make choices. Simple theories of motivation fail, and any simple hierarchy of motivation remains unproven (see Maslow, 1954, and the critique in Thompson and McHugh, 1995, p. 300). A number of recent authors have pointed to the importance of more complex factors, a regard for self-consistency, a need to maintain self-esteem and to reflect true identity, a need to help and support colleagues (Klein, 1989; Shamir, 1991). Of course, behaviour can be changed through fear. Thompson and McHugh quote the example of the supermarket checkout assistants who were monitored by closed-circuit cameras to ensure they smiled at all the customers. If *compliance* is required, it can be driven through control systems or training. But if people are required to think and act creatively, this cannot be driven through compliance; it requires attitude change, and attitudes are not simply conditioned responses they are the result of judgements and belief systems about 'how the world is', 'what will work' and 'what is my role'.

Individuals do not think or believe different things simply because they are trained to do so, or instructed to do so. We come to conclusions about the world through cognitive processes, through exploration, experience, analysis and reflection – almost all informal or social processes of learning, but all the more powerful for that. For each of us, what matters is the lived experience of building relationships with others into which we bring our own views, beliefs, attitudes and values, and through which we make sense of the world and create for ourselves a sense of value and purpose. Organisations are created through a process of subjective experience as individuals in lived relationships bounded by social, organisational and work cultures.

The workplace is inevitably part (although not the whole) of a process of forming individual and collective identities. Identity is not, as we explored in Chapter 3, fixed – it is a negotiated construct. Not only do we evolve our own identities, but we also create identities for ourselves in particular contexts. So, for example, we can create a 'work identity' which is appropriate to the situation we find ourselves in, and consistent with the expectations of others. Our constructed 'work self' can be nearer or further from the realities of our 'outside-work self' as we juggle personal identity (who we are to ourselves) and social identity (who we are to others). As we shall suggest later, we are creating additional stress and problems by forcing people into situations in which there is real dissonance between their sense of self in work and self in non-work.

Our work identity is created as we explore how the beliefs we bring fit with those around us, how the things we value about ourselves are valued by others, and how we explain what we do to others.

The meanings and identities that are created through this process of exploration may be favourable to the organisation's purpose, or they may not. People are not trying to simply adapt successfully, they are also trying to 'be themselves' to be true to their own values, to be a good colleague, a good father, a good teacher. How people take control over their work experience is crucial. Thompson and McHugh suggest a series of possible responses to change which include 'contradictory consciousness' – a deliberate attempt to create an oppositional identity (through antagonism, challenge, absenteeism, laddishness); unconscious resistance (when staff withdraw and develop a work personality outside the change, becoming cynical, passive, often simulating 'ritual helplessness'; a concentration on self (using the change process to develop individual learning and skills to move on); participation in collective action (such as trades union activity); as well as the conforming processes of exploration, understanding and integration.

The capacity of an organisation to change therefore rests on the results of these individual and interactive processes of identity-work. It is not therefore a simple process to 'gain ownership' or to motivate people to support change. To do any of these things means engaging seriously with people's reasons and beliefs, as well as their attitudes and behaviours.

The public manager as hero?

While in the private sector there is a considerable head of steam behind the idea of manager as hero, in the public sector the image of a manager has been seen as more problematic. The tendency to see managers as the bureaucrats, the 'suits', the system-wallahs – has often combined politicians, journalists, professionals and the public in an attack on managers as the problem. Hugo Young, on TV's Newsnight in June 1999, argued that the test of the new Director General of the BBC would be the extent to which the manager lost power to producers. And it is a political and media convention when discussing the NHS to celebrate the doctors and nurses and deprecate the numbers and the power of the managers. Cutting out layers of management is seen as synonymous with improving efficiency. Public managers during the 1980s experienced a real ambiguity – their numbers rose, their pay and status rose, but they were nevertheless vilified by politicians and the media.

The success of Hill Street Blues in the depression of 1980s Britain among middle-class professionals was due to the introduction of a new sort of cop in captain Ferillo – the public manager hero. He was never out in the field catching bad guys; he was in the office managing tensions and dilemmas, balancing accountabilities, holding things together. It was Ferillo who talked the stupid politician out of a short-term stunt that would endanger good policework, who calmed down community leaders after a shooting, who made PJ go to alcoholics anonymous as a condition of keeping his job. The beat policemen and detective heroes of other cop shows got results through bucking the system, by cheating on the paperwork, by lying to their boss. But Ferillo wasn't bucking the system, forgodsake; he was managing the system. He was making it work! How we all identified!

In the private manager as hero literature, the rules are all assumed. The rules of hierarchy enable him or her (but usually him) to 'make things happen'. But in the public sector the rules are not given – they are up for negotiation. Accountabilities are not simple. They conflict.

The public manager does not simply manage efficiently. He/she focuses effort on outcomes, inspires others, orchestrates resources, manages legitimacy, enables and empowers others, creates space for innovation – balances risk, manages conflicting accountabilities, listens to many voices – holds the system in balance. The public manager can never be a straightforward hero figure in the public sector, since power is not located simply with the manager. There are many powerful stakeholders. There are other sorts of heroes.

The role of the professional

The identity of the public manager is so fraught, and so contested, that many public managers don't see themselves as managers at all, but as professionals. It is through professional identity that many people in public organisations derive their sense of self, of belonging, of value. 'I am a public health doctor', a chief executive of a health authority will tell you. 'I am an engineer', says the director of a large local government department. The word professional carries a dual meaning – professional means high quality as in 'they did a professional job', but it also carries the status of a body of learning and a badge of accreditation. 'The professional class' implies upper-middle class – a 'professional qualification' implies university-level achievement. Each profession carries powerful reinforcing values, a sense of expertise and specialist knowledge, a place in the world.

Professions are self-regulating, with codes of ethics and independence of judgement. There is also a powerful cultural image of the professional as hero – the whistle-blower, the good teacher that chooses the children over promotion, the dedicated scientist, Florence Nightingale. But while the word 'professional' carries all these positive connotations, professionals can also be seen by the public as dangerously arrogant, deaf to individual choice or public opinion. New consumer organisations have been created to challenge professionals; 'SOS: NHS in Danger' is an organisation created to challenge the power of doctors to decide on behalf of patients. Self-help groups challenge the assumptions of medical and social-work professionals; community campaigns challenge the decisions of architects and planners; environmental campaigns challenge the 'expert' advice of scientists.

The professional is respected, but is feared. And the legitimacy of professionals is undermined by fast-moving technological change which makes it harder for them to 'know' on our behalf. The slicing up of knowledge into separate professional specialisms means that professionals seldom work well across boundaries or in the complexity of real-life problems. Who is best able to deal with a child excluded from school – an educationalist, a policeman, a youth worker, a social worker or a psychologist?

Professionals are often trained to trust their own expertise, and to *read* their clients' needs and aspirations through their own expert knowledge. But client needs and choices have sometimes been over-ridden. Professionals do not always know what other professionals would be able to offer, and are not always able to balance their own expertise with that of others. They can often unconsciously shape a client's demands to fit what they are equipped to provide. One manager said 'it's pot luck really. If they come to us first they'll get a home help, if they go to the health authority they'll get a district nurse. It make sense that we assess people as needing what we have got to offer.' Professionals are not always skilled in balancing their own knowledge against the knowledge of other professionals or the knowledge of citizens.

The conventional professional view that the management revolution introduced into public services in the 1980s was wholly bad is not tenable. Professional freedom has been fettered, but this sometimes happened in the interests of securing more efficient resource use, greater consistency of experience for users, or a better evidence base for practice. Managers sometime speak for users and customers, and challenge professional vested interests. The role of professionals in public services cannot be underestimated – the sense of being 'a professional' offers an alternative identity to people within public services, and a legitimate vantage point – that of scientist or expert – from which to challenge managerial decisions. Attempts by managers to prevent professional whistle blowing have not always succeeded. The alternative site of power occupied by professionals has acted as a block to daft managerial ideas, and helped to resist fads, but at the same time professionals also have vested and partial interests. They may be defending themselves.

The public servant

Managers and staff within public agencies often carry a powerful set of values around public service, values described by John Stewart (1981) as 'public service ethos'. Neutrality, equity, fairness and probity are vital if the system is to run efficiently to deliver the political goals of those elected politicians who have won democratic office. Respect for the democratic process and a willingness to accept the legitimacy of the decisions by elected officials is an essential part of the values system within public organisations. However, the public service ethos at its most dry can give way to a lack of interest in outcomes – the civil service mandarin obsession with 'service' to political masters, but without concern for results. Other values may be more contested – the values of confidentiality, for example, or of transparency. These values may conflict with those of management, or of professionals; or they may begin to merge. The concern with ethics within the health service is leading to a debate about wider sets of organisational values, about 'not doing harm', about 'truth-telling' and about 'autonomy' as principles for care. Public sector workers carry a set of values about the nature of public services which impact on their identity and work.

The emotionally committed worker

Some areas of public service command powerful emotions. Nursing, care for the elderly, work with the homeless or with people with HIV/AIDS, policing, teaching – all require emotional engagement and emotional resilience to cope with the tragic experiences that befall service users. We, the public, distance ourselves from the realities of human tragedy by relying on a dedicated set of professionals to whom we entrust the responsibility for caring. A fascinating book from practitioners at the Tavistock Institute explores this, and the extent to which, for example, the NHS is a service that 'keeps death at bay' on behalf of the rest of us; or the child protection service deals on our behalf with the unthinkable reality of child abuse; or the police carry on our behalf the responsibility for facing human evil (see Obholzer and Roberts (eds), 1994).

People often choose these jobs for the power of the emotional experiences available, for the personal, daily sense of little achievements. For these workers their daily life offers powerful experiences, of joy when cures or solutions are found, of despair when patients die, or the children you tried to help vandalise your car. The power of the emotional experiences within these workplaces and the importance they have in translating social and ethical assumptions into practice are seldom explored. Staff and managers are not encouraged to think or talk about the experience of managing these dangerous emotions on behalf of society, or about what their work represents to themselves, to others, even to clients. For many, the day-to-day experience is of failure, inadequate resources, poor systems, bad communications, rationing. The stress of the experience of failing those who depend on you adds to the stress of badly stretched provision, and overwork. Whatever the truth about the scope for efficiency savings, the lived reality of many front-line staff in these services is that they are caught between the demands of 'the system' and the demands of their customers – and this challenges their sense of well-being and value in the job they do. The public is unforgiving about failure, but does not want to hear about the problems. Government and media collude with punishing the individual when things go wrong, without understanding the systems failures that make it inevitable that things will go wrong again. The managerial paradigm offers no space to explore the emotions created by these tensions.

These identities do not sum up the whole list. There are others. But managers and staff within organisations are trying to make sense of change through all these lenses.

The specificity of the public service

The role of a public service organisation is almost always to explicitly intervene in the wider social, economic and political relationships of society, which means that the cultural assumptions that underpin the nature of those interventions are crucial. In other words, within a public organisation the belief systems that matter are not simply those about 'how organisations should work', but about what they are for. The belief systems and values that individuals hold about what they are doing, and why, impact both on what they do and how they do it.

Many people join the public sector because of preexisting beliefs that what it does is benign or useful, and because of a desire to help people. This does not mean that public servants are more ethical or moral than people who work in the private sector, but it does suggest that they may have higher expectations of what they may achieve in ethical or moral terms in their job. This creates a set of important conditions that impact on change within the public sector:

- As citizens we require public organisations to carry certain values – probity, honesty, integrity, accountability – that lead to a deeply ingrained 'rational-legal' practice. These are deeply embedded with public organisations as are expectations of neutrality and the replicability of public actions and public policy. Innovation inevitably challenges these values since experiments are bound sometimes to fail, and experiments, by their nature, mean treating different people or places, differently. The reality, therefore, is that experiments whether they succeed or fail are rarely 'rolled out' or applied to mainstream practice.

- We also rely on public organisations to carry social values on behalf of the rest of us. We no longer look after all vulnerable people within civil society; we have created public institutions to do this on our behalf. Much of the anger at examples of abuse within social services derives from the challenge to our moral comfort, when we discover that those we have charged to 'be good' on our behalf, have failed us. We often do not want to hear about, or explore, the reasons. We have very high expectations of the professional skill and expertise of public bodies, often an unrealistic expectation that they can solve social problems or prevent abuse, which they cannot.

- All staff and managers within public organisations are inevitably, also, users of the services provided by public organisations, and citizens who vote. They therefore are not simply interacting with the organisation as 'staff', but may also carry identities as users or citizens-authorisers or co-producers into the workplace.

- If local governance plays a role in securing the rules of engagement for civil society, then the nature of those rules is inevitably a subject for active exploration both inside and outside the organisation. Managers and staff play a role in enforcing and regulating social behaviour, and draw on powerful personal and professional values to do so, which are seen as legitimate in a work context. They are more likely than other workers to take industrial action to protect those professional values (for example teachers, nurses and doctors threatening action against changing work processes). However, the values and assumptions in play have not been, in the past, subject to challenge, or to open debate in civil society. Emerging relationships of governance change all this. If rules of engagement are negotiated freely within civil society, this impacts on the rules of engagement for managers and staff.

- The high profile of much public service means that managers and staff experience risk on a daily basis. We discussed in Chapter 4 some of the dimensions of public sector risk. Responses to risk, and the management of risk form an important part of working practice and culture in public service organisations. If the response to risk changes, then this will have important implications for individuals and working practice.

Multiple sources of power – multiple sources of identity

The idea of the manager as the only source of organisational power is as disabling in the context of governance as the idea of the politician as all-powerful. The political process is obviously a vital dimension of power within governance; so is community. But within organisations there are many sources of power, and the tensions between them can undermine any change process to enable the organisation to respond.

Staff and managers within public organisations are often trying to deal with change on many levels at once, trying to balance conflicting demands, trying to sustain a sense of personal worth and purpose within large and confusing organisations, to construct an identity out of the elements of professional, manager, citizen or activist that makes sense – trying to feel good about what they do. They are working within the constraints of organisations that don't work well with creaking systems and not enough money. For many staff and managers, old realities persist. They do not experience change as transforming the everyday job, simply as making it more difficult. They may be aware of the ambiguity that exists, that messages are mixed, and that politicians may change their minds. They may be factoring in the possibility that pilots often run out of funding, and too strong a commitment to new projects risks exposure. They may be worried about their own capacity to fulfil new roles. They may have given up learning a long time ago, and have found a comfortable niche carping from the sidelines. They may have checked out.

Organisations that publish a statement of 'values' often list values that are not experienced by staff or the public as real. They conflict with people's lived experience in the workplace or as customers. Value such as 'openness' or 'equality' or 'we look after our staff', if they are invented by councillors or top managers on an awayday without consultation, simply give rise to cynicism. If espoused values conflict with lived reality, they give rise to the experienced value of hypocrisy:

> ...the culture of this place is that we all waste time at poxy culture change programmes because it keeps the chief executive happy.

Often there is significant dissonance between the publicly stated culture – organisational goals and objectives, upbeat documents – and the disparaging comments made by senior mangers, councillors and staff in confidence. This is not to say that these organisations are necessarily failing, or even that they have worse problems than average, simply that there exists a massive perceived gap between theory and reality that is almost universally acknowledged and rarely talked about. In order to begin to make real change possible we need to recognise that,

1. Public agencies are trying to achieve social outcomes in the context of social and political ambivalence about the role of public services.
2. They are trying to reinvent themselves, without the tools or the time to do so.
3. The power to drive change is multilocated – powerful players include politicians, managers, professionals, citizens – and each of these different groups will think differently about issues of accountability and legitimacy.
4. No organisation works in isolation, but through its interactions with other organisations and individuals.
5. Change can neither be driven through command and control systems, or through a pretence that these do not exist.
6. Inequalities in society outside the organisation almost inevitably exist inside it and need to be openly explored.
7. Individuals bring their own values, belief systems and ideas to work, and do not easily shed them because of an imposed 'value process'.

It is important to work with-the-grain of reality, and to recognise that there are difficult and uncomfortable realities which are often ignored as dispiriting or demotivating. But they are real. They need to be faced up to and talked about, not as excuses for failure but as the operating context. In order to wire organisations together through effective relationships, the people within those relationships need space to explore the tensions and contradictions they experience in their work. These are inescapably part of the tensions and contradictions in the role of public service organisations, and there are no simple solutions. An organisational change process that pretends they are not there will not engage with the beliefs, and therefore with the attitudes and behaviours, of the people who make things work.

This is not the same as making space for whining, although there is often a stage of whining to be gone through. Organisational theorists have borrowed analysis from social psychological studies of bereavement, to track a process of denial, anger, acceptance and exploration to explain how people often respond to drastic and unforeseen change imposed from the outside. In the stages of transition from denial to acceptance, people often need to express their sadness, anger and frustration. But a social psychological explanation is flawed because it accepts as given that organisational change is like bereavement or divorce – something that fate (or the manager) does to you. But fatalism is a poor way to think about, let alone experience, change. The alternative is to engage with the belief systems that give rise to feelings of discomfort or anger – to share responsibility for solving the emerging problems – to explore seriously how else things could be. Power exists inside organisations as it does outside, and managers and staff have to come to terms with the realities of differential power, and to learn enough to make complex organisations work. The effective public manager is 'conscientious', bringing their whole human, ethical and intelligent self to their work, open to challenge, willing to justify decisions and actions, willing to learn, serious about achieving results.

If we look back at the case study at the beginning of the chapter, we can recognise that every individual manager or staff member within the authority saw change from a slightly different place. They were all trying to manage themselves, as well as responding to changing demands from the organisation. I do not want to argue that the issues in this hypothetical case are universal, nor that they would be recognised by all the players to be the case. But from the perspective of each actor, different things are real. The feelings and perceptions of each actor in an organisation play a role in change. The tensions they are experiencing are real ones; roles and responsibilities are unclear, and almost everyone feels pulled by contradictory pressures. The chief executive feels very isolated, the corporate directors feel beleaguered, the middle managers feel exposed, the staff feel under-valued. No one has said these things, except through jokes and ritual complaints.

Staff have never really had an opportunity to think or talk through the reasons for change, or to put their assumptions to the test. They don't know if spending has actually been cut – or redistributed. They don't know what users really think about the services they provide. They hold all sorts of opinions about the public, other departments, partner organisations – which have never been challenged or explored. They no longer know how to value their work, or whether others value it. They are disengaging. Managers feel unable to talk to councillors. Councillors are seen as exter-nal, alien, resistant to logic and unreachable. They are treated as a 'given' which means they are both feared because of their ability to punish, and infantilised since no-one bothers to tell them the truth. In the case study, there are no honest adult-to-adult conversations between councillors and managers.

The public is also seen as an external unknown force, capable of pun-ishing failure, but unable to be engaged in the realities of difficult choices that face the council. The managers have boxed themselves into a profes-sional corner where everyone else is 'a threat' and they alone are responsi-ble for getting things right. The only solution is to work harder. But because of the problems, much of their hard work is wasted. Partnerships are failing. But since so much organisational identity and profile has been built around a 'leading-edge' image, no-one dare say so. Within the part-nerships, relationships are worsening as frustration mounts.

The culture of organisational confidence and success is skin-deep. The organisation has coped well with a lot of change; there is much to cele-brate; there may well be enough time. But since no-one knows how to judge success or what counts as 'enough', the underlying emotion is that of anxiety – the timid wife trying to please a capricious and violent husband, treating moments of 'non-punishment' as calm opportunities for recovery, but having abandoned any sense of autonomy, or control. Good managers and staff achieve results despite the huge waste of energy they experience. They care a lot about what they are trying to do. Easier routes are closed off, so they clamber, exhausted but indefatigable, through long detours. They get the support they need outside, from family and friends. They get an occasional rare hit when a goal is achieved.

The culture of 'not talking about it' means that in meetings to discuss strategy or day-to-day problems, people remain cheerful and positive,

action plans are drafted and progress is charted. But there is no real dialogue that might enable people to face themselves, and others, with a reality
that is not all bad, but not good. Without such a dialogue it is impossible for
people to feel personally responsible for action, rather than simply cogs in a
machine. This frustrates them, but it lets them off the hook. It's not their
fault that services don't improve; they're doing their best. The perspectives
and assumptions of each individual go unchallenged. What is alarmingly
missing – looking in from the outside – is the time and space to explore, to
work through complex problems, to tell the truth, challenge assumptions
and feel confident that action might follow.

When we talk about 'human resources' it is often used as a technical
term describing the armies of staff to be deployed by managers. But there
are other human resources such as intelligence, energy, passion, commitment, identity and relationships that are also available to us, as individuals,
and which can be wasted. In the next chapter we will explore ways to stop
this happening.

8 Learning and Unlearning in Public Organisations

Managers, politicians and citizens are trying to operate with primitive tools, and to do so within tired old structures. We have identified the emergence of hybrid organisations, adapted in part to cope with partnership and an outcome focus, but bolted on to conventional bureaucracies. There is energy and capability inside local agencies but, if it is to be fully released, things have to be done differently. As we explored in the last chapter, change does not necessarily happen the way it was intended. Managers, staff, politicians – even community members – are not cogs in a machine to be 'changed' until they function correctly; they will have to change themselves. There is a Chinese proverb 'You can beat a servant all day, but you cannot beat them into doing something they don't know how to do.' Organisations, and individuals within organisations, only change if they learn how.

Management learning – from competent manager to explorer

Investment in training and development within the public sector remains very low compared with the private sector, and is concentrated on professional and post-professional training. For managers, training still predominates over other forms of capacity development, and is still concentrated in traditional skill areas (managing people, financial management, project management and so on). The majority of managers and staff within public agencies have less than ten days of personal development a year. Whilst local government has fallen behind the police service and NHS in human resource investment, there has been a recent flurry of investment in local government management development. Programmes such as Investors In People (IIP) have been introduced alongside a wide range of new management and leadership programmes and new competency frameworks. There has been new investment in leadership skills at the infrastructural level, with initiatives supported by the Local Government Management Board, the Local Government Association and the Improvement and Development

Agency (IdeA). Investment by local authorities in leadership programmes and capacity-building is growing.

The emphasis on management in the last two decades has succeeded in turning many thousands of administrators and professionals into competent managers. In every local authority, in every public agency, there are conscientious and hard-working middle and senior managers with a capacity to get the job done, a consideration for the needs of service users and an ability to listen to and respect their staff, which recent studies show is often missing in the private sector (see Knights and Collinson, 1987; and Watson, 1994). However, being a competent manager is not the same as being *effective*. The skills that many managers possess work only if the assumptions built into the training – about the organisation being well-aligned to strategy, having clear messages, simple tasks, sufficient resources, working systems, unambiguous targets and outcomes, homogeneous consumers – are true. Many managers, although well-equipped to manage people and manage performance, are nonplussed when they encounter the messy realities of governance.

The skills and capabilities that are expected of staff and managers in the twenty-first century are not those that have been required in the past. People with highly developed knowledge systems, adaptive behaviours and congruent beliefs are finding that these have become outdated. For some managers, the change is catastrophic. They were recruited and promoted because of their professional skills; public organisations were safe, offered good pensions, a strong value base, with emphasis on loyalty and tradition. Such managers like thinking in straight lines; like work to be well-ordered, one task to be completed before the next is begun. The confusing world of governance challenges the skills and knowledge they carry, and they do not have the belief or value systems that enable them to make sense of what is now asked of them.

Others, of course, are excited and energised by opportunities for change. In some parts of public service 'ducking and diving' has always been essential for survival, and in some services the ability to make things happen outside the system has been a characteristic of good front-line workers and good managers for decades. Skills were developed in begging resources and patching schemes together long before these things were given fashionable names and heralded as the new skills required of entrepreneurial managers. Those most able to respond to the new agenda are often those that did not fit well into the 'old' professional cultures, people from within disadvantaged communities, women, or people from the black and ethnic minority communities.

Routes into public services are changing. Fewer people work their way up through the ranks by serving in local government 'man and boy', and it is harder for people without a degree to get into public service. More women and black and ethnic-minority managers joined public agencies because of equal opportunities programmes in the 1980s. Also, the emphasis on learning from the private sector drew in managers with private sector backgrounds. Nevertheless, there are powerful glass ceilings within many of the professions, and many professional groups are still dominated by white men. At senior level there are still few black managers, and disproportionate numbers of men. Processes of recruitment and training are not yet sufficiently open or inclusive. Things are getting better, but only slowly.

And yet the need for a new sort of public services manager is clear. All managers need basic, core skills; but for public managers that is far from enough. Once the basic management skills have been laid down, public managers have to learn to function in the new world of governance. Managers have to juggle accountabilities, to create safe spaces within which their staff can get on with the job, to 'unmix' the mixed messages and translate them for staff into something that makes sense of conflicting roles. Managers have to be capable of balancing, negotiating, making choices and making judgements. They have to sponsor innovation, manage risk and manage legitimacy.

Civic entrepreneurship

Public managers have to work across boundaries, understanding that the capacity to solve the problems they encounter depends on an ability to draw on the resources and capacities of others. They are expected to put resources together in new ways that add value. Just as a private sector entrepreneur learns how to reconfigure resources differently to create added profit, a social or civic entrepreneur learns how to place resources (people, capital, technology, time, energy) in ways that better achieve social results. In a recent study we found that civic entrepreneurs are able to innovate, or to encourage others to innovate – they are creative but with a bias to action, they see change as opportunity, using the stimulus of externally-driven initiatives to make things happen. They are 'visionary opportunists' with a clear sense of direction but flexible enough to exploit opportunities as they occur. 'Civic entrepreneurship crucially involves making a public organisation aware of how it can respond creatively and positively to change' (Leadbeater and Goss, 1998, p. 59). However, they are not boffins or cowboys; civic entrepreneurs crucially work through relationships with others, through building trust and collective capacity. 'Civic entrepreneurs know they cannot succeed alone. In the organisations we studied, entrepreneurship did not depend on an individual but on a team, working entrepreneurially together' (*ibid.*, p. 58).

Managing risk

Public sector organisations are constantly managing risk. Social services departments, for example, are often managing extreme risks in child safety, and health care managers deal with the risk to life every day. Environmental risk, pollution risk, risk to communities and to children's education rub up against financial and organisational risk. Increasingly, the role of the public organisation is not simply to 'bear' or to take risks, but to negotiate risks with local service users and populations. One of the dimensions of new local governance is that risk becomes more apparent as the old systems for managing risk break down. Managers often feel very exposed – since politicians, public and media fail to take responsibility for their side of risk – and want someone to blame. Most public managers, particularly at very senior and very junior levels, work in circumstances that generate high risks, and do so within a risk-averse culture where the public wants certainty, safety and guarantees. The stress created can be intolerable. We have no good ways to respond to this, as managers, as politicians or as citizens. One of the most important capacities we require of our managers, but do not know how to help them develop, is the capacity to balance and manage risk.

Managing legitimacy

Senior managers in the public sector have to be highly skilled in managing the interface with politicians. For some local government officials and civil servants their political accountability is the only one that counts, but as networks of governance become more complex, managers become responsible for a wide range of relationships. A preoccupation with managing one's own politicians gives way to a wider process of balancing accountabilities to local and national politicians, to inspectors and regulators, to customers and to citizens (Parston, 1991). Mark Moore (1996) offers a persuasive case, based on evidence from the US context, that successful managers 'build legitimacy' – manage relationships with both politicians and the public to gain legitimacy for their actions and to renegotiate their mandate. Managers are constantly 'working the boundaries' between managerial action, professional expertise, political agendas, financial accountabilities, and creating relatively safe spaces within which to act.

Managers wishing to do things in new ways cannot simply go ahead. They need to win consent, persuade, explain, share responsibility. If public managers are to become 'explorers after public value', their job is no longer, if it ever was, to follow procedure. It involves exploration, experimentation and challenge. Such managers don't simply take the world as they find it, they shape the space within which they work. They are operating at the interface of professional, political and managerial knowledge systems – hearing the different voices of staff, service users, local politicians and central government. They see the dilemmas created when these different perspectives collide, and their job is to 'manage into' these dilemmas.

This does not only apply to very senior managers. Staff on local estates or in local projects are negotiating on a daily basis between community groups, listening to and balancing different views. They play an important role in orchestrating the spaces within which communities engage with each other.

Let us take a simple example. The housing manager on an East London estate turns up to discover that the chair of the tenants' association has locked the Bengali community worker out of the community centre. What does she do? Even a simple everyday occurrence such as this requires a capacity to create space for effective 'governance' in the context of racism, misunderstanding and community tension. Individual members of staff have to reflect on their practice, make judgments and negotiate solutions with local people. If they are to do this, they have to bring their whole selves, as complex moral beings, into the process of local governance. They need the resources, courage and support to examine their choices, question their assumptions, listen. Everyone who works within local governance should be willing to say why they think something is valuable, and subject that view to debate. 'Their most important ethical response is to undertake the search for public value conscientiously' (Moore, 1996, p. 299).

Professionals

The role of professionals changes alongside the roles of public managers. However, this does not challenge the importance of professional specialism or expertise. Indeed, in a world in which the total amount of knowledge grows exponentially, the acquisition of specialised knowledge is vital. But professional knowledge is less and less sufficient, on its own, to determine action; solutions seldom fall simply within the domain of a single profession.

Again, this is not new. Donald Schon, in his famous book *The Reflexive Practioner* in the 1970s, painted a vivid picture of the problems of conventional professional training in which university graduates were taught a body of theoretical knowledge which was then 'drawn down' over a lifetime to diagnose and intervene in specific situations (Schon, 1983). Professional knowledge is a guarantee of competence to practice, and as such is highly valuable, but since professional bodies also act as gateways to economic status and career advancement, professional knowledge is often carefully protected. In order to create 'a profession' it is necessary to limit access to knowledge, to guard the boundaries. The education of professionals includes not only a body of theory, but also an epistemology, theories about what *counts* as knowledge. For example, a doctor may see herself or himself as scientist, with scientific assumptions about experimentation and proof, while a social psychologist may have theories about the importance of emotional reactions. Planners and architects may carry 'professional' assumptions about aesthetics, which are not shared by the uninitiated. Schon argued that without a 'reflexive' professional response, able to listen to and learn from service users, good solutions would not be found. Service users have knowledge and expertise that is different from, but equivalent to, the knowledge of a professional – expertise about themselves and their families. Twenty years later, the voice of the service user is increasingly heard, but reflexive practitioners are not yet commonplace within every profession.

The Policy Action Team on Social Exclusion responsible for 'learning lessons' identified the current training of professionals as an important barrier to 'joined-up working'. The training of planners, housing managers, social workers, youth workers, health workers and the police is carried out mainly in isolation from other professions, despite the reality that on the ground collaboration is essential. 'The literature ... suggests that there should be far more cross-professional training opportunities to help practitioners work together more productively' (Cabinet Office, 2000, p. 49), and that

> Managers need training to manage complex cross-cutting operations. They need to understand neighbourhood renewal strategies and the role of their staff in implementing them. They need to know how to support their staff adequately. They need to be flexible enough to allow entrepreneurial team working to thrive. (*ibid.*, p. 50)

At the same time, the report warns against 'the dangers in the drive to "professionalise" all new skills and aptitudes' (p. 52). It recognises the historic glass ceiling which has meant that few women, members of black and ethnic minority communities or disabled people have progressed up the promotion ladder, and that many people with the skills and potential to lead communities do not have the educational qualifications to join professions, and recommends a more flexible approach to recruitment and promotion.

One fruitful approach is the development of multidisciplinary teams, which in some areas (such as hospital discharge) have become standard. At their best they do not dissolve professional expertise into a social science mush, but draw on the precision and illumination of each theoretical framework to create a creative dialogue which offers challenge, creativity and good thinking. The Northamptonshire Diversion Unit, for example, created a team that brought together police officers, social workers, probation officer and court staff to run a successful restorative justice programme. Each young offender worked with a caseworker who could come from any of the individual services – but each case was taken back into a dialogue between the whole team, and the ensuing dialogue used to find a best-fit solution which is then discussed with the individual offender (restorative action is always voluntary). The team was always made up of secondees – who stayed within their professions, and returned to them after a period of time working for the unit – both to sustain the creative tension between the professional groups and to optimise the networking between the agencies. The scheme achieved demonstrable improvement in outcomes compared to the traditional service.

The limits to training

An expansion of training in itself is to be welcomed, since it at the very least offers some space in which managers and professionals can think. It may, of itself, offer a sense of reward, since opportunities to learn are valued by many people. But the introduction of widespread new training courses and development programmes will not, on its own, be enough since learning and change are active processes. People learn when they choose to learn. In the public sector we have intensified training, but we have not yet paid enough attention to creating *reasons to learn*, and *reasons to apply learning*. Simply providing more and more training will not work unless we take account of how and why people learn.

People do not necessarily learn what they are taught. What happens inside a training programme or course involves the same complex set of interests and motivations as what happens on a daily basis in the workplace. People apply their own experience, history, prejudices, assumptions and beliefs inside any teaching situation, and read any new knowledge or skills through that experience. Thus, for example, a common response for many managers who have been sent on a course is not to turn up. If they did not see the value of the skill or knowledge in the first place, they will not put value on time spent to acquire it. Even when managers or staff are constrained to attend a programme, they do not necessarily engage. They may be too preoccupied, too tired, or too angry to make space for any new ideas. They may have experienced bad training in the past, and come with a closed mind. The training may be boring, or seem irrelevant. Even when they engage with and enjoy the learning, managers may still fail to use the new skills or adapt their behaviours because they have no valid reasons (in terms of their own beliefs) to do so.

In one urban authority the top management team had identified a set of management competencies which they believed all managers in the organisation should demonstrate, and were planning a development programme to ensure that all managers had training to develop the required capabilities – project management, finance management, leadership, innovation, coaching and so forth. In focus group discussions with the middle managers it became clear that many people had these capabilities, and had used them to a considerable effect in previous jobs. So what was the problem, we asked. 'There's no point trying to use your initiative here', they all said, 'you just get punished if anything goes wrong. It's not safe. Better to keep your head down and do what you're told. That way it's your managers' fault if things go wrong.'

Theories of learning

Many of the managers and staff within local authorities and other public sector agencies learn how to do their jobs through a process of university study followed by professional training. For workers such as teachers, doctors, social workers, architects and planners this formal education process forms a theoretical underpinning to the ways they do their jobs, and creates a body of knowledge that can be applied to each individual work situation as well as a body of people who share the same theory and learning experiences. These theoretical perspectives are acquired relatively early in life, and offer a powerful perspective from which to read situations. Technical qualifications are used to guarantee competence, but they also limit access to the profession to a narrow group who have acquired them. Universities have become more accessible and open over the past few decades, but many professions are still very limited in the range of backgrounds from which their members are drawn. Formal learning often defines the relationship professionals expect to have with their clients or their service users – for example the doctor–patient relationship is framed both by the independence of the medical practitioner and the Hippocratic oath, and is different from the relationship between social worker and client, or between leisure centre manager and customer.

Formal learning depends on the individual understanding of concepts and ideas, but formal processes are not the only ways we learn. Behaviourists have focused on associative or instrumental learning, and Pavlov famously suggested we developed conditioned responses to environmental stimuli. Behavioural theories of learning were demolished by Noam Chomsky, who argued that for adult humans there is never a simply stimulus–response process, since the active intelligence of the individual is always engaged in deciding whether and how to respond. By drawing on a combination of behavioural and cognitive theories, the concept of social learning has emerged which recognises the power of learning through the observation of others, a process known as modelling. People design their own behaviour by watching others; we do not follow the behaviour of others slavishly, but select those aspects of the behaviour we observe which we can usefully incorporate into our own repertoire of appropriately scripted behaviours. 'By modelling our behaviour in this fashion we avoid both indulging in wasteful and possibly embarrassing attempts to fit ourselves to our surroundings by trial and error while managing to exert some control and influence over our own activity' (Thompson and McHugh, 1995, p. 238). This modelling process helps us to understand the appropriate behaviour demanded of us in our organisational roles (see Biddle, 1979). Indeed, modelling is widely organised to help people to learn in organisational situations by providing 'role-models', mentors, buddies.

Alongside formal learning, which teaches us what to do, we are also engaged in social learning, which teaches us how to be. Social learning is often reinforced through a shared experience of formal learning, since people working together with a particular expertise will already have shared theoretical assumptions about the world and about their status within it, but these assumptions are reinforced on a daily basis by watching and working with others with a similar background and history. It is through social learning that we absorb both assumptions about our role, expected behaviour and status, but also, if we stay long enough, about the culture within an organisation. We absorb perceptions about what is wise, what works, what is possible and what are the limits to action. Managers and staff will often say privately, 'I used my initiative in my last job but when I came here I realised it would be dangerous'. Such comments are rarely officially said, and if they are they are probably denied. But they have been absorbed.

Social learning tells us how hard to work, whether or not to take long lunch hours, how to treat people in authority, how to treat consumers, how to deal with colleagues, who to listen to, who deserves respect and who can safely be ignored. Social learning reinforces our beliefs about our identity, our class, race and gender. It begins at school and influences how we see ourselves, where we fit, our ambitions, confidence and sense of belonging. It does not necessarily turn us into a carbon copy of 'organisational man or woman', since we bring to these processes of socialisation our own belief systems and values. We may learn to keep our head down while storing away knowledge to use in a more open or creative future, or we may learn how to safely challenge the rules.

Learning and unlearning

Recognition of the limitations of formal learning has led to a new focus on 'experiential learning'. Increasingly used as part of the learning process in both public and private organisations, experiential learning recognises the need to make a transition from theory to practice, and offers opportunities to test out new ideas in practice. Much of the recent work on experiential learning is drawn from the work of Kolb (1976) who suggests that learning has four interconnected stages in a learning cycle: action – concrete experiences; reflection – reflective observation of experience; theory – forming explanatory concepts; and experimentation – planning new approaches leading back to action (see Figure 8.1). By bringing the real-life context of individual participants into training courses, it is possible to complete the learning cycle, reflecting on real experiences, forming explanatory hypotheses, planning on the basis of this and then returning to work to test out actions – and then reflecting again. The use of case studies, live cases, role-playing and working on real problems enables participants in training courses to practice the application of new ideas, and to explore and resolve problems.

Figure 8.1 *Kolb's learning cycle*

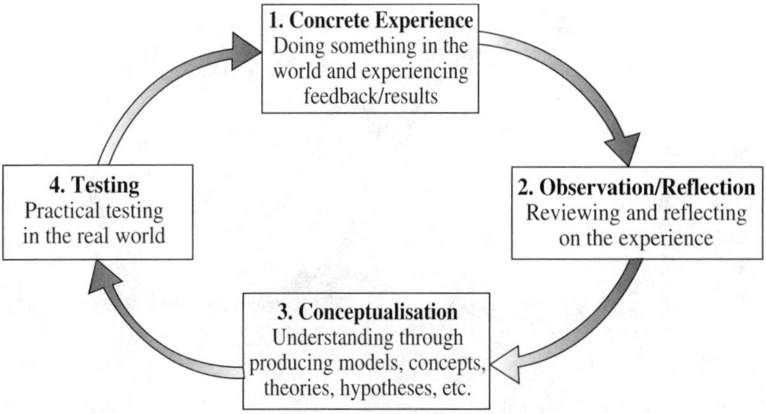

1. **Concrete Experience** Doing something in the world and experiencing feedback/results

2. **Observation/Reflection** Reviewing and reflecting on the experience

3. **Conceptualisation** Understanding through producing models, concepts, theories, hypotheses, etc.

4. **Testing** Practical testing in the real world

Source: Based on Kolb (1976).

However, if these experiences are boxed into learning events, the danger is that they are not translated into everyday practice. Back in the workplace things look different, the boss may not be sympathetic, day-to-day problems may push people back into old ways, colleagues may be discouraging. A crucial next step is therefore to ensure that learning events are connected into day-to-day work, through designing new projects to apply the skills that someone has just learnt, or by undertaking to try out new ways of doing things, or allowing a newly-trained colleague to 'act up' or to take on new responsibilities. Action-learning sets or commissioned projects enable managers to practice new skills at work, and draw on the support of colleagues to think about new problems. Experiential and action learning marks a real step forward from much conventional training (it does, of course, form a part of formal training for doctors, teachers and other professionals who spend their last years of training 'on the job'). But managers and staff within public agencies have few opportunities to continue to learn. For example, in one district council a formal training programme ran into the ground as managers found it hard to apply their learning within a tense atmosphere of cuts and reorganisation. By abandoning the formal modules and translating learning processes into the daily work of the managers, it was possible to develop the capabilities of managers individually and collectively to grapple with their real-life problems. Managers and staff need time to think, and spaces within which

Figure 8.2   *Breaking out of old paradigms*

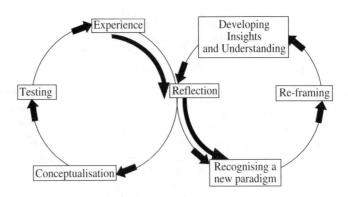

Source: Douglas, R., unpublished paper.

to try out new ideas, to experiment, to test themselves. The absence of thinking time drives out innovation.

It is hard to experiment within existing mind-sets, and to test beliefs among like-minded people. Change requires the stimulus of difference, the experience of 'otherness' to jolt us into seeing the problems in our own frame of reference. A crucial element in learning is curiosity about how other people do things. Holidays often offer the only chance most public sector workers have to learn outside the organisation, and we underestimate the results. Learning by working alongside others, by visits, job-swaps, secondments, by locating an office somewhere else or by working alongside others, all helps. Robin Douglas has developed a diagram of the learning process that recognises the need to break the cycle of old assumptions and old evidence, and to recognise the need to draw on outside knowledge to make a breakthrough (see Figure 8.2). For Douglas, the learning process involves both the Kolb cycle of experience – reflection, theorisation, planning – but the second round of learning does not simply repeat the loop. Outside experience enables a revised set of reflections, a new theory, a different experiment. (Douglas, 2000).

Since people have reasons for doing what they do, there must be a space for exploring and testing out those reasons, a process of dialogue. Socrates did not invent dialogue, but it was he who introduced the idea that individuals could not easily test their own assumptions:

> His brilliant idea was that if two unsure individuals were put together, they could achieve what they could not do separately: they could

discover the truth, their own truths for themselves. [They could learn] by questioning each other and examining their prejudices, dividing each of these into many parts, finding the flaws, never attacking or insulting, but always seeking what they could agree between them. (Zeldin, 1998, p. 33)

It is remarkable how few the spaces are within conventional public agencies for shared exploration. But for public managers, the beliefs that they carry and the assumptions they make about the world are an important part of their role. Since public services impact on the wider community, it is important that the assumptions that underpin those impacts are tested. As 'explorers after public value' public managers draw constantly on their own values, integrity, sense of purpose, understanding of the world and their belief systems. These are worthy of respect, but can be subject to challenge.

If local governance is to work, then the acquisition of new knowledge, new skills and new capabilities needs to be accompanied by 'unlearning' – a process of challenging and rethinking the theories that underpin personal and organisational interventions, testing out assumptions about conventional ways of doing things, about constraints and the likely actions and perspectives of others. Some of the most exciting recent developments have been ones that offer space for mutual exploration and challenge. In the London Borough of Newham, for example, the ambitious three-year whole authority pilot for Best Value, was accompanied by some equally ambitious learning. Each Best Value team was commissioned to review a service, or a theme or group of services, to client groups. Regularly, they would meet in groups of four teams and each team would present their work to their peers. The other teams would act as discussants – to challenge what they had done, explore the ideas, challenge assumptions.

Throughout the process, outsiders of different sorts came to work with each team, to check out their progress, to make sure the different groups were working congruently, to offer other ways of seeing the problems they were grappling with and to give support. At the end of each year, the project leaders of teams that had finished work met those that were about to begin, to exchange learning about the process, to debrief about what went well and badly, to help design a new and better process next time. A conference of all the participants in the new teams heard from a panel of 'old stagers' – to question them about their mistakes and successes – and were able to make their plans in the context of learning done by their colleagues.

Finally, however, it would be foolhardy to assume that beliefs change simply through a rational process of dialogue. There is an emotional world of work, the social and personal spaces within which work takes place.

We need both to understand the impact that powerful systems of reward and punishment have on individuals from the outside, and the ways people cope with and respond to the constraints, stresses and contradictions on the inside. This means recognising the importance of the emotional stratagems that lock people into patterns of behaviour, and into safe routines. We know from the developing theories of psychology that these are not lightly abandoned.

All of these shape the way individuals form relationships with others. Some professional groups learn about relationships in their professional training – but this is seldom exchanged with other groups. For relationship organisations little time is spent on learning about how to do relationships. In the last chapter, we examined the emotional component of some of the work carried out within public agencies. People often choose public service jobs because of a desire to help, and yet if they identify emotionally with everyone they see they cannot cope. The risks of failure are very great, and the capacity of the public to blame failure is unlimited. This leads to the development of coping strategies, routinisation of decisions, or procedures to protect against too great a responsibility such as involving large numbers of people in each decision to spread the load. Often these are at odds with the organisation's primary task and may negatively affect patients or clients.

A variety of emotional pressures and anxieties give rise to taken-for-granted routines. Organisational change – even new learning – is sometimes experienced as highly threatening. Inside organisations, people have found ways to deal with anxiety, and change makes them anxious that coping strategies will be disrupted and fears and anxieties that form part of the job will become overwhelming.

The day-to-day work involved in local public services is often in areas of life where emotions run high – crime, education, riots, children's safety, child abuse, illness, accidents, pollution, drugs, family relationships, death. And yet in few public service organisations is it easy to talk about and handle feelings appropriately at work. Often the learning absorbed within conventional training courses doesn't make sense – new values don't relate to the lived experience of managers and staff, and many of the problems and difficulties remain unspoken and therefore unsolved. Since in most organisations 'how I feel' is not appropriate data – the feelings that get in the way of good performance are never explored. In order to achieve change, staff need space to explore the tensions involved in the work, and to evolve conscious strategies for coping with anxiety at the same time as improving the service to users. 'By putting into words what had previously been too dreadful to talk about and therefore impossible to think about' (Obholzer and Zagier Roberts, 1994, p. 119) it is possible to begin to plan lasting change.

Part of feeling comfortable in a complex and changing world is the development of a personal map of values, beliefs and choices within changing roles and functions, a self-conscious process of managing into, and shaping the space to make decisions, and self-awareness about individual identity and capacity in these changing roles. Through exploration of feelings as well as theories, it is possible to manage dissonance – to make sense of the contradictory things that are being asked of public managers in a society that is unclear about their role. Managers and staff within local governance need to be self-aware about the skills, knowledge, attitudes, behaviours, values and belief systems they bring to work, and to bring all these into play as they make judgments alongside the public. This is a different sort of 'knowledge' to either conventional professional or conventional managerial knowledge – and it is acquired in different ways. As local agencies attempt to equip their managers and staff for the future, there is a place for formal training, but alongside this must go experiential and emotional learning, space to reflect on and to test out beliefs and values, and an active curiosity about perspectives from the outside.

None of this is difficult to achieve. Many experiments in learning across the public sector show the elements of effective learning:

- Learning is built into everyday tasks. Day-to-day work includes opportunities for reflection, debriefing, practicing things, giving and receiving feedback.
- Managers and professionals routinely seek and use evidence to test ideas, to learn from new practice and to evaluate progress. Assumptions do not go untested.
- Good 'maps' of the environment are developed and constantly updated. All staff are involved in analysing and exploring the reasons for change, and the ways the organisation can respond to changing circumstances.
- There are constant challenges to fixed assumptions – managers have access to mentors and coaches, are able to visit other agencies and see how things are done differently, and work across boundaries.
- There are opportunities to practice new ideas and new skills in comparative safety.
- There is scope to invent and innovate without immediate pressure to turn emergent ideas into action. Research and development is carried out routinely.

- Individuals have help to develop self-awareness, feedback about how they act within situations and the impact they make on others.
- Public managers and staff have workspaces within which they can digest and examine new situations, to explore their feelings and to find a way of dealing with problems they encounter. A careful balance is struck between organisational and individual needs.

Learning organisations

While there is a considerable literature that describes how individuals learn, much of it in the field of psychology, there is less agreement and certainty about how organisations learn. Much of the theory of organisational learning is translated directly from theories of individual learning, but an organisation is not an individual. And while it is possible to use phrases such as 'the organisational brain' or 'the organisational memory' as metaphors, we know that an organisation is in reality a group of people working together, and not a single organism. This has important consequences for the possibilities of organisational learning.

One response has been to argue that organisations cannot be said, in any meaningful way, to 'learn', and that therefore what is important is the individual learning of staff within the organisation. If individuals are given every opportunity to improve their own learning, then the organisation will benefit. Some private sector organisations have taken this up by encouraging their staff to learn anything that interests them – and by providing opportunities for lifelong learning in the expectation that this will help them to learn the things the organisation needs them to learn. Professions carry the implicit assumption that organisational performance is based not on systems or structures, but on the knowledge held by professional staff.

But people do not simply learn in isolation from each other. Much of the literature that deals with the learning organisation (Argyris and Schon, 1978; Lewis, 1984; Senge, 1992) suggests that certain sorts of organisations are better at enabling learning to take place. The learning organisation is characterised by an emphasis on self-management, matrix-type structures, dedicated training and learning support and flexibility in working practices and environmental response (Sims *et al.*, 1993, p. 198). These mechanisms make it easier for people to exchange learning and to apply learning in practice. The concept of the 'learning organisation' has achieved wide currency, although some commentators suggest that in reality it is used in organisations that are not structured like this at all, and is used loosely to describe almost any human resource management (HRM) initiative (Thompson and McHugh, 1995, p. 316).

Argyris and Schon (1996) argue that if members can act collectively or for an organisation, then they can learn for it. Knowledge becomes organisational knowledge if the organisation is able to act as a 'holding environment for knowledge'. One possibility, therefore, is that an organisation encourages the acquisition of knowledge, rewards it and creates opportunities for it, so that more and more people within the organisation are able, individually, to learn things that will contribute to organisational success. A second possibility is that the structure and systems of an organisation can contribute actively to organisational learning, by creating methods for diffusing or storing knowledge. If knowledge is simply stored in the heads of individuals, this may make it difficult for learning to be transferred. One team may work brilliantly alongside another team that is failing, simply because learning is not transferred. If an individual or team discover, through experiential learning, that something works well, and are rewarded for changing, the change will become embedded into practice. But if there are no mechanisms for others to learn about it, it will not be transferred.

An important dimension of a learning organisation may therefore be the relationship between the individual and the collective. If individuals feel that their knowledge is their own intellectual capital which can be used to win advancement over others, or if the organisation believes that the only things worth knowing are those that are taught in formal ways, they are unlikely to share knowledge. Separate professional departments and silos reinforce the sense of private or specialist knowledge. By creating opportunities for knowledge to be made collectively available, it can be diffused and spread throughout the organisation.

The vast literature on knowledge management shows how urgently managers feel the need to improve the transmission of knowledge. Traditional methods of knowledge storing such as data warehouses, procedures, policies and statistics tend to only store 'formal knowledge' dealing with the theory of how things are supposed to be, rather than the tacit or social knowledge about how things are. Inside organisations there are informal mechanisms for transmitting knowledge, through gossip, conversation, myth, stories, jokes and so on. There are haphazard ways of storing valuable social and experiential knowledge – through 'old hands' who hold a memory of organisational history, or managers who are considered a safe pair of hands because they have tried similar things before. But organisations are seldom self-conscious about the ways that they store and transmit the soft or tacit knowledge that individuals have accumulated through practice, nor about examining the robustness of the assumptions that are gathered along the way.

A third way in which an organisation can be said to support learning is by creating an environment within which there are reasons for applying knowledge. People may learn new things, but they are unlikely to apply that knowledge unless there are rewards for doing so, or at least no disincentives.

We have already suggested that managers may acquire new skills but fail to use them in their organisational context because they believe that it will be fruitless, inappropriate or risky. If organisations remain stuck, or if messages are mixed, it may seem safer to carry on in old ways than to risk practicing untested skills. If, despite the rhetoric of 'empowerment', a series of day-to-day disasters drives top managers back to command and control, middle managers and staff will learn to simply do what they are told. If managers are pulled off training courses about corporate working to sort out operational issues within their departments, they will learn that the organisation really values operational performance more. Public managers are asked to change deeply engrained habits of action in a context of considerable uncertainty, and it takes considerable courage to do so in a culture where courage is seldom rewarded. In many public organisations, the complexity of the task, the number of new initiatives, the scale of the change agenda creates a 'no time to learn, got to get on' mentality. Time is so tight, the round of activities is so great, that there is no possibility of allowing time to reflect or think. Indeed, the culture instinctively sees reflection as slow, and as wasting time.

The distinction that Argyris and Schon have made between single and double-loop learning remains a useful one. They argue that within organisational contexts there is always a 'theory-in-use' – a theory about what will work in certain circumstances. They suggest that this theory-in-use can only be constructed from organisational observation, since in reality the implicit theory could be contrary to the espoused theory. The theory-in-use may be tacit or indiscussable – it may, for example, be a theory that 'nothing ever works around here so the important thing is to look busy but not to try to achieve anything'. Behaviour that can seem to an outsider as bizarre – seeming nonchalance about serious service failures, for example – may make sense within the theory-in-use inside the organisation. For those who have been inside organisations for some time, the strangeness of some of the lived assumptions may have faded, and organisational behaviours will seem normal. Argyris and Schon (1996, p. 20) warn that people can learn collectively to maintain patterns of thought and action that inhibit learning. Single-loop learning is therefore learning that changes strategies of action in ways that leave the theory-in-use unchanged. Double-loop learning, by contrast, is learning that challenges and changes the values of the theory-in-use – for example, assumptions about what is possible, or how change can be made to happen.

While the characteristics of a learning organisation set out by theorists are seldom all in place, it is possible to hypothesise some minimum requirements. A learning public organisation is one that creates new spaces for learning, and some of the examples of learning exchange and storage are:

- Deliberately giving managers and staff time to think and reflect.
- Development time spent not acquiring new skills but exploring the wider environment.
- Valuing of diversity of perspective, experience and background. Including people in teams because of their difference.
- Designing challenge and discussion processes into new initiatives and everyday work.
- Including practice exchange into all day-to-day work, scheduling visits, job swaps, secondments as well as workshops and conferences.
- Developing 'creativity spaces' either using the internet or intranets, or setting up improvisation or innovation workshops.
- Accessing ideas from outside – turning data from users into easily accessible information; using user-consultants.
- Creating 'learning laboratories'.
- Storing knowledge in easily accessible ways.
- Linking the organisation to other organisations' data systems.
- Ensuring easy access to the internet for work purposes – creating internal networks, intranets, chatlines, on-line discussions and problem–solving groups.
- Building-in debriefing and reflection time to all meetings and projects.
- Debriefing all projects and initiatives carefully; identifying learning points, sharing them and storing them to learn from next time.
- Developing effective evaluation systems.

A bubbling-up of learning sets built around experimental projects, cross-departmental project groups, 'challenge' groups, external visitors, influences, user-feedback, research and development opportunities, job-swaps and learning laboratories looks fruitful. The imposition of a top-down learning programme is more doubtful. Evaluation is often neglected in busy public organisations. There is too much going on to stop and look at the past, too many new initiatives to explore the successes of old ones.

But without effective processes of evaluation, even the first learning loop is never completed. Robust evaluation processes requires a strong evidence base, but it cannot be left to external inspection and audit; managers and staff need to constantly reflect on the effectiveness of what they are doing. Evaluation requires clarity about what was supposed to happen, and time spent as part of the work process in analysis and diagnosis – whether it happens or not. It is important to explore the reasons for success as well as the reasons for failure, to assess not simply whether progress has been made, but whether enough progress has been made. Good evaluation moves away from a blame culture of 'who was at fault?', towards the explorers' question – 'what didn't we know?' Proper evaluation helps the organisation to understand itself, to understand the patterns of behaviour and of obstacles it encounters, to explore the impact of the wider environment, to test assumptions and to rethink strategy. We explored in Chapter 5 the waste caused by a failure to evaluate, and in the absence of real evaluation the organisation cannot learn anything.

Network learning

While there is an industry of consultants trying to teach tools and techniques that contribute to organisational learning, we have argued here that networks of governance take place not inside individual organisations, but between organisations and between public agencies and citizens. The question is therefore not simply, can organisations learn? But can networks learn? Can networks become 'holding environments for knowledge'?

In the private sector the concept of a network is a dynamic one, and many writers enthuse about the potential of interorganisational networks to provide the exposure to external knowledge essential to the innovation process (see Sayer and Walter, 1992). But in the public sector, partnerships and networks have been slow to capitalise on the potential for shared learning. This may be because a sense of shared purpose and trust is still evolving, or it may be because the 'terms of engagement' have not yet been established. It may be that shared learning is hampered by the differences in culture, attitudes and language between agencies and professions. We may find very different theories-in-use in different parts of the public sector – and since they are often unstated and invisible, they are unlikely to be explored. It may also be that networks and partnerships in the public sector have been very task-focused and very driven to achieve narrow objectives – a written strategy document, a bid for funding, a project plan.

We said in Chapter 5 that a network has none of the command-and-control mechanisms that enable organisations to function without the voluntary commitment of individual members to everything that happens. For a network to learn, several conditions have to be in place. The agencies and individuals have to want to learn across boundaries, have to be able to build a network capable of storing and exchanging learning, and have to be able to create reasons to apply learning outside an organisational context.

If instead of developing task-based partnership, we developed open-ended networks and treated them as laboratories, or sites of exploration, we would structure them entirely differently. In the first place, we would encourage not the narrowing of focus to a single strategy document, but the widening of experimentation. We would create a community of explorers interested in hearing about experiments and about work in progress, not through formal report-backs, but through active dialogue – the partnership would be a place where learning could be tested, digested and exchanged. It would be possible to value the knowledge of different participants so that instead of power struggles, processes would be developed to hear from and learn from the different participants. All participants could draw from the knowledge within each of the participating groups without any group imposing their own assumptions about what was important. The range of expertise would be put to constructive use. Instead of a rush to solutions, time would be spent understanding and analysing problems, trying to fit interventions together and to understand how and why things happen. Networks and partnerships could then build up a shared body of knowledge through analysis and discussion, instead of replaying old territorial arguments.

Networks are not always effective at learning. A recent Institute of Personal Directors (IPD) study showed that individuals could get overloaded by emails and communication (IPD, 1999). Public services still focus on policy development but avoid reflecting on implementation; the next step is to move to processes where networks can begin to reflect on their own effectiveness, and are able to learn about how the network functions. It is possible to do this not by stopping the machine of interagency working, but by watching it in motion. Through interactive learning it is possible for a wide range of agencies to experience in comparative safety the ways they interact, interpret each other's actions, and track the patterns of organisational behaviour that result.

In Chapter 5 we explored whole-systems thinking. My colleague Laurie McMahon has developed over many years the technique of open simulation to enable groups of organisations within a locality or a sector to come together to explore the working of a whole system in action. A whole systems event, which could last from one to three days, creates the conditions and features of a potential future in which participants can learn about how they and other participants might respond. Since there are no formal rules for the simulation, participants are able to explore how and when rules are made, how agendas are set, where power drifts and what are the real priorities of different players in different situations. By watching the actions of others and debriefing collectively about strategy and intent, people within agencies are able to harness shared purpose and learning to understand each other's constraints.

Open simulations are able to model the diversity and apparent randomness of major change because it is possible to generate and renegotiate the rules and conventions that govern intra- and interorganisational relationships (McMahon, 1994). Simulations and open negotiations increasingly form part of the way that real organisational work is carried out at local level; 'Large scale behavioural simulations can help whole systems to handle inter-organisational change' (McMahon and Arnell, 1998). Open negotiations take the idea of an interactive workshop a stage further and enable groups of stakeholders to work together for one or two days to carry out all the negotiations necessary to reach a decision. This requires considerable advance preparation to ensure that people are ready to negotiate, and it is important that all key players are present and have authority to act. However, they offer an exciting acceleration of what is often a time-consuming process of checking back and deliberating before action is taken. They are both learning events and 'real work' simultaneously. The boundaries are beginning to blur.

9   Learning and Unlearning in Civil Society

It will not be enough simply to develop learning – and unlearning – inside public organisations. If local governance is what happens when managers, politicians and citizens meet, then learning is equally vital within politics and within civil society. And, of course, the same obstacles to change exist here too. Politicians and citizens will not behave differently unless they see compelling reasons to do so, and learn how. They, also, have to change themselves. Given the analysis in the previous chapter about how people learn, it must follow that politicians, lay governors and citizens also have to engage in a process of unlearning, as well as learning. If it is challenging to see how this might happen inside organisations, it is even more challenging to conceive of ways it can happen in broader society.

In this chapter I want to explore possible ways to generate learning – and unlearning – in three different contexts: within politics, within lay governance structures (quangos, voluntary bodies, neighbourhood and regions) and within local communities. Finally, I want to consider whether or not a 'new politics' might be emerging.

Political learning

There has been a debate about the capacity of local councillors to carry out governance ever since the introduction of local democracy. The debate about 'councillor calibre' has often encoded a concern about working-class men and women gaining access to public office. The local government reforms of the 1960s and 1970s were justified, in part, by an argument that larger authorities would be more likely to attract business executives and better-educated councillors.

The new debate about councillor calibre is about their capacity to adapt to changing roles. The argument is made that while the old committee-style council required only limited skills and knowledge, few existing councillors can cope with the requirements of modern governance. But there is a fundamental dilemma at the heart of a debate about councillor competence. On the one hand, the modern council is a complex business with multi-million pound budgets managed by senior and highly-paid executives. The temptation has been to extend management training to councillors, a fast-track course to enable them to manage the local authority. On the other hand, the basis of local democracy has always been that local councillors are ordinary members of the public, working on a semi-voluntary basis, with expenses paid, but not full remuneration.

Local politicians represent their communities after a hard day's work, bring experience as housewives, or have a lifetime of work behind them. Councillors bring a more diverse set of skills and experiences than many middle managers, and considerable personal talent. Creating full-time paid politicians will not necessarily solve the problems of capacity; politicians should not simply replace managers. The skills politicians need are different from those needed by managers, and the skills they have often go unrecognised. Managers often lack the skills that politicians, even relatively junior ones, learn early. It can be an education just watching a skilled councillor 'work the room' in a tenants' meeting or a school fete, shaking hands, remembering names, making a serious political point, defusing tension, making a fuss of the oldest committee member, and thanking the catering staff. It is not just smarm, or fakery. There are skills in connecting to people, making them feel involved and important, honouring contributions, recognising lived experiences. These are seldom described or taught, but they are nonetheless real.

The skills of politics are learnt on the job. Unlike other powerful social leadership roles, such as that of a priest, there is no intensive period of reflection, training and testing, no challenge to individual motivation and purpose. In the absence of a formal learning process, informal learning is all-important.

But what, exactly, do politicians learn by watching, by copying, by modelling the behaviours of others? Ordinary people are often horrified by the soap-opera glimpses they get of day-to-day politics – the briefing and counter-briefing, the angry exchanges, the absence of generosity, the ever-present fear of betrayal, the bitterness and backstabbing. It is as if ordinary rules of behaviour are suspended and the self-discipline required in other walks of life is abandoned. Of course real-life politics is seldom like the tabloid caricature, but there is some truth in it; enough to deter many with passionate beliefs from a career in politics. The social learning about politics differs from place to place. In many rural councils, politics is convivial even across parties; while in some cities it is a tense and frightening business, even within a single party. Hardened politicians often argue that this is a useful testing process and 'if you can't stand the heat, get out of the kitchen'. But we need to consider what we are asking of our representatives, and what sorts of human beings we want to represent us. If politics is a domineering and selfish business, it will attract domineering and selfish people.

Councillors are often asked to carry almost intolerable burdens, to make decisions about life and death issues, to cut badly needed services in order to meet budget deficits, to face community anger when they close failing schools, to make the difficult choices everyone else has ducked. They have to face public anger, but they also lie awake for long lonely nights trying to square their principles with harsh realities. It is not a process that encourages people to open up, or to let down their defences. Of course fewer and fewer people choose to carry these burdens. Why should they? What support do they get? The skills of survival are those of talking rather than listening, of defending rather than exploring, of 'covering your back' rather than building consensus.

And yet, there are many good-hearted and serious people in all political parties, with a strong sense of duty and a passion for their neighbourhoods. A recent development programme for councillors across parties asked them to identify their personal values; the room came alive. On the flip charts around the room they wrote, 'belief in community, cooperative, fairness, trying to do one's best for society, socialism, loyalty, belief in human potential, tolerance, ending poverty, community empowerment, democracy, equity, honesty, integrity, a desire to serve ... '. Many councillors genuinely enjoy their daily activities and their busy schedule of meetings, but many others live their day-to-day lives in a simmering state of frustration.

The skills that would enable politicians to play the most positive roles within local governance are not rewarded by our current political system. A politician who is seen to listen to or agree with outsiders can be seen as weak, allowing the opposition to gain credit. Councillors have often gained recognition and promotion through assertive and aggressive behaviours – fighting their way to the front, either within a political party or within a tenants' association, in a voluntary organisation or as a school governor. Representatives are often chosen as 'someone who will make a fuss for us', someone who cannot be ignored. The struggle to be heard is often important in representing excluded groups, and people who represent minority communities often have to learn to confront and challenge those who don't want to listen.

These behaviours are reinforced by the way politicians are dealt with by the public and the media. Politicians are people from whom explanations are demanded, who are challenged by journalists to justify their actions, who are accused of dithering, buck-passing or wasting time if they try to consult or listen to others. Politics is seen as a 'telling' sort of job – politicians are constantly challenged to 'answer the question' – or to allocate blame. Effective local democracy is probably not simply something within the gift of politicians; we get the politicians we deserve. The activity of civil society, the level of public debate, the extent to which we are informed, the role we create for politicians and the expectations we have of them will also shape the political culture within which local governance takes place. What is missing is a culture in civil society that can both honour the service of representatives and challenge abuse of power. Unless voters can be clear about what they have asked local politicians to do, and can hold them to account, they will not value them.

There has been a recent spate of investment in training for councillors, particularly linked to new roles. This is invaluable, but it is important to recognise that while formal learning is helpful, social learning also has to be tackled. Councillors will also have to *unlearn* political practices that have become out of date. The day-to-day pressures of councillor roles and the relentless rhythm of agendas makes it hard for councillors to step back and reflect. The transition to new roles at least offers a chance to 'stop the clock' and to rethink ways of working. When asked to think about the political process, the ways that meetings are managed and the way their time is spent, most councillors express considerable frustration. They often feel that they are deluged with information or get the wrong information, that they have little time to think, insufficient background knowledge, that meetings are interminable, dull, pointless. But little time is spent on designing effective meetings or good decision-making processes – these are not, after all, 'political' issues. Councillors are beginning to stop and think about how best to use their time, to explore the best ways to do things, to understand their colleagues' frustrations and find ways to make work more enjoyable, and more productive.

They have begun to use away-days and workshops to develop strategy; and similar workshops can be used to develop agreement about how best to work to achieve that strategy. Some local authorities have developed job descriptions for councillors, performance measures and processes of evaluation and feedback. Councillors can work together to reflect on the effectiveness of individual and group behaviours, to develop agreement about codes of conduct not simply dealing with the issues dealt with by scrutiny committees, but identifying helpful ways to behave to each other. One council group developed a code of conduct which included: 'I will always listen carefully, and not assume I know what my colleagues are going to say in advance', and 'I will reflect on whether my speech is necessary and not waste time if it has already been said'. Councillors can discuss the ways they behave to officers, explore the effectiveness of current patterns of behaviour, and explore the expectations they have of officers. Joint councillor/officer workshops can begin to explore relationships in practice – to use role-plays and scenarios to consider the roles and relationships needed in the future. New select committee and scrutiny and review arrangements create scope for councillors to visit other areas, investigate what is happening outside the town hall, invite in experts and community leaders as part of a process of active problem-solving. It is as true for politicians as it is for managers that learning works best when it is directly connected to 'real work'. Processes for reflection, observation and problem-solving could be built into the day-to-day jobs of councillors.

Of course, admitting to 'learning' can create tensions. Feedback is always difficult when there are rivalries and old scores to settle. In an adversarial environment, it is dangerous to admit weakness, and foolhardy to give opponents new weapons. A councillor who exposed to colleagues their personal failure to understand finances could find the revelation in a local newspaper under a headline 'unfit to serve'. Learning needs to be made safe, which may mean activity within party groups, or action-learning sets or project teams. Team-building in a conventional sense may not be appropriate – since roles are unique and political sensitivities have to be acknowledged – but 'group'-building may make sense. Councillors may need individual support, and there is little yet done to offer mentoring or twinning schemes for politicians. Leaders can find themselves almost entirely unsupported except, if they are lucky, by a good chief executive. And they may feel reluctant to go on training courses with the colleagues they are supposed to lead. But there is scope to use one-on-one coaching, mentoring and learning sets in the ways that many chief executives do. Individual councillors can be offered the sorts of development help that managers routinely get, support in working out a personal development plan, access to a range of training and development activity.

There are none of the usual levers to make politicians learn. Many councillors value new experiences and choose council work because of the opportunities afforded to find out about different worlds. But other councillors find learning hard. Councillors also come with their own democratic mandate. They have no necessary reason to adopt new skills, attitudes and behaviours just because they learn them on a course. The very assertiveness and debating skills that lead individuals to become councillors, also equip councillors to challenge any training they receive. There is little to encourage councillors to learn to do things differently, and nothing to force them to do so.

We have suggested that unless there are new ways of rewarding and validating the roles of councillors and other elected and appointed people, recognising their contributions, understanding the dilemmas they face – little will change. Only so much can be done at local level, and much depends on national political parties. Future politicians need to learn skills in listening, facilitating, negotiating and brokering. Unless selection processes begin to recognise different abilities to those of 'talking well' and ways are found to reward the bridge-builders rather than the Machiavellians, there will be little incentive to learn new skills, or for those who have them to enter politics. If new structures such as elected cabinets or mayors are to succeed, political parties will need to pay attention to how councillors develop different ways of working and to see learning and exploration as an essential part of politics. If political organisations become merely vote-catching organisations, based on telephone and television, the links that might create or develop political learning will disintegrate. But perhaps, although this is the subject for another book, the current roles of political parties are themselves dissolving. We have suggested that processes of governance inevitably create politicians in a wider sense, not simply speaking on behalf of a political party but struggling in their communities to balance outcomes, negotiate between different interests, mobilise consent and create spaces in which people can come together to resolve problems. It is to these emerging 'governors' that we now turn.

New roles in governance

A wide range of citizens have been put on the boards of governance organisations, from tenant management organisations to community development trusts, from task forces to regional development agencies. Businesspeople, voluntary-sector activists and community leaders are working, often alongside politicians and public managers, in new organisations and new governance structures. Regional development agencies, skills and enterprise councils and neighbourhood initiatives all have non-executive boards that include lay people. Health authorities have non-executive directors taken from the community; housing associations often have tenants on the board. Citizens are beginning to take decisions about resource use in neighbourhood initiatives, and in strategic partnerships. And yet there is little or no direct education for these new governance roles. Citizen governors have few opportunities to explore what their roles mean, or to develop good governance behaviours. Business people are often chosen for their financial or business acumen, but the problems they face in planning public intervention are entirely different to those experienced in the private sector. In health, there is increasing attention to a selection procedure that chooses people who have the right abilities, but the abilities needed for good governance have never been defined.

We do not yet have a strong civic understanding of what responsibilities these roles carry, and how to perform them; the assumption is simply that if you put together a board of people with different experiences they will somehow be able to govern. In reality, there is no guarantee that they will be successful. There is no shared knowledge about what governance roles involve, or what has to be learnt. The boards of voluntary organisations, community projects and quangos may have budgets that vary from a thousand to several million pounds, but they all struggle with the issues of governance. Board members are often invited to join because of their experience in business or in the community, but the cultures and the organisations they come from are often very different to those in which they are expected to work. As one board member of a new partnership organisation remarked, 'some lunatic put this board together. There are private entrepreneurs, politicians, civil servants and environmentalists. We haven't got anything in common. How will we ever work together?' Nor do they necessarily have any shared idea about what the partnership or organisation is intended to achieve, of the resources at its disposal or of the best ways of working. Board members do not necessarily have a clear idea about what governance means, or whom they serve, or about how the conflicting interests they encounter can be accommodated. There is little space for reflection about outcomes. New boards often face externally-driven pressures to produce glossy strategy documents before they have been able to agree any real strategy.

In a housing association board, a row had developed to boiling point between the city financiers and the tenants. The financiers accused the tenants of selfishness because they argued against plans to build more houses that would be cross-subsidised by their rents. From the financier's perspective, the duty of a business was to expand, and the rents represented a source of revenue that could be used to fund expansion. The tenants, on the other hand, knew that rents were already a high proportion of weekly expenditure, and were worried that if rents rose, tenants in work would leave the estates, leaving the community entirely made up of pensioners, single parents and the unemployed. Ten years ago, tenants would not have been on the board to put their point of view, but even now it was hard for other board members to value their perspective. And yet tenant worries about community sustainability and tenant consent were as important a contribution to future strategy as the expertise contributed by business executives. By hearing both, the board could work to win consent from tenants for a strategy of limited expansion, that met their aspirations for the community and did not simply strengthen the balance sheet of the organisation.

The skills that enable people to 'do' governance are not innate, and yet despite the expansion of governance roles there is no expansion in learning. Governing bodies have to become very self-aware of their own backgrounds and interests; they have to make explicit the difficult choices they have to make and create a sensible evidence base from which to make them. They cannot simply expect to command the legitimacy to make decisions, they have to build legitimacy through their ability to mobilise consent. They come from very different backgrounds and have to unlearn their assumptions about the right way to do things.

In the early stages there is often a furious row between the desire of businessmen and women to be fast, directive and results-focused; the concerns of public managers to win allies, smooth paths to government and fill in the right forms; and the determination of community representatives to listen to local people. Boards can easily become adversarial, with entrenched conflicts, or become cosy clubs in which assumptions are not challenged. There is nothing necessarily to drive a focus on results, or to strengthen strategic thinking. Unelected boards seldom pay sufficient attention to issues of accountability and legitimacy.

It is possible, however, for new governance bodies to be creative, radical and accountable. A board combining businesspeople and civil servants, community leaders and politicians can often do things that are almost impossible back in their home cultures. By drawing on the different ways of seeing of each member of the board, by making use of the networks and communication channels each brings, by learning from each other rather than just arguing – they can begin to innovate. By learning about the differences in the legitimacies they bring, they can build in ways to secure consent. But to do this requires radically new ways of working. Citizen governors will need to learn new skills as they take on new roles. This needs investment. There are sources of support for individual board members which can be borrowed from management development – personal development plans, coaching, mentoring, shadowing schemes and 'role swaps' with access to learning sets or reference groups – but there is also a need for shared exploration and strategic thinking. Governing bodies or boards need to set aside time without long agendas to reflect together on what they are trying to do.

In one charitable organisation the board set out to identify goals for the future. They had been in existence for five years and spent millions of pounds. The goals they came up with were about efficiency, better delivery systems and national reputation; but no outcomes were mentioned. When this was pointed out, the board decided to set aside time to discuss them. While the overall aims of the organisation were easily established, a fascinating discussion exposed real tensions – for example about the balance between fitting in with government objectives or acting independently, between filling gaps other organisations didn't fill or adding critical mass to other initiatives, between playing safe and taking risks. Finally, the issues were thrashed through and an agreement emerged, one which most of the board found exciting and compelling. 'No wonder we have always been reactive', said the chair thoughtfully. 'We never had time for any thinking before'.

The questions: 'whom do we serve'; 'in whose interests are we working'; 'what are we trying to achieve'; 'what is at stake'; 'how do we balance accountabilities'; are as important for citizen governors as they are for politicians. The replacement of political structures by quangos or voluntary groups does not solve these problems, it simply transfers them to another group of 'governors'. Pluralism in governance may be good, but it must be accompanied by a civic culture that understands what is asked of governors, what is expected of them, and offers support and learning in how to make it work. These are civic roles, not purely private ones, and they carry, inevitably, a wider civic responsibility. Until we learn to expect the role of governor to be an ordinary dimension of citizenship, and learn the basics of governance as part of the wider repertoire of citizen behaviours, governance is always open to abuse.

Learning in communities

Learning and unlearning are not simply important for managers and official governors; increasingly citizens need to learn to work alongside each other and powerful agencies, and they need the skills to do so. The knowledge, beliefs and values of citizens and communities are as important as those of the managers and politicians they encounter.

There has been a flurry of recent interest in community capacity building. At local level this has predominantly centred on building the skills of voluntary-sector managers and staff, and creating access for local people to education and training. A number of initiatives have also been set up to support entrepreneurship within communities, and to support community leaders. The Community Development Foundation, the National Council for Voluntary Service, The School for Social Entrepreneurs and the Community Action Network are actively promoting community education,

---

Box 9.1 *Community Links*

Community Links is a network of projects run by local people, including playgroups, supplementary education, advice services, counselling, training and management of a café and shop in Canning Town. Among the courses which are run, the First Steps course assists those involved in establishing small voluntary groups. It is a two-year practical management course which helps groups plan, develop, evaluate and promote quality services. It is accredited by the University of East London. Thirty-five small minority ethnic groups were represented on the 1999 course. New forms of support are being developed for new arrivals to the UK to enable them to make their contribution to the area they are living in.

Box 9.2 *The School for Social Entrepreneurs (SSE)*

The School offers various training modules, practical experience and customised training and aims to encourage entrepreneurial talent among people who work in the public, voluntary and community sectors and in partnership with the private sector. Its emphasis is on personal development.

The SSE believes in a just-in-time approach to learning for social entrepreneurs, with students offered individual learning accounts. Skills training must be relevant to current needs and be applied as soon as possible. Students gain experience from working within entrepreneurial, community-based projects. The school is developing an open-learning course using new technology, and is also developing courses for those living and working in deprived neighbourhoods.

Box 9.3   *The Community Action Network (CAN)*

The Community Action Network was set up in 1998 by a group of successful social entrepreneurs. It is developing an on-line intranet with a target of 2000 social entrepreneurs linked up by the end of the year 2000. The network aims to link individuals and organisations so they can learn from and support each other. Participants see CAN as a marketplace, where members can trade ideas and support; and CAN offers IT training and technical support. Within the Network, CAN is developing cells of ten members so that the relationship between them works effectively. These ten by ten groups link up electronically and receive support and joint training sessions.

---

and a number of innovative local schemes have been established such as Community Links in East London. (Examples taken from Social Exclusion Unit: National Strategy for Neighbourhood Renewal: *Report of Policy Action Team 16, Learning Lessons 2000*).

Local and central government support for community-learning initiatives is growing, but these initiatives are still only operating at the margins. Even if local people are interested in these schemes, they may have family committments or lack confidence, or time. For many people, learning does not come easy. But if we are to develop active, self-aware and self-managing communities, what is needed is not simply the acquisition of formal knowledge, but participation in a process of exploration and discovery about how communities could be. Individual members of the public also have social unlearning to do. As individuals we all carry powerful assumptions about what our roles are, what our responsibilities are, how we 'fit', what is important and what is possible. We may have written off public organisations or professionals years ago; or we may have had bad experiences or bad neighbours, lost trust in our abilities or lost faith in others. Any real process of learning must involve testing assumptions, examining prejudices and rethinking.

For people who consume public services, the powerful social learning absorbed during their lifetime constantly reinforces assumptions about officialdom or other communities. The learning experience of ordinary people is often very different to that of the graduate managers and professionals they encounter. Perhaps most significant, there is often a difference of view about what counts as evidence, or as knowledge.

Let us take one example. A recent set of focus groups with residents in an ethnically diverse inner-city area revealed that participants from the white population believed strongly that housing allocation favoured the Asian population, while Asian participants believed equally strongly that housing allocation favoured the whites. The local authority response was to produce a statistical chart, which demonstrated that allocation was in fact fair, that it matched the proportions of each community within the total population. The overwhelming reaction of the focus groups was to disbelieve the council's statistics. Here we have a classic example of different sorts of belief about evidence – trained professionals put their faith in the written word, in statistics, while to local communities not all of whom even read or write well in English, statistics can always be 'fiddled' by officialdom.

Within personal and family life, it is the story, the anecdote that is used to explain things, that carries the currency of common sense. Professionals often discount personal experience or illustrative examples, since they are used to a professional training that looks to quantitative rather than qualitative evidence. The many frustrating encounters between professionals and service users or between managers and community groups often have, at their heart, different assumptions about what counts as knowledge – with professionals offering statistics and recorded data to inform discussion, while community members are offering stories or feelings. There is no 'right answer' – since quantitative data cannot be seen to be a more important source of knowledge than stories or individual experience. Many professionals fail in their work because of an inability to empathise or to be imaginative, and many community groups fail to persuade government because of an absence of academically recognisable 'evidence'. We need to build shared capacity to learn from both.

It is here that difference – the problem worrying so many players when we encountered it in Chapter 3 – becomes one of the most valuable assets within a community. The break-up of old communities and the coming together of people with different experiences offers a chance to break out of old patterns of thinking by accessing other people's pasts, other memories, other experiences. The development of oral history projects, the accessing of stories, myths and histories, enables people to learn to tell their own story and to see where they collide and diverge from other people's stories. The scope to explore one's own beliefs is as important in building consensus as the scope to hear about others.

If communities have available to them the perspectives and experiences of others, then false assumptions can be dislodged. Tensions and conflicts can be looked at clearly, with all the different ways of seeing in play; and it may be possible to build new options or solutions that have not been explored before. It may take time, and requires equal access to at least some baseline knowledge on all sides. Not everyone has to know the same things, since each participant can offer their knowledge and experience into the discussion, and learn from each other. But it requires sufficient respect for other perspectives and trust in the other participants to enable thinking to move forward, rather than simply restate starting positions. Crucially, it involves the possibility of open, unstructured conversation. An important part of any process of engagement is the space and time to be creative. The more innovative the solutions we need, the more carefully the space has to be designed to engender creativity.

But where are the places where such learning can take place? It is not realistic to assume that our society will spend millions of pounds on training courses for the public, since it invests so pitifully little in adult education. It is probably not realistic to expect ordinary members of the public to commit themselves to learning programmes without some powerful motivation or reward. The challenge, then, is to build learning into everyday life, into existing encounters and relationships. One possibility is that public agencies change the ways they interact with citizens in order to create learning. Local managers and politicians could treat these interactions differently, defending less; valuing the early stages of decision-making more; exploring the question, before rushing to answers; engaging users and citizens in active thinking; listening hard, challenging, testing and working on solutions together.

There is one obvious potential learning space. By making learning part of the everyday work of consultation and communication with the public, it is proving possible to create a dialogue which can change assumptions and beliefs on all sides. We looked in Chapter 3 at the significance of public consultation, but traditionally public organisations have simply used consultation as data, using public opinion to inform organisational decision-making. Surveys, interviews, focus groups and meetings tell us about the initial responses people make – often with little thought or reflection and with only partial information. Opinions can offer a baseline, a way of gauging the support a particular action might have, to understand the factors that motivate people's choices or actions. But opinions can be dangerously ill-informed, or based on unexamined prejudice, and for this reason they are often ignored or overridden by better-informed politicians or professionals. But professionals and politicians are also guided by untested opinions. If public opinions continue to be ill-informed, and therefore continue to be ignored, there is no real basis for a relationship of more serious engagement.

The processes used in managerial, professional and political learning can be translated into community learning. Whole system events can bring together large numbers of stakeholders within a community to explore the reconfiguration of services or to plan action on crosscutting social issues. Negotiation workshops, simulations and hypothetical exercises, all offer scope for local people, politicians and managers to work together to understand their environment and resolve problems. New techniques such as citizen juries, community workshops, interactive conferences and open-space events are often seen simply as more interesting or more fashionable ways to gather opinions. But they can go beyond this, and offer spaces in which managers and citizens can engage together in active thinking, where citizens acquire new knowledge, test assumptions and prejudices, explore different ways of doing things, propose solutions. The problems that face managers, professionals and politicians, face us all – changing roles, mixed messages, social complexity, fragmentation of old communities, challenging of old assumptions. How do we equip ourselves to be citizens in the twenty-first century?

New processes are being developed constantly. There are visioning techniques such as 'Imagine', or community discovery techniques in which large groups of people explore the sorts of services they would like to see (Bennett, 1999; Parston and Cowe, 1998). Future search techniques created by Marvin Weisbord (1992), and the search conference devised by Merrelyn Emery (see description in Bennett, 1999) have been used by many local authorities, community groups or partnerships to create self-managed community conferences which review the past, explore the present and create possible desirable futures, trying to identify common ground between participants and agreeing action plans. 'Planning for real' is a well-known approach to involving communities in developing ideas about a geographical area using a three-dimensional model of the area. Local communities are also working with theatre and visual techniques to make participation more immediate and more meaningful (see for example, the descriptions of Act Create Experience (ACE) and participatory theatre in Bennett, 1999). And open-space events allow participants to discover and build their own shared agenda. A number of authorities are experimenting with the use of new technology – using interactive techniques to gain instant feedback about the views of a large group of people and to track how views change as people learn from each other.

A number of techniques of community consultation draw on processes of deliberation, of dialogue based on new knowledge. The deliberative opinion poll, pioneered by Professor James Fishkin, has been used in the

USA both at national level for the Presidential Election, and at local level. Fishkin (1991) argues that communities of individuals can be trusted to make judgements if three elements are present, absence of tyranny, equality of knowledge and scope for deliberation – or 'rich speech'. Citizens' juries attempt a similar process on a smaller scale; a relatively small group of people comes to a conclusion over several days about an issue of local government or public policy. The jury has usually around 12 to 20 members, and meets over four or five days. The jury hears evidence from a variety of expert witnesses, and can ask for further information or clarification. Once it has heard all the evidence, the jury draws up its conclusions in a report to the council (Hall and Stewart, 1997). Community workshops and community issues groups use the same deliberative approach to citizen's juries, but are less-intensive. Community workshops enable a group of people to meet over a longer time rather than in a concentrated few days, to reach conclusions; they are shorter, drawn from relatively homogeneous groups so that people can think about issues with others who share the same experience, and are facilitated to help each group formulate suggestions (Clarke, 1999). Workshops are run in clusters to enable a wide range of different perspectives to be gathered, and then the different workshop groups exchange views and test out possible solutions.

Advocates of deliberative methods (see Barber, 1984; Cohen, 1989) suggest that 'politics should involve reasoning, open debate and reflection on the opinions of others' (Stoker, 1997, p. 166), rather than instrumental bargaining. Bottom-up schemes of regeneration have been developed which engage local communities in dialogue and deliberation (see Thomas, 1995; Gibson, 1993; Taylor, 1995), and Taylor suggests that for processes to work, solutions and action plans need to begin from resident's own priorities, meetings need to be organised in ways that allow 'non-joiners' to participate and 'require training and facilitation' (Taylor, 1995). There is scepticism about the extent to which new methods of participation are able to empower the disempowered, about the 'real' role of public agencies and the difficulties that emerge (Stoker, 1997, p. 181). On the ground, managers, staff and citizens say that current experiments feel different to those of the 1970s and 1980s, but much depends on whether fundamental change takes place inside public service organisations and whether current experiments move into the mainstream. If the new cocktails of relationships we have explored throughout this book begin to interact, we could imagine a chain reaction which would make local governance radically different.

New techniques for engaging the public could be seen as simply better and better forms of decision support, or they can be built into processes which take the decisions themselves. In the past, the process of judgement has almost always been handed back to local government or to professionals. But there is the prospect of using processes of dialogue and consensus-building to create shared spaces for negotiation and decision-making; for helping communities to make good use of the facilitators and professionals they have within their midst; to use the services of professional experts and facilitators; and to begin to build a capacity to design decision-making rather than simply participate in the processes designed by others. Ways are being built to establish what Parston and Timmins (1998) call 'a license to operate', which has been agreed by a wide cross-section of the community as a best-fit compromise to take forward. As we discussed in Chapter 3, this would require more rather than less attention to processes of transparency and accountability.

The behaviours and skills to make these processes work are all-important. In South Africa where public engagement within a democratic context has had to be built almost from nothing, and where community relationships are to say the least tense, they have begun to train skilled facilitators within communities and to build an acceptance of the skills needed to help build consensus, to defuse tension and to help create the conditions for agreement. The ability to design and create moments of dialogue, of exploration, of judgement will be abilities necessary on all sides and at all levels in local governance. Within civic education, as well as within the education of managers and professionals, we will need to find spaces for learning, for exploration, for experimentation, and for reflection.

Is there a new politics?

Academics have begun to suggest that we are witnessing the emergence of a 'new politics'. Stoker argues that the emerging new vision of local governance is premised 'in part on a critique of existing democratic politics and in part on a fuller recognition of the richness of democracy' (Stoker, 2000). Writers such as Giddens (1991) and Beck (1997), as we saw in Chapter 2, see a changing international role for governance. Giddens argues that the politics of distribution of risk is beginning to replace the politics of distribution of resources, and suggests that a more active process of social formation is emerging, a 'dialogic democracy' in which individuals and communities actively negotiate meanings and identities and boundaries through which collective action can be arrived at. Beck suggests that 'the authoritarian decision and action state gives way to the negotiation state. Stoker and Young (1993) suggest that 'third force' organisations may play an increasing role in representation and decision-making.

The initiatives that are underway are radical and creative, but we should be cautious about the speed of change. The 'spin' is always capable of destroying the reality. We should be careful of assuming somehow that a benign process is inevitably underway through which public agencies will be able, through efficiency savings, to meet user needs; that the mixed economy will solve the problems of demand and supply; that better-informed citizens will make demands that can more easily be met; and that service users will become more-market focused, less dependent and able to negotiate between themselves to tackle the remaining problems. Formidable obstacles remain.

The old politics is failing. The politics of the right has always been a politics of the protection of privilege, and of the authoritarian right of the limitation of privilege to a narrow group, excluding women, ethnic minorities, working people and 'outsiders'. The politics of the left has also, historically, been a politics of protection and exclusion, protecting the 'respectable' male, white working class from the demands of poorer people, while the politics of the far left has been a politics of scism and repudiation.

Old political allegiances no longer fit changing lives; identity is fragmented, overlapping, complex. 'Identity work' takes place in communities just as it does at work. Any new politics has to take account of this, and has to create spaces within which there can be a negotiation from difference, a recognition of the value of diversity, and a capacity to generate many solutions rather than one dominant solution. In a truly pluralistic politics, networks of governance would be concerned with political behaviour, as well as statements of policy:

> We need to create an overt politics of inclusion, one that recognises the partial nature of identity and builds a series of connections between diverse interests, creates a logic that links the concerns of different and fragmented groups... this will mean a new language of shared exploration, of learning from experience, of experimentation, of tentative rather that fixed conclusions, of joint endeavour, and of listening to other perspectives to understand rather than to refute. (Goss, 1995, p. 175)

Politics is always a process of story-telling, but it must also be a process of investigation, of listening.

Politics is always and inevitably about inequalities of power, and any negotiated or dialogue democracy has to include negotiation and dialogue about power. If there is to be a new politics, then it cannot simply be a politics of pragmatism which assumes away unequal life chances, nor one that talks about exclusion but fails to act on it. That is the challenge for any new politics. There is optimism in the formulations of 'dialogue democracy' that has yet to be justified. Social formations in the past have not found reasons powerful enough to persuade the powerful to enter into meaningful dialogue with the powerless, and unless the powerless are able to articulate their own desires and to act, within the political process, the 'new' politics will remain rhetoric.

Politics does not simply reside within official institutions and structures, and is not limited to the actions of political parties. Local politics has always included powerful economic players, local employers and potential investors, who achieve their objectives through business lunches and on the golf course. There have always been social movements, from Chartists to eco-warriors, that work outside the formal political processes. New forms of political expression include consumer action, the internet, networks, global networks, opinion polls, referenda, direct action, lobbying. Local papers played a powerful political role a century ago, but over the past half-century there has been a steady media abandonment of local politics.

But mass political parties have played an important role for a century, acting to organise ideas and interests into alliances capable of winning majority support, to create solidarities and communities of interest and difference, to create a discourse of interest alignment. Party politics, at its best is the process of building public support for a shift in the fundamentals that shape our society, creating radical alternatives, binding support from many different interests for long-term investment in change. It can make choices clear, between different future possibilities, between different ways for society to be. At its worst, it is pork-barrel pandering to the immediate moral panics and preoccupations of selfish constituents, inward-looking, self-obsessed about personal ambition and not public goals. It was ever thus. The importance of the role of politics cannot be narrowed to the current performance of political parties, nationally or locally. There is little fundamental political debate between parties and movements at present, little clear allegiance between class or interest and party. But this state of affairs may not be permanent. The 'end of ideology' has been celebrated several times this century, without any justification in fact. Formal politics can and should offer a vital process of exposing and interpreting different powerful interests so that debates between them can be carried out in the public domain. Without active political debate, powerful interests will continue to influence policy, but in secret. Politics is the mediation of power, and if it is not done visibly it will be done invisibly. The danger then is that without effective political parties, civil society will dissolve into apathy.

There are other possibilities, however. If political parties cease to be able to relate to the experiences and interests of significant sections of the population, social movements may take over and new political forms are likely to emerge. The new information society and access to new forms of political organisation through the internet may change our assumptions about how politics works. We may, for example, be able to envisage a highly-politicised civil society without the dominance of political parties. Alternatively, political parties and collective activism may revive, although in modern forms.

Democracy is not simply the structures and systems of government decision-making, but the wider range of rights and obligations that accrue to the citizen, the power of local representatives and the extent to which they can be held to account. An effective democracy depends on the scrutiny of the press, on the existence of effective human rights, rights to redress and access to information. It should be judged not just by levels of voting, but by levels of citizen information, transparency and accountability among all the agencies involved in local governance. The slow death of documentary and news media makes it harder and harder in the UK to explore issues outside the immediate agenda of spin-doctors. Politics should be capable of bringing into the public domain the real questions of the age. The political debate about governance should not be confined to a preoccupation with performance indicators and service delivery. The themes that have driven this book such as 'What is a community?', 'What is the relationship between representative and direct democracy?', 'What is the relationship between neighbourhood interests and strategic concerns?' or 'What is the role of a Councillor?', are not technical, they are political. We should be able to vote, not simply between different political parties based on how often our bins are emptied, but on what sort of local democracy we are offered. Any 'new' politics would need to be capable of exploring the choices available to citizens about the sort of democracy we want to have.

10   Conclusion

Box 10.1   *An example of governance working ...*

As the door opens, you can hear the noise, not shouting, but a low, deliberate hum of urgent conversation. People are working furiously in small groups, some with flip charts, some around tables. The walls are lined with paper, on which are hundreds of post-its, some organised into a huge wall-sized project plan, others interspersed with scribbled writing, cartoons and drawings. There is even a poem. The groups working together seem incongruous; pensioners working alongside managers in sharp suits; teenagers discussing issues with local policemen or doctors. It is possible to meet people who you would never talk to in your everyday life.

You can see very important people who command multimillion pound budgets talking to people who would not think of themselves as important at all. There is a lot of laughter and enthusiasm. People are talking directly and honestly, and you can catch people no longer able to edit what they say, and saying it anyway. There are some heartstopping moments when people say the unsayable and a moment's silence while it sinks in, but then there is the capacity to handle it. The police superintendent confesses that the police have mishandled things, and asks for help. The local authority chief executive agrees that their systems failures have been stopping progress, and promises action. If you had told these people yesterday that they would be saying these things in public, they would have been horrified.

At the same time, the people from the local community stay realistic and practical, and are not blaming anyone. They understand the problems. The vision they come up with is not fanciful or romantic. Difference is OK, and people recognise that they don't have to hold hands at the end of the day. If some people remain unhappy it's important just to acknowledge that. No single person or organisation is in charge of the event, but the process remains realistic and useful,

(*continued*)

and many people are helping to make it work. It is, as a colleague points out, a 'leaderful' situation, and there is capacity within the whole set of relationships in the room for leading. No one looks simply to the local council to implement the action plan they have created. People are standing up and pledging money, time, hours and commitment – some community members are even volunteering money to help get things going. At the end of the day, things aren't closed, but everyone gets the sense that they can take things forward, and recognises that it's only going to lead to anything if they do something personally.

The changes we have been exploring throughout this book are not wishful thinking; they are happening. Not everywhere, not evenly. In the most advanced local councils there are pockets of jobsworths and failed systems. Inside the biggest dinosaurs there are creative middle managers making things happen that their bosses probably know nothing about. In some places the politicians are backward-looking while the managers have embraced modernisation, in other places the opposite is true. Some agencies have forged effective partnerships but are struggling to change themselves. In one city, the housing department has built a relationship with local communities while their neighbours in social services or health struggle. A hundred miles away, it's the other way round. The obstacles are great and people scramble over them at different speeds and with varying confidence.

The changes needed now in local governance rely on active energetic, courageous managers and staff, politicians and citizens. The new system of local governance is not either failing or working – it is *being worked* by the men and women within it. They are trying to make sense of their lives, of their organisations, of their work in a new world. What is perhaps surprising is the extent to which change has been embraced, and the large numbers of politicians, managers and staff within and across organisations that are energised by change, and are willing to take risks with their own jobs and careers to make it happen. Given the weakness of the levers at the government's disposal, there is an extraordinary amount of change underway. It is not driven by government, and indeed it is not necessarily going in the ways that central government would choose. Politicians, managers, community leaders and staff are often doing what they can, within dispiriting systems and obsolete structures to make new ways of doing things happen. They have limited ambitions. They often 'fall back' on bureaucracy and single-agency solutions through sheer exhaustion. They do not simply do what they are told; they do what they can to make sense of a confusing world. It is this active process of making and shaping governance which offers the opportunity to break out of sterile traditions of administration and government, into new and uncharted relationships.

People act as managers, professionals, workers, citizens or politicians with the past locked up inside them. They have built ways of seeing and belief systems over many years. The limits and constraints on new ways of thinking are our assumptions carried from the past:

> Nothing influences our ability to cope with the difficulties of existence so much as the context in which we view them; the more contexts we can choose between, the less do the difficulties appear to be inevitable and insurmountable. The fact that the world has become fuller than ever of complexity of every kind may suggest at first that it is harder to find a way out of our dilemmas, but in reality, the more complexities the more crevices there are through which we can crawl. (Zeldin, 1998, p. 13)

The conventional view is to see social fragmentation, the break-up of communities, as a problem. But these things are also the beginnings of solutions, since they break us out of old ways of doing things. It is in this breakdown of past aspirations and certainties that learning is most possible. It is probably only when old ways no longer work that people are willing to try new ones and it is through difference that we can learn the most. In any examination of local governance we should not try to 'close the edges' – to define systems and boundaries in such a way as to constrain what is possible, to build models in which some agents are in and some are out, to create frameworks that close down the possibilities that, in the real world, governance could become something else.

Emerging examples of practice

There are many live examples of new practice. Since practice evolves so fast, and because each experiment is very different, it is as important to learn from each example as to try and generalise. Some partnerships, for example, are beginning to develop into real locations for governance at the regional and local level. Council leaders and chief executives in many of our cities already spend more time working with the police, with health chiefs and with the leaders of private companies than they do managing services. In Newcastle, Manchester, Birmingham, Sheffield, Leeds – the sense of city governance carries far beyond the boundaries of the local council. Managers and politicians gather as a matter of course to resolve regional problems – either through shadow assemblies, or bodies such as the Thames Valley Partnership. In London, regional and subregional initiatives such as the Thames Gateway Partnership are important locations of decision-making. Regional and subregional governance is here to stay, whether or not new formal elected structures are created.

Box 10.2   *A working partnership*

Herefordshire covers a vast swathe of glorious rural England and became a unitary authority in 1998. The health authority, police authority and local authority cover the same area and many of the problems faced are not within the scope of any single agency. A partnership board brings together these three organisations alongside the voluntary sector and business. The board has worked together to agree a vision and 'ten ambitions' for the county – and then agreed protocols and ways of working. Set up as part of the Local Government Association's New Commitment to Regeneration, the partnership board has begun to work out protocols for joint working and to connect up the plans, projects and partnerships that exist piecemeal across the county. The hope is to begin to create a single integrated plan for the place – integrating and agreeing the community plan and the council's performance plan, the health strategy and the community safety strategy. The new one-stop shop is not badged by the local authority, but involves all the agencies, and is called Info.Herefordshire. Already resources have been pooled and staff seconded to the partnership full-time, and these seconded staff are beginning to network – creating a virtual organisation (the e-mail address for the partnership is *oneplan@herefordshire*).

At the local and neighbourhood level, relationships between public agencies and ordinary citizens are also evolving fast. In Lewisham, a panel of 1000 citizens is consulted regularly about all sorts of things – council tax, housing issues, community safety and health plans. The people on the panel are not simply treated as 'data' they are kept up-to-date with a regular newsletter which tells them when action has been taken as a result of consultation. As they understand more about the council, their views become more carefully judged and they are able to explain things to their friends and neighbours. They are invited to take part in a range of meetings and workshops to solve practical problems or explore the future. They often accept.

Box 10.3   *Community discovery in Lewisham*

In 1998 a group of 65 residents from Lewisham's community panel (broadly representative of the social class, age, sex, ethnic and disability profile of the borough) came together in a community discovery event for a day and a half. The group began by identifying the issues they wanted to investigate, formed small groups to discuss different issues that interested them, 'mapped' their ideas and experiences, thoughts and comments and then worked on suggestions for change. They looked at health, learning and community safety, and did so by opening up the narrow definitions of service delivery and began to build integrated pictures of public service.

> Despite the cynicism of some public service professionals, people are able to think holistically across service boundaries and build 'big pictures' of space? community outcomes. Artificial service boundaries are rooted largely in the organisation of service delivery... the public do not have separate relationships with discrete service systems, rather, they have lives that they experience as being comprised as many connected parts...local people can help us build greater understanding about how services failure in one area can have consequences in another, and thus about how to make more effective use of public resources. (Parston and Cowe, 1998)

The experiment contributed important learning for all the agencies involved. However, the report of the event warns 'not all the messages are easy to hear. Some pose hard challenges to what policymakers and managers do'. But there was no evidence here of participation fatigue. 'People enjoy authentic engagement around these issues, and the opportunity to connect with each other, stimulate their thinking and feel part of an active community' (*ibid.*).

Box 10.4 *Experiments in Watford*

Watford borough council has been attempting to build a different sort of relationship with their community over many years. They have set up a whole series of local experiments – community-visioning conferences on community safety, pilot schemes with coordinators in local neighbourhoods local areas to bang heads together and help local people access the system. The Watford Best Value pilot was a similar experiment including the local community in a complete rethink about the local area.

Led by former chief executive Carol Hassan for eight years, the project is continuing in 2000 under the new chief executive, Alan Clarke, her colleague for most of that period. He states that, 'It's about creating the environment in which we can build community self-esteem and ability to self-organise'; 'building the community inside the organisation, and bringing the community in, at the same time as we turn the organisation outwards and into the town'. He recognises that 'you can't manage change, you can only manage the context that makes change possible, just like you can't make plants grow, you can only create the conditions in which they can grow'. Asked how that is done, he explains

'by drawing explicitly on theory and underlying ideas which help us understand what is happening, by involving everyone in exploring the wider systems of interaction, understanding how organisations work, and by creating spaces where it feels safe to take risks so that you can experiment with different ways of working.'

Box 10.5 *Neighbourhood forums in York*

In York, neighbourhood forums have been working since 1992. The first pilot was so successful that they spread until there were 21 in the city, each covering between 3000 and 8000 people. The forums cover small neighbourhoods, and have had £3 per capita – which works out at between £9000 and £24 000 a year to spend in the local area. Each forum has an open membership, and despite initial doubts they have continued to be well attended and successful. But there have been some important factors leading to success.
(continued)

The agenda (well designed with photos and bold graphics, on one side of paper) is posted through every letterbox in the neighbourhood. It is built from both forum member's concerns and council issues, and meetings are lively and well organised. Sometimes forums hold 'travelling meetings' where the group walks around the streets to look at problems and residents are welcome to meet them at the corner of their street – 7.45 outside the Kings Arms, 8.15 outside the primary school, etc. The councillors who chair the meetings have had intensive training and coaching to help them carry out their new role.

York became a unitary authority in 1996 and its new boundaries took in 31 parish councils. Under a set of policy proposals entitled 'Valuing Communities' the council set out to work positively with the parishes granting them the same £3 per capita and collectively calling parish councils and neighbourhood forums 'local assemblies'. Now the modernisation of political arrangements includes the setting up of 'ward committees' so that local ward councillors able to 'sign off' decisions at local level and the level of developed resources has been increased to £6 per capita.

In the early years, the neighbourhoods spent their money on predictable things like fencing or dog-dirt bins, but as the years have progressed they have begun to extend their thinking. Now the initiatives include an after-school club, a 5-a side football team, detached youth work and an arts-based scheme to involve young people.

Rory Barke head of democratic services at the City has been guiding the process since 1992:

> 'We need to let people organise themselves, keep paperwork to a minimum, allow different approaches evolve in each area. It gets more exciting as local residents get a feel of what they want to achieve for themselves. In the first instance they saw it as coming to a public meeting to meet the councillors now its our neighbourhood forum – we'll decide what to do with it.'

Rory began his career in the voluntary sector asked whether the new initiatives will fade out the way that the 1970s and 1980s initiatives did, he says no:

(continued)

'The 1980s was about decentralisation rather than devolution. This time we are trying not to bureaucratise everything, recognising that it has to be bottom up, taking a more organic approach to design, not imposing things. We are taking a longer term perspective about what we are trying to achieve.'

The need for diversity

Local governance works, when it works, because of the energy and commitment of key managers, community leaders and politicians. Diversity is inevitable, since what works in one area does not work in another. There are tensions between strategic direction and local priorities, between the long and the short term, as well as struggles for resources and conflicting interests. But where progress is being made, these dilemmas are managed, creative solutions are found and new approaches are tried. Managers in one innovative organisation say that their symbol is the post-it note – invented because someone discovered a glue that didn't stick properly. 'Post-its are rooted in the way we think – nothing is fixed, everything is moveable, you can shape and reshape, repattern things until they work'.

Public policy is not implemented by buildings or systems or procedures; it is implemented by people. The active dynamic in relationships between the state and civil society is human imagination. We cannot achieve the relationships we need by harnessing a few highly intelligent imaginations at the centre and crushing hundreds and thousands of others into the semblance of a machine. It is the energy of human imagination in every encounter that will create the relationships we need for the future.

Looking into the future

It is dangerous to write too confidently about the future in times of transition, since issues and preoccupations fast become obsolete. But there are no other times. Over the next few years, networks of local governance will be transformed. The experience of executive mayors, first in London – but perhaps later in other cities such as Birmingham or Liverpool – will transform city government. While the mayors have few powers, they have huge legitimacy and considerable influence. Their role as 'skilled orchestrators' can begin to create city identity, and bring resources together across organisational boundaries.

The political landscape of UK local governance will be transformed as the fortunes of the main political parties begin to change. A switch of major cities to conservative control, a renaissance for the liberal democrats, a revival of the greens, the arrival of new political forces – are all possible. Proportional representation at local level would change things too. The map of local governance in the UK is likely to be characterised by far greater political diversity – and tension – than has been true for the past decade. But the most dramatic changes will be due to the technology revolution inside public organisations. One-stop shops and call centres may become intermediate technology; and most of us will expect to transact our business with government through a PC, a television or a phone within five years. Information about many services is already on line, and many councils are already doing business over the internet. But we are just at the beginning. As governance moves into cyberspace, many of the problems that have beset local councils – departmentalism, silo thinking, systems failure, communication breakdown – could be tackled. Technology offers extraordinary possibilities for public access, for dialogue, for on-line exploration.

But there are dangers also. In the rush to get on-line, local agencies could hard-wire old relationships and ways of doing things. Knowledge management systems, for example, could follow existing information flows, kept tightly within single agencies with limited access. Alternatively, they could become open-access, available to other agencies or to the public. Policy information could be carefully limited to those with passwords, or it could be open to comment and suggestion from ordinary members of staff or consumers. Delivery systems could be wired up separately for each service, or pathways could be built between them.

The gap between the information 'haves' and 'have nots' may widen. Indeed, the challenge for local governance, as for national governance, will not be whether they continue to provide an acceptable level of basic services for middle England; it will be whether social cohesion and collective decision-making can be sustained in the face of growing diversity and inequality.

The role of central government?

The Blair government has set out a modernisation programme for public services, and it can at times look as if progress is painfully slow; and it has

been easy to blame the managers and staff for the failures in public services. National government, impatient for results, understandably wants to
keep 'pulling the levers' for change in the hope that things will speed
up. But it has yet to live up to its own rhetoric. Government cannot yet
relate to the networks and partnerships that are emerging at local level and
civil servants insist on trying to drive performance through individual
agencies. But good partnerships have negotiated objectives, shared strategy,
pooled resources and mutual 'contracts' and need the flexibility to negotiate these locally.

The most important insight I can offer from many years in the field is
that real change takes a long time. The evidence from the civic entrepreneurship study suggests that it takes about ten years to turn an organisation
around. The factors that make the greatest difference seem to be sustained
and consistent leadership throughout a ten-year period, a clear and simple
message, and leadership at many different levels with space for everyone
in the organisation to explore and innovate.

Greater and greater pressure does not necessarily speed things up. After
a while, pressure becomes counter-productive since it spirals into panic
and hyperactivity. The most difficult aspect of intervention is 'courageous
patience' – the confidence that any levers that exist have been pulled, and
that pulling them again will only make matters worse.

Constant structural change can be a dangerous distraction. Crude uniform solutions dictated from the centre will not help, since there are no
uniform problems. Even targeted intervention has to be planned very carefully, since hit squads, penalties and sanctions cannot make people different, (although, if they are smart, they will learn to look different). While it
is true that there is a need to increase capacity and to change the culture,
these things are not straightforward; there is a process of 'becoming' that
is just as important as the process of finding out. Government itself is one
of the forces that shape the wider environment within which local actors
'become'.

Despite the introduction of many management development programmes, training programmes and culture change programmes, the reality
is that people cannot be changed in any simple way. They have to change
themselves. In the process of making governance work, we need to concentrate on unlearning as well as learning. We need new learning processes
that are helpful in this difficult process of 'self-changing': creating space
for challenging and recreating ideas about what is possible. Learning has
to take place in daily life rather than boxed away in training programmes;
and the ordinary work of local governance itself has to offer space to

explore new ideas, to see connections and linkages, to build consent, to explore ourselves, and to shape and change the environment within which we find ourselves. The real work of change is long-term and sustained, and involves reflection and dialogue, not simply paperwork or plans.

There are things that could help. Investment in cross-boundary working at the centre could begin to create a national government able to do business with local governance. Partnerships at national level could work directly with networks and partnerships at local level. Government departments could model effective engagement with citizens, and explore the implications of engaging with citizens as authorisers and co-producers, rather than simply consumers. Government could begin to reward courage – to make sure that timid authorities understand that it is better to experiment than to play safe. Government could recognise and honour effective strategy at regional and local level, and continue to withdraw irksome controls and monitoring systems. Where competition or bidding systems waste resources, they could be abandoned. Process compliance should be treated as valueless; results should be measured in terms of outcomes, not processes. The exchange of experience between civil servants and local manages, between quangos and public agencies and between local government networks should be encouraged. Training should be properly funded. Secondments and job swaps should become an essential element in promotion and government should insist that, where possible, information systems should be open-access and all possible knowledge shared with local citizens. Of course individual confidentiality must be preserved, but much of the information in the public domain could be made accessible. Perhaps the single most important thing that government could achieve would be an open dialogue – not just within government, but within the media and within civil society – about the nature of public organisational cultures, about the roles and relationships emerging within governance. We need better theoretical and practical tools to understand the changes we are living through.

The generation of shared 'tools' for understanding is necessary, not simply to watch from the academic sidelines but to actively support managers, politicians and community leaders as they find a way forward. If we are to make sense of the future, then theorisation has to cease to be the property of academics and become a day-to-day tool of those who make change happen. Everyone involved in local governance needs to be able to stand back and reflect on practice, and to embark on new conversations. The trend towards 'reflexive modernisation' is not simply a matter of observation and study, but a matter of creating new spaces for dialogue in public life.

Bibliography

Argyris, C. and Schon, D. (1978) *Organisational Learning: A Theory of Action Perspective* (Reading, Mass.: Addison Wesley).

Argyris, C. and Schon, D. (1996) *Organisational Learning II* (Reading, Mass.: Addison Wesley).

Arnstein, S. (1971) 'A Ladder of Citizen Participation in the USA', *Journal of the Royal Town Planning Institute*.

Audit Commission (1996) *Streetwise* (London: Audit Commission)

Audit Commission (1996) *Misspent Youth: Young People and Crime* (London: Audit Commission).

Bachrach, P. and Baratz, M. S. (1962) 'Two Faces of Power', *American Political Science Review,* vol. 56, pp. 947–52.

Bains Report (1972) *The New Local Authorities: Management and Structure* (London: HMSO).

Ball, C. (1994) *Bridging the Gulf*, European Foundation for the Improvement of Living and Working Conditions (Luxembourg: Office for Official Publications of the European Communities).

Barber, B. (1984) *Strong Democracy* (Berkeley and London: University of California Press).

Baker, A. (1999) *Ruling by Task Force* (London: Politicos/Democratic Audit).

Beck, U. (1997) 'The Reinvention of Politics', in U. Beck, A. Giddens and S. Lash *Reflexive Modernisation; Politics, Tradition and Aesthetics in the Modern Social Order* (Cambridge: Polity Press).

Bennet, A. (1999) 'Building a Common Vision of the Future', in S. Goss (ed.), *Managing Working with the Public* (London: Kogan Page).

Beresford, P. and Croft, S. (1993) *Citizen Involvement; A Practical Guide for Change* (London: Macmillan).

Biddle, B. J. (1979) *Role Theory: Expectations, Identities and Behaviours* (London: Academic Press).

Blair, T. (1999) Foreword to *Modernising Government*, White Paper, CM 4310 (March).

Brennan, A., Rhodes, J. and Taylor, P. (1998) *Evaluation of the Single Regeneration Challenge Fund Budget: A Partnership for Regeneration – An Interim Evaluation* (London: Department of the Environment, Transport and the Regions).

Brown, A., Jones, A. and Mackay, F. (1999) *The Representativeness of Councillors* (York: Joseph Rowntree Foundation).

Budge, I. (1996) *The New Challenge of Direct Democracy* (Oxford: Blackwell).

Burns, D., Hambledon, R. and Hogget, P. (1994) *The Politics of Decentralisation* (London: Macmillan).

Burton, P., Forrest, R. and Stewart, M. (1987) *Living Conditions in Urban Areas,* European Foundation for the Improvement of Living and Working Conditions,

(Dublin and Luxembourg: Office for the Official Publications of the European Communities).

Cabinet Office (1999) *Modernising Government*, White Paper, CM 4310 (March).

Cabinet Office (2000) National Strategy for Neighbourhood Renewal, Report of Policy Action Team 16, *Learning Lessons.*

Charteris, S. and Carrigan, P. (1999) *Developing Your Council's Scrutiny Role* (York: Joseph Rowntree Foundation).

Carchedi, G. (1997) *On the Economic Identification of the Middle Classes* (London: Routledge & Kegan Paul).

Castells, M. (1996) *The Rise of the Network Society,* vol. I (Oxford: Blackwell).

Castells, M. (1997) *The Rise of the Network Society,* vol. II (Oxford: Blackwell).

Clarke, R. (1999) 'Involvement in Deliberation and Decision Making', in S. Goss (ed.), *Managing Working with the Public* (London: Kogan Page).

Clegg, S., Boreham, P. and Dow, G. (1987) *Class Politics and the Economy* (London: Routledge & Kegan Paul).

Cockburn, C. (1977) *The Local State* (London: Pluto).

Cohen, J. (1989) 'Deliberation and Democratic Legitimacy', in A. Hamline and P. Pettit (eds), *The Good Polity* (Oxford: Basil Blackwell).

Coleman, J. S. (1990) *Foundations of Social Theory* (Cambridge, Mass.: Harvard University Press).

Commission for Local Democracy (1995) *Voting in Local Elections* (London: Commission for Local Democracy).

Corrigan, P., Hayes, M. and Joyce, P. (1999) *Managing in the New Local Government* (London: Kogan Page).

Dahl, R. (1957) 'The Concept of Power', *Behavioural Science,* vol. 2, pp. 201–15.

Deetz, S. (1992) 'Disciplinary Power in the Modern Corporation', in M. Alvesson and H. Wilmott (eds), *Critical Management Studies* (London: Sage).

Department of the Environment, Transport and the Regions (1998) *Modern Local Government: In Touch with the People* (London: DETR).

Department of the Environment, Transport and the Regions (1999) *Local Leadership, Local Choice* (London: DETR).

Department of the Environment, Transport and the Regions (1999) *Participation in Best Value* (London and University of Warwick: DETR).

Department of the Environment, Transport and the Regions (2000) Social Exclusion Unit Policy Action Team 17. *Joining it up Locally, the Evidence Base* (London: DETR).

Douglas, R. (2000) Unpublished paper.

Dowson, S. (1999) *Keeping it Safe – Self-Advocacy by People with Learning Difficulties and the Professional Response* (London: Values into Action).

Dunleavy, P. (1995) 'Policy Disasters, Exploring the UK's Record', *Public Policy and Administration,* vol. 10, no. 2.

Fishkin, J. (1991) *Democracy and Deliberation: New Directions for Democratic Reform* (Yale: Yale University Press).

Foster, A. (1999) 'Pressure points and priorities: the challenges to the public sector', in *Community, Opportunity, Responsibility and Accountability*, Report of Symposium on the Future of Public Services (London: Office for Public Management).

Fordham, G. (1995) *Made to Last, Creating Sustainable Neighbourhood and Estate Regeneration* (York: Joseph Rowntree Foundation).

Geddes, M. (1998) 'Achieving Best Value Through Partnership', Warwick and DETR Best Value series paper no. 7 (Warwick: The Local Government Centre).

Gibson, T. (1993) 'Estates Regeneration on Meadowell', Housing Research Findings no. 97 (York: Joseph Rowntree Foundation).

Giddens, A. (1991) *Modernity and Self-Identity* (Cambridge: Polity Press).

Giddens, A. (1997) 'Living in Post-Traditional Society', in U. Beck, A. Giddens, and S. Lash, *Reflexive Modernisation; Politics, Tradition and Aesthetics in the Modern Social Order* (Cambridge: Polity Press).

Giddens, A. (1998) *The Third Way* (Cambridge: Polity Press).

Gillanders, G. (1999) 'Models of Resident Controlled Housing' (London: Housing Corporation).

Goss, S. (1989) *Local Labour and Local Government* (Edinburgh: Edinburgh University Press).

Goss, S. (1995) 'Language, Identity and Power', in *Renewal*, vol. 3, no. 3 (July).

Goss, S. (1996) 'Redrawing the Boundary between State and Civil Society – The Role of the Voluntary Sector', in *Renewal*, vol. 4, no. 2 (May).

Goss, S. (1996) *Leading Local Government, The Changing Role of Chief Executives* (London: Office for Public Management).

Goss, S. (1998) 'State, Business and Civil Society – Rules of Engagement', in *Renewal*, vol. 6, no. 4 (Autumn).

Goss, S. and Corrigan, C. (1999) Starting to Modernise: developing new roles for council members: a practical guide (York: Joseph Rowntree Foundation).

Goss, S. (ed.) (1999) *Managing Working with the Public* (London: Kogan Page).

Goss, S. and Parston, G. (1989) *Public Management for New Times* (London: Labour Co-ordinating Committee).

Goss, S. and Sharman, N. (2000) 'Neighbourhood Governance', *Renewal*, vol. 8, no. 4, Autumn.

Habermas, J. (1971) *Towards a Rational Society* (London: Heineman).

Hall, D. and Stewart, J. (1997) *Citizens' Juries: An Evaluation* (Luton: Local Government Management Board).

Halpern, D. (1998) 'Social Capital, exclusion and the quality of life: towards a causal model and policy implications', Unpublished paper given at a Nexus conference 1998.

Halstack, E. G. (1936) *Local Government in England* (Cambridge: Cambridge University Press).

Hambledon, R. and Taylor, M. (1994) *People in Cities: A Transatlantic Policy Exchange* (Bristol: School of Advanced Urban Studies, University of Bristol).

Hambledon, E., Essex, S., Mills, L. and Razzaque, K. (1995) *The Collaborative Council: A Study of Inter-Agency Working in Practice* (York: Joseph Rowntree Foundation).

Hambledon, R. (1996) *Leadership in Local Government* (Bristol: University of the West of England).

Hambledon, R. *et al.* (1997) *New Perspectives in Local Governance* (York: Joseph Rowntree Foundation).

Hambledon, R. (1997) 'Strengthening Political Leadership in the UK', *Public Money and Management*.

Handy, C. (1984) *The Empty Raincoat* (London: Hutchinson).

Handy, C. (1989) *The Age of Unreason* (London: Business Books).

Hart, R. (1992) *Children's Participation: From Tokenism to Citizenship* (New York: Unicef).

Held, D. (1997) *Democracy and the Global Order* (Cambridge: Polity Press).

Hennessey, P. (1990) *Whitehall* (Fontana).

Higgins, J., Deakin, N., Edwards, J. and Wicks, M. (1983) *Government and Urban Poverty* (London: Basil Blackwell).

Higgins, J. (1998) 'HAZs Warning', *Health Service Journal*.

Hodge, M., Leach, S. and Stoker, G. (1997) 'More than just the Flower Show: Elected Mayors and Democracy', Discussion Paper no. 32 (London : Fabian Society).

Holman, B. (1999) *New Connections: Joined up Access to Public Services* (London: Community Development Foundation).

Honey, P. and Mumford, A. (1982) *Manual of Learning Styles*, (Honey).

Hutton, W. (1995) *The State We're In* (London: Cape).

Ignatieff, M. (1996) 'Belonging in the past', in S. Dunnant and R. Porter (eds), *Age of Anxiety* (London: Virago, Little Brown).

Judd, D. and Parkinson, M. (1990) *Leadership and Urban Regeneration; Cities in North America and Europe* (London: Sage).

Klein, H. J. (1989) 'An Integrated Control Theory Model of Work Motivation', *Academy of Management Journal,* vol. 14, no. 2, pp. 150–72.

Klein, H. J. (1989) 'An Integrated Control Theory Model of Work Motivation', *Academy of Management Journal,* vol. 14, no. 4, pp. 163–88.

Knights, D. and Collinson, D. (1987) 'Shop Floor Culture and the Problem of Managerial Control', in J. McGoldrick (ed.), *Business Case File in Behavioural Science* (London: Von Nostrand).

Kolb, D. A. (1976) *The Learning Style Inventory: Technical Manual* (Boston, Mass.: MacBer & Co.).

Kooiman, J. (1993) *Modern Governance* (London: Sage).

Labour Coordinating Committee (1988) *Labour Councils in the Cold: A Blueprint for Survival* (Labour: LCC).

LGMB (1995) *Portrait of change* (London: LGMB).

LGMB (1998) *Survey on Councillor Profile Post-1998 Elections* (London: LGMB).

Lansley, S., Goss, S. and Wolmar, C. (1987) *The Rise and Fall of the Municipal Left* (London: Macmillan).

Leadbeater, C. and Goss, S. (1998) *Civic Entrepreneurship* (London: Demos Public Management Foundation).

Le Grand, J. (1990) *Quasi Markets and Social Policy* (Bristol: School of Advanced Urban Studies, University of Bristol).

Leiper, R. (1994) 'Evaluation: Organisational Learning from Experience', in A. Obholzer and V. Zagier Roberts (eds), *The Unconscious at Work: Individual and Organisational Stress in the Human Services* (London: Routledge).

Lessem, R. (1986) *The Roots of Excellence* (London: Fontana).

Lewis, R. (1984) *Open Learning in Action: Case Studies, Open Learning Guide* (London: Council for Education Technology).

Lindbloom, C. E. (1959) 'The Science of Muddling Through', *Public Administration Review*, vol. 19, pp. 79–88.

Lowndes, V. (1998) 'Management Change in Local Governance', in G. Stoker (ed.), *New Perspectives on Local Governance* (London: Macmillan).

Lowndes, V. *et al.* (1998) *Enhancing Public Participation in Local Government* (London: DETR).

McMahon, L. (1994) 'Learning from the Future – Using Behavioural Simulations for Management Learning', *Future Management,* issue no. 1.

McMahon, L. and Arnell, G. (1998) *Practising for Partnership. A Report Based on Seven Whole Systems Simulations* (London: NHS Executive).

Maud, Sir John (Chairman) (1967) *Report of the Committee on the Management of Local Government* (London: HMSO).

Maslow, A. H. (1954) *Motivation and Human Personality* (New York: Harper & Row).

Martins, L. and Miller, C. (1999) 'Empowering the Disempowered', in S. Goss (ed.), *Managing Working with the Public* (London: Kogan Page).

Miller, C. (1999) *Managing for Social Cohesion* (London: Office for Public Management).

Moore, M. (1996) *Creating Public Value, Strategic Management in Government* (Harvard, Mass.: Harvard University Press).

Moore, M. (1999) 'The Job Ahead', in *Community Opportunity, Responsibility, Accountability – Report of Symposium on the Future of Public Services Office for Public Management* (June).

Morgan, G. (1986) *Images of Organisations* (Beverly Hills: Sage).

Obholzer, A. and Zagier Roberts, V. (eds) (1998) *The Unconscious at Work: Individual and organisational stress in the Human Services* (London: Routledge).

Offe, C. (1984) *Contradictions of the Welfare State* (London: Hutchinson).

Office for Public Management (1998) *Consultation in Hammersmith and Fulham, Better Government for Older People* (London: OPM).

Office for Public Management (1999) *Consultation in Consort and Friary Wards, Southwark* (London: OPM).

Office for Public Management (1999) *Consultation with Local People in a London Borough* (London: OPM).

Parkinson, M. (1998) *Combatting Social Exclusion: Lessons from Area-based Programmes in Europe* (Bristol: Policy Press).

Parsons, T. (1951) *The Social System* (New York: Collier Macmillan).

Parston, G. (1991) *A New Framework for Public Management* (London: Public Management Foundation).

Parston, G. and Timmins, N. (1998) *Joined-Up Management* (London: Public Management Foundation).

Parston, G. and Cowe, I. (1998) *Making the Connections – Citizens mapping the Big Picture.* (London: Public Management Foundation).

Perri 6 (1997) 'Social exclusion: time to be optimistic', in *The Wealth and Poverty of Networks: tackling social exclusion* (London: Demos).

Perri 6, Leat, D., Seltzer, K. and Stoker, G. (1999) *Governing in the Round; Strategies for Holistic Government* (London: Demos).

Peters, T. J. and Waterman, R. H. (1982) *In Search of Excellence: Lessons from America's Best Run Companies* (New York: Harper & Row).

Phillips, E. (1993) *Consultation? I thought We Did that Last Year: Consultation with Black and Ethnic Minority Groups in the Preparation of Community Care Programmes* (London: Research Centre).

Portes, A. (1998) 'Social Capital, its Origins and Applications in Modern Sociology', *Annual Review of Sociology,* vol. 24, pp. 1–24.

Poulantzas, N. (1975) *Classes in Contemporary Capitalism* (London: New Left Books).

Prasha, V. and Shan, N. (1986) *Routes or Roadblocks? Consulting Minority Communities in London Boroughs* (London: Runymede Trust).

Putnam, D. (1993) *Making Democracy Work* (Princeton: Princeton University Press).

Rao, N. (1993) *Managing Change: Councillors and the New Local Government* (York: Joseph Rowntree Foundation).

Rao, N. (1998) 'Representation in Local Politics, a Reconsideration and Some New Evidence', *Political Studies,* vol. 46, no. 1.

Rhodes, R. (1997) *Understanding Governance, Policy Networks, Reflexivity and Accountability* (Buckingham: Oxford University Press).

Richards, S., Barnes, M., Coulson, C., Gaster, L., Leach, B. and Sullivan, H. (1999) *Cross-Cutting Issues in Public Policy and Public Service* (London: DETR).

Roberts, U., Russell, H., Harding, A. and Parkinson, M. (1995) *Public Private Voluntary Partnerships in Local Government* (Luton: Local Government Management Board).

Russell, H., Dawson, J., Garside, P. and Parkinson, M. (1996) *City Challenge Interim Evaluation* (London: The Stationery Office).

Rutherford, J. (1990) 'A Place called Home; Identity and the Cultural Politics of Difference', in J. Rutherford (eds), *Identity* (London: Lawrence & Wishart).

Sayer, A. and Walter, R. (1992) *The New Social Economy; Reworking the Division of Labour* (Oxford: Blackwell).

Schon, D. A. (1983) *The Reflexive Practitioner* (New York: Basic Books).

Senge, P. M. (1990) *The Fifth Discipline* (London: Century).

Senge, P. M. (1992) 'Building Learning Organisations: The Real Message of the Quality Movement', *Journal for Quality and Participation* (March).

Seyd, P. (1987) *The Rise and Fall of the Labour Left* (London: Macmillan).

Shamir, B. (1991) 'Meaning, Self and Motivation in Organisations', *Organisational Studies,* vol. 12/3, pp. 405–24.

Sills, A. and Desai, P. (1996) 'Qualitative Research on Ethnic Minority Communities in Britain', *Journal of the Market Research Society,* vol. 38, pp. 247–65.

Sims, D., Fineman, S. and Gabriel, Y. (1993) *Organising and Organisations: An Introduction* (London: Sage).

Skelcher, C. and Lowndes, V. (1998) 'The dynamics of multi-organisational partnerships: an analysis of changing modes of governance', *Public Administration,* vol. 76 (Summer).

Skinner, B. F. (1971) *Beyond Freedom and Dignity* (New York: Alfred A. Knopf).

Skocpol, T. (1979) *States and Social Revolutions* (Cambridge: Cambridge University Press).

Social Exclusion Unit (2000) Report of Policy Action Team 16: *Learning Lessons* (London: SEU).

Steele, J. (1999) *Wasted Values: Harnessing the Commitment of Public Managers* (London: Public Management Foundation).

Stewart, J. (1981) *Local Government: The Conditions of Local Choice* (London: Allen & Urwin).

Stewart, J. and Stoker, G. (1988) 'From Local Administration to Community Government', research series no. 351 (London: The Fabian Society).

Stewart, J. (1995) *Innovation in Democratic Practice* (Birmingham: The Institute of Local Government Studies).

Stewart, J. (1996) *Further Innovation in Democratic Practice* (Birmingham: School of Public Policy).

Stewart, J. (1997) *More Innovation in Democratic Practice* (Birmingham: School of Public Policy).

Stewart, J. (2000) *The Nature of British Local Government* (London: Macmillan).

Stewart, M. and Taylor, M. (1995) *Resident Empowerment in Estate Regeneration* (Bristol: Policy Press).

Stewart, M., Goss, S., Clarke, R., Gillanders, G., Rowe, J. and Shaftoe, H. (1999) *Cross-Cutting Issues Affecting Local Government* (London: DETR).

Stewart, M. (2000) 'Local Action to Counter Exclusion', in Policy Action Team 17, *Joining it up Locally, the Evidence Base* (London: DETR).

Stoker, G. (1991) *The Politics of Local Government* (London: Macmillan).

Stoker, G. (1997) 'Local Political Participation', in R. Hambledon *et al.*, *New Perspectives on Local Governance* (York: Joseph Rowntree Foundation).

Stoker, G. (1998) 'Unintended Costs and Benefits of New Mangement Reform in British Local Government', in G. Stoker (ed.), *New Perspectives on Local Governance* (London: Macmillan).

Stoker, G. (ed.) (1999) *The New Management of British Local Governance* (London: Macmillan).

Stoker, G. (2000) 'International Trends in Local Government Transformation' (draft paper).

Stoker, G. and Young, S. (1993) *Cities in the 1990s* (Harlow: Longman).

Szreter, S. (1999) 'A New Political Economy for Labour: the Importance of Social Capital', *Renewal*, 7.1, pp. 30–44.

Tarplett, P. (1999) 'Changing the Organisation to be Effective at User Engagement', in Goss, S. (eds.) *Managing Working with the Public* (London: Kogan Page).

Taylor, F. W. (1947) *Scientific Management* (New York: Harper & Row).

Taylor, M. (1995) *Unleashing the Potential: Bringing Residents to the Centre of Regeneration*, Housing Summary no. 12 (York: Joseph Rowntree Foundation).

Taylor, M. (2000) *Top down meets bottom up: Neighbourhood Management* (York: Joseph Rowntree Foundation).

Thake, S. (1995) *Staying the Course: The Role and Structures of Community Regeneration Organisations.* (York: Joseph Rowntree Foundation).

Thake, S. and Zadek, S. (1997) *Practical People – Noble Causes; How to Support Community-based Social Entrepreneurs* (London: New Economics Foundation).

Thatcher, M. (1993) *The Downing Street Years* (London: HarperCollins).

Thomas, D. (1995) '*A Review of Community Development*', Social Policy summary no. 5 (York: Joseph Rowntree Foundation).

Thompson, P. and McHugh, D. (1995) *Work Organisations: A Critical Introduction* (Basingstoke and London: Macmillan).

Tsoukas, H. (1994) 'From Social Engineering to Reflective Action in Organisational Behaviour', in H. Tsoukas (ed.), *New Thinking in Organisational Behaviour* (London: Butterworth & Heinemann).

Urban Task Force (1999) *Sharing the Vision; Summary of Responses to the Urban Task Force Prospectus* (London: DETR).

User Centred Service Group (1993) *Building Bridges between People who Use and People who Provide Services* (London: National Institute of Social Work).

Wainwright, H. (1994) *Arguments for a New Left* (Oxford: Basel Blackwell).

Walsall MBC (1999) 'Neighbourhood Governance in the Borough of Walsall', in *Background Notes on Walsall's Local Committees* (Walsall: Walsall MBC).

Watson, J. B. (1930) *Behaviourism* (New York: Norton).

Watson, T. (1994) *In Search of Management; Culture, Chaos and Control in Managerial Work* (London: Routledge).

Weber, M. (1984) 'Bureaucracy', in F. Fischer and C. Sirriani (eds) *Critical Studies in Organization and Bureaucracy* (Philadelphia: Temple University Press).

Weir, S. and Beetham, D. (1999) *Political Power and Democratic Control in Britain* (London: Routledge).

Weir, S. and Hall, (eds) (1994) *EGO TRIP: Extra-governmental Organisations in the UK and their Accountability*, Democratic Audit Paper no. 2 (Human Rights Centre, University of Essex and Scarman Trust Enterprises).

Weisbord, M. (1992) *Discovering Common Ground* (San Francisco: Berrett-Koehler).

Willke (1992) *Des Ironie Des Staates* (Frankfurt: Suhrkamp).

Willmott, H. (1994) 'Theorising Agency: Power and Subjectivity in Organisational Studies', in J. Hassard and M. Parker (eds), *Towards a New Theory of Organisations* (London: Routledge).

Young, K. and Rao, N. (1997) 'Public Attitudes to Local Government', in R. Hambledon *et al., New Perspectives in Local Government* (York: Joseph Rowntree Foundation).

Zeldin, T. (1998) *An Intimate History of Humanity* (London: Vintage).

Index

Note: references to *boxes, figures* and *tables* are indicated in *italics*.